The
Strength
to
Live

Published and printed by Ignite Publishing, a division of JBO Global Inc.
5569-47th Street Red Deer, AB
Canada, T4N1S1 1-877-677-6115

Cover design by Dania Zafar
Book design by Dania Zafar and JB Owen
Edited by JB Owen, Mimi Safiyah and Zoe Wong.
Designed in Canada, Printed in China
ISBN: 9798987212110
First edition: January 2023

Ordering Information: Quantity sales. Special discounts are available on quantity purchases by corporations, associations, and others. For details, contact the publisher at the above address. Programs, products, or services provided by the author are found by contacting them directly. Resources named in the book are found in the resources pages at the back of the book.

Author Details: Cindy Tank-Murphy
Website: www.thestrengthtolive.com
Facebook: www.facebook.com/TheStrengthToLiveBook
Instagram: @thestrengthtolive
Email: cindy@thestrengthtolive.com

The
Strength
to
Live

Clarity ~ Compassion ~ Courage

Finding healing and hope after a loss from suicide

CINDY TANK-MURPHY

FOREWORD BY
GLEN WAGNER M.DIV
Pastor, Leadership Coach, and Entrepreneur

Published by Ignite Publishing, a division of JBO Globle Inc.
IGNITEYOU.LIFE

Contents

Testimonials

"Cindy Tank Murphy's book, *The Strength to Live*, takes on this most personal and challenging topic with heart, compassion, and sensitivity. She keeps it REAL for all of us. This book needs to be read by everyone who wants to deepen their understanding of themselves and those around them. Truly a compelling and beautiful read."

Wendy Hayum-Gross, LCPC, MS, Co-Founder of Grow Wellness Group

"Author Cindy Tank-Murphy gives her personal account of the death of her father by suicide. Intrigued by the many suicides that plagued her hometown, along with the recent death of her father, Cindy began a mission to save others from the fate of suicide, educate loved ones on prevention, and help survivors to cope with their loss. Fortunately, her passion for this subject helped her see the signs of suicide in her daughter, and she got her the help she needed.

I can appreciate this book because I, too, lost my dad to suicide due to the torturous pain of cancer. Her writing helped me to see my dad's death from a perspective that removed any shame I felt. This powerful book removes the negative stigmas concerning suicide. It shines the spotlight on mental illness and the need to take the disease of suicide as seriously as illnesses such as cancer. She also encourages the reader to see their deceased loved ones for the life they lived, not how they died.

I recommend this book to all, whether or not you've lost someone to suicide. This book will help you to possibly identify suicidal ideations that those who are close to you may be experiencing. I appreciate the author's transparency concerning her dad and daughter. I can feel her heart on each page and her strong desire to bring healing to those who need it."

Elder Curtis Ghee, author, speaker, and fellow suicide loss survivor

"Exquisitely raw, heartfelt, powerful, and beautiful.

The Strength to Live by Cindy Tank-Murphy is quite simply the best and most important book I have read in years. If you, or someone you know, have lost a loved one to suicide, or perhaps you know someone who is struggling with mental illness and possibly suicidal thoughts, this book is a vital and powerful guide to help you and to equip you to help others. Cindy shares gracefully and passionately from a position of deeply personal experience. However, this book provides so much more than sharing other people's raw, heartfelt experiences of death by suicide. This book offers the most relevant, insightful, and impactful guidance and support to help you and those you care for to navigate unfathomable grief and a myriad of turmoiled emotions carrying you gently yet powerfully to the point of acceptance and love, which you may have believed impossible. In today's world, this is vital reading for us all."

Tracy Stone, Cl.Hyp, CPPD, ARTT, GHR (Reg.), Executive trainer, transformational coach, clinical hypnotherapist, international bestselling author, and inspirational speaker

"Cindy Tank-Murphy's The Strength to Live is a book like no other on the crucial topic of surviving suicide. As a psychotherapist, I would recommend this book to survivors and urge other clinicians and people with depression in the family to read it. In a time when suicidality is reaching unprecedented levels in this country and an ongoing mental health crisis, this book helps people understand the nuances of depression and anxiety and how they can (and sometimes do) lead to suicide. Often, the parents I counsel ask what to look for and what to do when their teen is struggling with suicidality – I would feel confident that Cindy's book would provide an excellent guide for these families.

What I love about the way this book is presented is that it is easy to jump directly to the chapters that best align with where a person is in their grief journey. Grieving people can't always read long books, so the easy-to-read format allows people to learn and heal at their own pace. As a therapist, I plan to bring this book into my sessions to work on the exercises along with my clients on this difficult journey. Cindy chooses wonderful vignettes and masterfully describes each stage of healing from a loved one's death by suicide. For those looking for something to "do" to facilitate their healing process, her easy-to-follow exercises at the end of each chapter will give people many opportunities to apply the strategies she so clearly illustrates. I am thrilled as someone who lives with depression, as a parent of a child who has been suicidal, and as a clinician to finally have a powerful book that takes suicide out of the darkness and into the light."

Jennifer Curtin, LCPC, Therapist & Practice Owner

"It was my honor to read Cindy's book about suicide. It is generally not a subject that people like to discuss, but this book is very cathartic to those who have lost a loved one to suicide. I liked this book for several reasons. First, it gave a lot of insight into those you care about that might be suffering from the emotional trauma that could lead to them taking their life. Next, it gives step-by-step activities to consider and use. The interactive quality of this book allows one to work through these activities immediately, almost like using a workbook! I could feel the emotional release Cindy obtained by writing this book. I experienced suicide by one of my best friends from high school. Too many times, as a teenager, I tried to talk him off his emotional cliff. He finally achieved what he had tried many times—his death. In retrospect, this book would have been very helpful back then, for me and maybe for him. Cindy—hold your head high because this book is a much-needed read for many people."

Melanie Summers, M.A. Education, Certified Health & Fitness Coach, International Best Selling Author, and fellow suicide loss survivor

"Cindy has shared such thought-provoking information on suicide and mental health in a fashion that speaks directly to the reader. This book brought to my attention many aspects that survivors of suicide deal with. It has helped me understand how my behavior, actions, and words can impact someone positively or not. The many faces of mental health and the toll it takes on families are far-reaching, and this book is an inspiration, and hopefully, it will enlighten and inspire readers to shift their perceptions."

Cheryl Viczko, Co-author and alignment coach, Co-founder, All In Alignment, Essential Feng Shui Practitioner

"Having gone through the loss of my brother to suicide, I was eager to read Cindy Tank-Murphy's book, *The Strength to Live.* I sometimes had difficulty reading it, realizing I've yet to fully deal with my brother's loss. It brought up many feelings that I didn't know what to do with, but Cindy's book relays extremely practical advice on understanding, coming to terms with, and healing from this loss.

I highly recommend this book to anyone who has been touched in any way by suicide or is seeking understanding about this complex topic shrouded in shame, guilt, and misunderstanding. Be prepared to work through your grief with the help of Cindy's healing techniques."

Sharon Eistetter, Author, Speaker, Coach, and fellow suicide loss survivor

"Cindy Tank-Murphy is more than an author and mental health advocate. She blends her soulful healing energy with what was a riveting life-altering event in her own personal family, and unfolds excellence that will resonate in the halls of health and mental wellness for decades to come."

Dr. Jo Dee Baer, Holistic Nutritionist, Certified Health Coach, Speaker, Consultant, Author & Trainer

Dedication

To Mom, who gave selflessly to us kids and whose endless love and devotion made our home feel safe and full of happiness. To my siblings, for always believing in me and supporting my crazy ideas and dreams. To the grandkids, the ones lucky enough to ride the golf cart with Grandpa, and those who will learn about him through our family stories by which we continue to share his caring heart, joyous laugh, and generous spirit.

I also want to dedicate this book to those who are no longer with us:

In remembrance and honor of LeRoy, Morgan, Mark, Erica, Jay, Lourdes, Tyrone, Mandy, Todd, Keith, Bill, Mark, Roy, Travis, Erin, Bruce, Ryan, Corey, Isaac, Lucas, and so many others unnamed who were on my mind while I wrote this book, including the 47,000 lives we lose annually in the United States to suicide. If I could list them all, I would.

WORDS FROM THE PUBLISHER

As a publisher, one likes to take on *sure things*; books that are sought after and topics that follow the trends. When Cindy came to me in the winter of 2021 to write a book about suicide, I'll admit I was a bit trepidacious. I knew nothing about suicide, never having experienced it firsthand myself. I felt it was slightly morbid to address the act and deeply personal to talk about the overwhelming grief. At first glance, it seemed awkward to create a book addressing such a private and unimaginable topic and then highlight the painful and tragic loss.

It didn't take long after listening and working with Cindy to see the importance and necessity of this book. Her deep understanding of suicide and personal experiences with its devastation gave her a perspective that few have. Losing her father to suicide and having her child attempt to follow the same path yielded a kind of wisdom and strength that was impossible to deny. Cindy also had unparalleled compassion for those going through the same situation and a fire in her soul to help prevent others from experiencing the same fate she had gone through. Her unique vantage point, years of personal growth, and deep dive into the subject made her the perfect candidate to write a book of this magnitude.

As the months went on and Cindy submitted her drafted manuscript, I became both enthralled and deeply invested. I could see from the first chapter that she not only knew what she was talking about but also brought the level of grace and empathy that needed to be shared. She was tremendously vulnerable about her personal loss and candidly truthful about her grieving process. She had done the work to overcome the pain and developed tools to find some solace in the healing process.

While working with Cindy I learned and found a greater understanding of how suicide carries stigma, judgment, and aversion. I began seeing the loss of a loved one by suicide in a different light, with compassion, empathy, and heart. Cindy opened my eyes to the growing problem with detection, support, and treatment. She peeled back the layers surrounding the silence, shame, and ignorance many of us commonly feel and gave voice to the survivors dealing with the grief.

I loved her title for the book, *The Strength to Live*. The sharing throughout her chapters regarding those that chose suicide, and those that were left living in the aftermath, showed tremendous courage and strength. Cindy also reflected on her own inner strength and the strength of many others as she spent close to two years interviewing those that have survived the loss of a loved one. She gave faces to the names of victims and voices to those who were shadowed in silence. She addressed the emotional, physical, and mental impacts and devised ways to not only move through the pain but heal it. Her steps, ideas, and strategies were so heartfelt and practical that I knew they would not only help others but empower them in the ways they required it most. Needless to say, within a very short time, I knew this book would not only be helpful but a fundamental *must-have* for anyone going through this experience.

While editing this book and collaborating with Cindy, I learned things about suicide that I didn't know, but needed to gain knowledge on. Her book educated me in ways I now feel everyone should be informed of. Not only regarding the grief of suicide, but also the signs beforehand, the triggers, the common generalizations, the social stigmas, the insensitivities, the barriers to help, and the mental health challenges that many of us ignore. I felt ignorant toward an issue that affects millions of people. Cindy helped to educate me and brought forth a level of compassion and responsibility that all of us should have, not just for ourselves but for the many others who need our support.

I am deeply proud to be the publisher of this book. I feel both a sense of duty and pride to support this great work in being available for the family, friends, and survivors of those who need it most. I also feel privileged to have watched Cindy take on this brave and courageous task. I have witnessed her not only grow as a writer but become an advocate and leader in this fight. She truly is a champion and a healer. She fought through her own grief, overcame her own setbacks, and rallied forth to not only heal herself but to heal you and the millions of people who will read this book. I know that because of this book people will see that through suicide comes great strength: the strength to not only live, but to love and support those that need it the most.

Wherever you are in your journey of healing from a loss by suicide, I know this book with help bring you forward, overcome the grief, and assist you through the pain. I am certain that Cindy's words will speak directly to what you are going through and open your heart toward solace and peace. Her gentle words and helpful *Healing Moments* will move you from where you are currently to where you want to be in the future. And, the many people she has gathered to create a community of support will prove you are not alone but surrounded by grace.

I offer my deepest compassion and condolences for your loss, and as Cindy has taught me, I share that you are not alone but supported in all the ways you need. This experience in your life is a gift in its own right, and I applaud you for the strength you have to champion through it and become the hero in your life and the beacon of hope for someone else.

The Strength to Live is a phenomenal book, and Cindy Tank-Murphy is an author I am honored to know, and you reading this book is a gift I feel blessed to share.

Many Blessings,
Lady JB Owen, ROC

FOREWORD

GLEN WAGNER M.DIV

PASTOR, LEADERSHIP COACH, AND ENTREPRENEUR

It is an honor to write the foreword for Cindy Tank-Murphy's new book, *The Strength to Live.*

I'll never forget the first time I was asked by a family to do the memorial service for their son whose life had ended in the deep tragedy of suicide. Normally the difficulty of death is faced by calling those endings a 'celebration of life' service. As a young pastor,

I didn't know what to say to this family that had just discovered their beautiful twenty-one-year-old boy dead in his college dorm, laying lifeless from self-inflicted wounds.

They shared with me his tortuous journey through adolescence and young adulthood while struggling with depression, anxiety, and various mental health issues. Years of working with doctors, therapists, psychiatrists, substance abuse counselors, and social workers all committed to finding answers to the debilitating weight of daily living that their son had experienced throughout most of his days on earth. I sat holding back tears, wondering how in the world I could possibly help this family find healing in a very sad, dark, and grief-filled season that will forever mark their lives and the story of their family.

That emotional struggle was complicated by my own lived experience, which included many of the same dynamics I heard described by these kindhearted parents when talking about their son. I have spent years in therapy and continue to do so to this day. I wrestle with my own demons that have manifested through trauma, borderline personality disorder, and a life filled with addictions and tragedy. Therefore, I am familiar with the 'brokenness' that these trials leave in their wake. I knew one thing that day at the funeral: I had to find a way to help, make a difference, and change how we as a culture deal with mental health and the deep shame and stigma that permeates our world. I knew then, and even more now after 35 years as a pastor, that there are better ways to change the narrative of shame and hopelessness surrounding mental health and suicide.

During these past 35 years, I have also been an executive coach, working with marketplace leaders, entrepreneurs, and executives on leadership and strategy issues in growing companies. I can tell you that every single one of my ninety-plus corporate clients has been touched in deep and profound ways by mental health issues and, in some cases, by the tragedy of suicide. These dynamics are at play in individuals, families, organizations, and the wider culture from top to bottom; no one can ignore the tide of mental agony that ripples as a constant current through the world in which we live.

Sooner or later, you, someone you know, or someone you love dearly will struggle against the inner battle of desperation and search for relief from the darkness that is mental illness. The issues are very real indeed.

So, when my friend Cindy Tank-Murphy asked me if I would consider writing a foreword for the book you now hold in your hands, I was honored beyond belief. As a daughter, a mom, a survivor, a marketplace leader, and an author, she has given us a gift beyond measure in her book, *The Strength To Live*. From the depths of her own experience and grief, the hope she offers is palpable, the wisdom is deep, and the practical tools are invaluable. This work is filled with touching, heart-wrenching, and truthful stories of families, survivors, and healers that the world so desperately needs to hear from now, in this way, and at this time. Cindy's book is a true work of up-close knowledge gained from lived experience and written with the compassion of a kind and generous soul who knows what it is like to walk through these issues in the daily ebb and flow of family life.

The reader will find stories of real people and families from every walk of life that have seen mental illness up close. Stories of families that have faced the ultimate grief of losing a family member to suicide. Ways in which to work through that grief and shame, and examples of people still wrestling the demons away on a day-to-day basis. There is also advice and guidance on how loved ones can help while at the same time dealing with the very real fear of what the future may hold. Cindy moves us deftly through the intricacies of hopelessness, helplessness, and worthlessness that often precipitate suicidal ideation. She provides insights and wisdom that quite honestly can be life-saving and life-giving. We are indebted to her for this act of mercy and love.

I know this project has taken many hours and days of tear-filled typing, remembering, and researching to get it just right. That has been and is her passion. To talk, discuss, wrestle with, find answers, be helpful, and offer insights that are grounded and, at the same time, ultimately practical to get us moving toward healing in this strange journey of mental health and suicide.

Her 'Healing Moment' exercises at the end of each chapter are worth reading and sharing with every family, every small group, every place of worship, every neighborhood, every community, and every organization for their practical insights and applied wisdom. I am working my way through all of them with a whirlwind of emotions, as I think about the hundreds of families I know personally that have been and continue to work through these issues in their lives on a regular basis. Being human is sometimes the most difficult thing to be. Life is filled with both joy and sorrow. Nothing is sweeter than the intimacies of love, friendship, and family. Nothing is more tragic than the way mental health and suicide are surrounded by a shame and stigma that is capable of tearing our souls to shreds in the slow drip of debilitating depression. Or, the sudden knowledge that a life once viewed as so vibrant and alive is gone, in an instant, leaving questions, doubt, and sadness in its wake.

This book is for you if you care about your loved ones.

This book is for you if you wrestle with mental health issues.

This book is for you if you have lost someone to the tragedy of suicide.

This book is for you if you are a healthcare worker or a therapist.

This book is for you if you are a corporate leader or employee.

This book is for you if you have ever considered suicide.

This book is for you if you are a religious leader or belong to a religious organization.

This book is for you if you are an atheist and wrestling with the meaning of life.

This book is for you if you are a mom, a dad, or a sibling and need answers.

This book is for you if you are...human.

My hope and prayer is that Cindy's book will be read by many and open doors for her to share her stories, her wisdom, and her humanity with anyone who will listen. These are strong words, kind words, and words filled with tender mercies. The world needs these deep words of compassionate wisdom, practical insights, and hope-filled inspiration.

I know I benefited tremendously from reading this work of the heart. I know you will too.

Glen Wagner M.Div
Pastor, Leadership Coach, and Entrepreneur
Chicago IL. Christmas 2022

WHO THIS BOOK WAS WRITTEN FOR

I've given much thought to whom I have written this book for. There is not just one person I thought about during my writing process. In fact, if you asked me today who should read this book, I'd say, "Everyone."

I wish that every person, no matter whether or not they've been touched by suicide, picks up this book and finds a chapter that is meant for them to read. I hope they gain a nugget of wisdom to share with the world. However, I realize this is not a topic that everyone can comprehend. Not everyone is ready to delve into the abyss and bring themselves back to the surface, transformed, with a newfound compassion and understanding of suicide.

I wrote this book for those who have lost a friend or family member to suicide. The ones who are grieving in silence, dealing with shame and guilt, and are trying to put the pieces of their lives back together.

This book is for those whose grief is so profound they are in crisis themselves, barely holding on and needing reassurance that the fog will lift. For those who fear a loved one is suffering with such intensity that they fear they may lose them to suicide and are desperately trying to navigate the sense of helplessness that comes with not knowing what to do to save them.

And finally, *The Strength to Live* is for anyone willing to explore complex grief, self-imposing fear, limiting beliefs, mental health, and what causes someone to want to end their life; this book will shed some light on the many questions surrounding suicide.

This book is for courageous individuals who want to do the work to become mental health advocates and help change the trajectory of mental health around the world. If it is in your hands right now, this book is for you.

PREFACE

Eight hundred thousand people around the world die from suicide every year.

Forty-seven thousand deaths are in the United States alone, making it the 10th leading cause of death and claiming more lives than war, murder, and natural disasters combined. It's estimated that there are 1.3 million suicide attempts made every year.

Many grieve the loss of someone they know in silence, and few share the devastation it has caused. For every suicide death, at least ten people are impacted and suffer from the immense grief associated with losing that loved one. Recent studies have shown this number is much higher, and it is likely that we can not truly calculate the number of individuals tormented by such a loss.

Suicide is so prevalent that it's become almost impossible to find someone who hasn't personally been touched in some way by it, yet the pain associated with it is rarely discussed. Many survivors of suicide live in the shadows of guilt, shame, anger, and amidst millions of painful unanswered questions. It's a community no one wants to be a part of, but a community nonetheless.

Although there are many statistics regarding suicide, there is little information about those left behind reeling after the fact. If 800,000 people worldwide die from suicide every year, imagine the staggering number of wives, husbands, siblings, children, relatives, co-workers, and friends left in the wake. The number is too large to comprehend and proves how many individuals live in the darkness and aftermath. This issue affects us all, and I am one of those numbers.

In 2014, I lost my father to suicide after his lifelong on-and-off struggle with mental illness. He was a loving, devoted, sensitive, generous father, an amazing person, and his death by suicide does not define him as a man. My reaction to the complex grief I was dealing with was to seek a way out of the darkness. I knew I couldn't allow his beautiful life to be erased by this one final act, but trying to comprehend how to wade through the loss was more difficult than I anticipated. Everywhere I turned I was reminded of him and his death. It wasn't until I processed the grief, through a series of steps that I will share with you, that I began to smile, laugh, and find the strength to enjoy life again.

If you are reading this book, I can only imagine that suicide has somehow touched your life. You, too, may be reeling in the shame, anger, and guilt that plagues many of its survivors. If you are a survivor of a loss due to suicide then my heart goes out to you, and I applaud that you are here, reading this book, and willing to step into the next evolution of this process. Together we are bonded by something more profound than ourselves; something we may wish was different, but something that, as we move throughout this book, will bring us closer and touch a part of you that is ready to move forward.

This community of survivors we are in is a group that needs to lean into the support of one another now more than ever. We have a mental health crisis happening worldwide, and the trajectory will not decline until we begin to have open and honest conversations about the correlation between mental illness and suicide.

I believe that together we can heal one another, raise awareness of the mental health crisis, find support, offer help to those who are still grieving, and be a light for any other loved ones who may be struggling to survive the feelings of suicidal ideation (also referred to as suicide thoughts, ideas, or preoccupation with death and suicide). We must focus on how we can all move forward and begin rebuilding our lives.

When I first had to deal with the loss of my father, I lacked the knowledge of how to heal, and resources on the topic were limited. I found myself searching the internet for answers about how someone could bring themselves to take their own life. It was unimaginable to me how that could happen when I first began my search for answers. More information has been available in the last eight years since I committed to healing. You can now find Facebook and Instagram survivor pages and support groups, local Survivor of Suicide chapters, and more survivors willing to share their stories to ease the stigma. What I didn't find was a direct path or clear instructions on how to overcome the complex grief, navigate it, and ask for help for myself, my children, and my spouse. My mom and siblings all needed support as well. I spent a long time waiting for adequate resources to show up, only to find myself time and time again searching for a book or website that would give me some practical steps to help me and those around me. With little available, I was led and inspired to write this book for all the people who, like me, want to understand the depths of their loved one's pain and come to terms with their loss. I also wanted to do something to honor my father, and I felt compelled to make what I had gone through better for another person, family, or friend going through a suicide loss. I didn't know how to approach this subject initially, but I allowed myself to be open and vulnerable to finding a way. I just knew there needed to be something that I could do to help.

Since then, my daughter has fallen into her own abyss of suicidal ideation that began at the age of 15. Her journey of suicidal tendencies and my journey to support and find the cause has led me down a winding and often frustrating road to dead end after dead end. I have had to study her diagnosis as if I were a medical student to get her the right treatment while living in fear for the past several years, leading to the pinnacle moment where I knew this book *had* to be written. I felt called to share my story because anyone in my situation needs a support system. Any parent dealing with a child who's been diagnosed with a serious life-limiting illness lives in fear of losing their child. Still, a parent who has a child experiencing continual self-harming thoughts doesn't always know where to go for support. People didn't know my daughter was living day by day, and we didn't know if she would live to see her next birthday. I lived in fear every day, with very few people knowing what our family was going through.

My experience with both my father and my daughter has given me a frame of reference to provide an important viewpoint beyond the clinical and objective understanding. It has enabled me to see suicide through a much-needed perspective, one that is up close and personal. My reality has given me a strong desire to help others see the view from this same position.

My hope is this book will help empower those who feel helpless after a suicide loss and that it will educate those who fear they know someone who might be at risk of suicide. Most importantly, the ideas on these pages will motivate anyone feeling helpless or fearful to react and take measures due to this new perspective. It is designed to expand your mindset and help reframe your feelings while challenging your current thinking. The good news is, I believe you are strong enough to read this new perspective, or you wouldn't have it in their hands right now.

Along with supporting you on your healing journey and helping you find the tools and support you need should your child or loved one show signs of emotional struggle, I feel very passionate that by educating you throughout this book I can prepare you for the next time you come across someone who is experiencing suicidal ideation

15

or a mental health crisis. A World Health Organization statistic states that 1 in 4 adults will be affected by a mental health disorder in their lifetime, and in the United States alone, that statistic increases to 50%. With statistics like that, it's not whether or not you'll be confronted by someone experiencing a mental health crisis, but rather when it does happen, will you be prepared to initiate a positive outcome to the situation? The knowledge of these facts and figures has compelled me to dig deep to tell you not just my story but many other stories of survivors of suicide loss and how they managed to turn their loss into something positive. All the people in this book share one thing in common. They've lost a loved one to suicide, and through their healing, they've learned how to move forward and are now brave enough to share their stories with you. Each story is here to provide you with the knowledge that you are not alone, that what you're going through is understandable considering the type of loss you've been through, and that there is a light at the end of the tunnel once you begin to work on healing yourself.

Their stories may be similar to yours and touch upon themes like alcohol/drug abuse, violent behaviors, traumas, and symptoms both seen and unseen. The desperate desire to turn back the clock and save them that we all share. They each bring together the common thread of hope and are here to help you begin to turn your pain into something positive. I hope that through your tragedy, you can find clarity and that this book will prevent another person from going through what we have endured. If more of us are educated, then we can possibly prevent another suicide and save a life. A precious life. A life meant to be lived. Suicide is preventable. *If you or someone you know is in crisis, please reach out for help.*

I understand reaching out for help can be scary, or you may even feel like you aren't really in that much need to call a crisis line, but this is important for you to know. If you are feeling an intense emotion surfacing and struggling to keep calm as you read this, you

Suicide Crisis Lifeline:
Dial 988 in the United States

**(formerly the National Suicide Prevention Hotline
800-273-8255 / 800-273-TALK)**

or Text TALK to 741741

For International crisis numbers:
https://findahelpline.com/i/iasp

may be in crisis. There may be thoughts flooding your mind that can help you realize you need to act and reach out for help. Someone who has been in this situation, unable to understand the severity of their emotional state clearly, has provided these questions, which you may also be grappling with and could be clouding your judgment. If you're thinking thoughts of...

There are probably people who need this crisis line more than me.

What do I even say?

I don't want them to call 911 on me.

What if no one answers?

I'm not 'suicidal enough' to call this number.

If you are thinking any of these thoughts or something similar, please know that this is your sign to pick up the phone and call for help. The person on the other end of the line is waiting and wants you to call. They will listen and help.

INTRODUCTION: STRENGTH

The strongest people are not those who show strength in front
of us, but those who fight battles we know nothing about.

- UNKNOWN

To some, suicide is an ugly, repulsive word. The mention of it can elicit a sharp sting in the chest, a hollow void in the gut, and takes your breath away for a split second. There are times you might feel dirty and nauseous just at the thought of its presence. Those of us who have lived through the loss of someone by suicide know this feeling all too painfully well. There is immense grief felt with any death, but layered on top of suicide is an indescribable sorrow, a dark, heavy suffering that feels as if your heart is literally about to explode. It is an agony that leaves you in a cloud of darkness and deep despair with no end or light to guide you, and just when you think the darkness is slowly lifting, it pulls you back like a riptide. The lingering loneliness can be more profound than any other intense loss. Images of the act of their demise flood your mind playing over and over like a video loop. The loss leaves you so stunned that you are unable to comprehend who your loved one ever was to you. You keep asking yourself, what happened to that amazing person you adored with all your heart and thought you knew everything about?

How could I have missed the signs? Was it my fault? What were their final thoughts? Why didn't they reach out? Why couldn't I have saved them?

All these emotions paralyzed me and left me feeling numb, incapable of expressing compassion for myself or anyone else when suicide gripped me in its unforeseeable talons. I remember the first time I was asked how my father died. The disorientation in my mind caused me to stutter, "his heart just gave up." I could not even utter the word suicide. The confusion about what had happened trapped me in a dark maze with dead ends and no escape. I didn't know how to process or explain it to the outside world.

It took years to come to a place of peace with his passing. Now, I have decided it's time to tell my story in the hope that I can shed some light on this complex issue, understanding both the horror and the healing. I want to share my story so that others can begin to lift some of the ugliness from their stories. I believe by exposing the fear that keeps us quiet, survivors like you and me can gain our voices back and understand the mental illnesses, such as PTSD, bipolar disorder, depression, schizophrenia, borderline personality disorder, and others that are the underlying problem behind this epidemic. There are many additional factors beyond some of the medical conditions I've listed, which can also contribute to a mental health crisis, such as environmental, lifestyle, stressful life situations, and even brain injury, which makes it difficult to compare any two people's circumstances, and often it's a combination that creates the 'perfect storm.' What causes one person to take their life may not be the same for someone else, and that is why the answers often remain elusive; the survivors are left whirling in confusion.

Once we can get past the idea of suicide as a dirty word, we can talk freely about these mental conditions without shame, we can begin to have honest conversations on how we can impact and improve mental health outcomes. Our voices can break through the clutter and help change the narrative regarding suicide as not a result but the effect of a disease. Understanding it as a disease allows us to release our contempt for the act itself. We no longer have to hide in shame; instead, we can accept that the illness created the end result. Then the many of us who have experienced it firsthand can be more compassionate and accepting of what our loved ones went through. And, together, we can bring hope to those experiencing the same devastation and loss. But first, we must heal and surrender to the tragedy we have experienced, so we can begin to re-emerge stronger and finally free.

If you are like me, you may be searching or even yearning for answers. I want you to know that what you did or didn't do had no impact on why your loved one made that painful decision. Some secrets are so deep and agonizing that we will never be able to comprehend them. At least not in this lifetime. Some might say that I've been cursed with growing up in a family that has struggled with mental illness and that I have known several people who have died by suicide. I see it differently. I view my life experiences as my calling to help others see suicide death from a different perspective. I want them to gain a similar understanding that I've come to accept; one of compassion and understanding. I won't claim to have all the answers, but I have done much inner work to get to a place of peace and acceptance. I developed a growth mindset which allows me to look at situations from diverse perspectives. What I know to my core is that my father and your loved one didn't want to hurt us and didn't mean to cause us this tremendous pain. They likely wrestled for a long time with demons inside their mind telling them death was their only way out, perhaps without anyone realizing their struggle. They shielded you from their unbearable suffering because they wanted to spare you the burden. The only way they knew how to stop their inner torment was to leave this earth and find another realm where their pain was no longer felt.

Looking back, there may have been signs or indications that they were going through enormous stress, emotional instability, confusion, and anger. In hindsight, you may now see some of those signs more clearly. They may have been diagnosed with a psychiatric disorder, such as major depressive disorder, generalized anxiety, bipolar disorder, or another very real and debilitating mental illness. There also may have been the opposite; maybe they were working daily, attending to their affairs, and going about their life without warning before the tragedy. You may have never known the internal struggles your loved one experienced, those that they had lurking in an all-consuming darkness. Whether you knew something was wrong with them or not, I'm here to tell you from my personal experience and the experience of others I've spoken to that the only thing your loved one knew at that moment was that they needed to end their pain. Dis-ease devours the mind and soul like ravenous cancer devours the body. And, just like untreated heart disease can lead to a heart attack unknowingly, untreated serious mental illness can lead to suicide.

This may be hard for you to hear right now, but it took your loved one all the strength they had to live, to continue forward... to keep hope alive. That force kept their loving presence on this earth for as long as they could hold on. I believe that strength is a gift. A gift they graced you and everyone around them with. I want you to hold onto that knowledge of their fortitude and understand that the love they had for you allowed them to survive for as long as they did. It takes immense strength and courage to fight the demons of suicidal thoughts and impulses. Your loved one fought for as long as they could.

I know it may not feel possible right now to agree, comprehend, or accept this idea, but I am here to help you get to a place of true understanding and, most importantly, peace. I will help guide you on this journey of gaining the strength to live through the pain, anger, shame, guilt, and other complex emotions you may be feeling. I'll show you how to change your thought patterns and redefine your loss so you can move forward with hope. The work will not be easy, and you will have moments of intense sorrow while working through your grief, but I promise you can and will emerge with a new perspective. It will be possible to smile once again, laugh, and enjoy life as you did prior to this tragedy.

In this book, you'll learn how other people, just like you, have survived the aftermath of losing a loved one and heroically found a new beginning. I will introduce you to beautiful individuals, sharing their stories of moving from deep despair to a life of hope once again. Their stories will help you realize you are not alone. The feelings you are going through are legitimate and real, but they do not have to define you. You will be inspired to transform and grow and see how much you have to live for.

As we work together, I will introduce you to six phases I developed in my healing process. When I look back at how I was able to move forward, I realize six fundamental phases became turning points in my recovery. The steps I went through and wish to share with you are Yearn, Educate, Surrender, Empathy, Emerge, and Share. I know from personal experience that once you have moved through these six phases, you'll feel a greater strength and awareness about yourself. You will feel more at peace and able to freely and openly discuss your loss, and you'll have breakthrough moments that will propel you to the next level of acceptance and understanding. Eventually, I assure you, your feelings will dissipate, and you'll notice a shift in your grief journey. Don't worry if you forget some of the steps along the way because I'll review them for you in the book's final section.

Before we get started, I want to be honest about a few things -- I am going to share the raw and honest details that lie within the depths of suicide from my personal experience and the perspective of other survivors of suicide loss. You may find my language explicit and harsh at times; I don't mean to offend you. I believe in honesty, straightforwardness, and empathy. I only speak what comes from my heart because the only way to support you in an authentic way truly is to speak without sugarcoating, or placating you.... I also believe you don't want to be patronized about something so important. If I were to keep things safe and comfortable, thinking you are too fragile to read the rawness you've just experienced, you might speculate that I don't know the depth of your pain, but I do. I'd also venture to say that someone you know taking their life may have been the most traumatic day you have ever experienced; it was for me. That is why my frankness is both honest and sincere, in the hope of making a relatable connection with you.

Please know I'm not trying to open additional wounds. You are here to heal, and that's what we will do. If something emotionally triggers you, feel free to put the book down and return when you are ready. I encourage you to be compassionate with yourself. I'm allowing you to judge what feels right for you on your own terms and at your own pace. My job is to be the one person you can trust to uncover your fears, give you the confidence to seek your truth, and help you heal.

As you read this book, you will find mini-activities called "Healing Moments." Healing Moments are meant for reflection, self-discovery, and self-care, which I've found successful in aiding my recovery and ability to move forward. I will share them throughout the chapters at times when it's meant to provide you with an emotional anchor and ground you from the effects of any distress. You can continue to do these techniques multiple times as much as you like to help solidify your healing. They are meant to break your old thinking patterns and create new patterns that you can use to change your current state. Some Healing Moments may not resonate with you or feel right at first, which is okay. I suggest you go back and try them a second or third time to see if they start to feel more comfortable. Feel free to write your thoughts, feelings, and emotions within the spaces provided in the book or a journal. If you are truly ready to improve your well-being, then please commit to trying all of the Healing Moments at least once. You will find by doing these Healing Moments, you will begin to find clarity and ease into a more peaceful mindset.

We can both agree that your life has been forever changed, and I'm not here to tell you to move on, but rather I'm here to tell you it is possible to move forward. It will take time and effort on your part, but I can guarantee you that it's possible to find the strength to move beyond your grief and find the strength to live. I am with you. I'm ready to help you. I will be here every step of the way.

It's time to start your healing. Let your Strength to Live begin.

1

CANDIDLY

*"Healing comes from owning
your story and sharing it freely."*
- CINDY TANK-MURPHY

Since becoming a mother at 30, I have felt the strong urge to write a book. Over the years, I've had a few ideas, but nothing that ever felt exactly right; until now.

I am enamored by authors. I admire their bravery in telling stories with such vulnerability. Even in fiction, the author's thoughts are poured out on a page for everyone to see. They are naked, right there in front of us. That exposure and vulnerability has always impressed me, so when I started to have this innate knowing that I was meant to write this book, it not only felt respectable, but it also scared the sh*t out of me. I was being called to expose my thoughts and feelings on paper, *and* asked to unearth two of the most controversial and frightening topics in our society: suicide and mental illness.

It wasn't until a midlife shakeup, and what I refer to as *my leap of faith*, that the vision of this book started to become apparent. That spring, I left behind a corporate job that paid well, but no longer fulfilled me personally or professionally since the loss of my father. I was searching for answers. I grew up in a small northeastern Iowa town, with a population of just 3413. Over the span of my life, I'd known so many people who had taken their lives by suicide; a cousin from a neighboring small rural town, classmates' brothers, a friend's boyfriend, and as you already know, my own father. The first suicide I was ever exposed to was my elementary school principal. I was eight, and the news left me feeling scared and confused about why someone would want to die.

I have often asked myself, *why have so many suicides occurred in my birthplace?* I can easily count over 10, 15, maybe even 20 deaths I had known about over the years. Curious and struggling with the remnants of unanswered questions, I went where most of us go to find answers. I asked Google, "Why have so many people died by suicide in New Hampton, Iowa?" I know, it was sort of a strange request for the 'Tech Guru,' to reply to, but I was desperate to find answers. Asking Google seemed like the best technique to use when looking for clarity on something impossible to solve on my own. However, that one search on Google sent me down a road of self-discovery, and ultimately became the catalyst that saved my daughter's life a year later. (I promise to share more about this in upcoming chapters.) Thank you, Google!

The reason why that search became so important was because two years earlier I had lost my father to suicide, which was influenced by his own struggle with mental illness. Since then, I began to witness similar mental illnesses amongst my closest family. My 15-year-old daughter had been struggling with anxiety and depression for almost six years. We began therapy for her in fourth grade, when she started having panic attacks. *Why did mental illness plague my family?* I asked myself, *why was this happening to my daughter? What the f*ck do I do?* So, I typed into Google... "Why have so many people died by suicide in New Hampton, Iowa?"

The search came back with *an* answer at the very top of the page. A speaker was coming to my hometown of New Hampton, Iowa, that very evening, May 10th, 2016. The post read...

We are SUPER EXCITED to bring Christine (an Iowa mom!) and her message to the New Hampton Community. We are a community and the children in it are worth it. The 'It's All Love, Only Love' Coalition travels to communities and schools to speak to students, parents and school administrators about the importance of healthy self-care for mind and body and the importance of always being kind. By being educated on the signs and symptoms of depression, particularly in children, we can have a greater chance of seeking professional help fast and giving our children the childhood they deserve; one without the sometimes paralyzing depression, sadness and anxiety.

Christine Schmidt was the speaker presenting that evening. I learned through further investigating online that Christine was a mother, my age, and also a survivor of suicide. She had been traveling throughout Iowa on a mission to educate students about the effects of bullying and suicide. Christine, I found out, was coming to share her message after losing her 12-year-old daughter, Morgan, to suicide in April, 2014. *Heartbreaking.* The coincidence was too hard to ignore. What were the odds that someone who had lost a child to suicide was going to be speaking in my hometown that evening – *the very day I typed those 12 words into my computer?* I felt as if the Universe had spoken directly to me and God had answered my prayer. There was no denying the signs. It was loud and clear. I had to meet and speak to Christine.

Over the next few years, I developed a friendship with Christine and the topic she was sharing. I was passionate to learn more of what she knew on the subject of suicide. I felt everyone needed to hear this tragic story of how a mother lost her child to a misdiagnosed mental illness. "It could happen in your family," I would tell them.

I became so obsessed that I started telling random people at inappropriate times about Christine's story of losing her daughter to suicide. I began a business venture to help save teens from the effects of bullying, social media, and suicide, which provided me the opportunity to speak to both small groups and large international audiences. I told Christina's story to anyone who would listen, at every opportunity, even if they weren't interested. I made them listen. I knew her story like it was my own because deep down I felt Christine's story closely resembled my own. If I didn't take immediate action to help my own daughter, I feared Christine's story would become mine, and I could lose my daughter who was the same age as Morgan would have been if she had survived.

The following fall, I knew my daughter was feeling suicidal. She was disconnecting from herself, her friends, and her life. I could see the dissociation in her eyes as she would blankly stare into space. Her irritability was intense, sometimes angering at the most insignificant things. After trying unsuccessfully to get help for her, I prepared myself. I took a course and earned a certification in Mental Health First Aid. I knew the statistics of just how many teens took their life and could rattle them off instantly. I also knew the year Morgan and my father died by suicide, so did 42,771* (American Association of Suicidology) other loved ones. As much knowledge as I had accumulated, I still struggled to confront my own daughter.

The Halloween of my daughter's sophomore year of high school was the turning point. I could no longer wait for someone to step in and help me. I had been unsuccessful in my quest to find a clinician who would take my concerns seriously. We had taken her for mental health assessments, only to be told she didn't need help. To them, I was the overzealous mother frantically trying to get answers to something they deemed unnecessary. My daughter was very good at hiding her illness from the outside world and anyone she didn't want to know. But, I knew the inevitable truth; *My daughter was suicidal and I needed to act immediately.*

Halloween day, I had gone into her room several times trying to get her out of bed, as I had to do many times before. She ended up staying home from school because her depression and anxiety had kept her paralyzed in bed. She couldn't physically move. She was going downhill fast. There was no turning back. I had to do what no parent ever wants to do; *I needed to ask her if she was contemplating taking her own life.* I went into her room, sat beside her on her bed, and asked the dreaded question. She responded, "yes." I asked the following question, which I'd been trained to ask, "Do you have a plan?"

"Yes, Mom." She then detailed how she planned to end her life.

That day was one of the most challenging days of my life. It ranks amongst the most horrifying moments I have had to endure, next to the moment I found out my father took his life by suicide.

Looking back, sitting beside my daughter on that bed was the beginning of many more horrific moments. Including the times my daughter made attempts to harm herself, the multiple times she's been suicidal since then, and the years of struggle, trying to find the right diagnosis, therapy, and medications to help her. It's been five years since the day I asked her that question, and we are still searching for the right treatment to end her suicidal thoughts.

I share my story with you so you know that I have both experienced the emotional impact of suicide from someone who has succeeded, my father, and the anguish of keeping it a bay from someone who is contemplating it, my daughter. I know the fears that come from both ends of the spectrum and understand it from a perspective that enables me to be a lifeline for you and where you are right now. My goal is that, together, we can explore your experience so that we find a way to uncover the wisdom within your story.

Over time, what you have been through will begin to shift from a fearful place to a safe place, and that shift will enable you to share your new perspective with someone with the intention of enlightening and enhancing their life. Telling our stories and sharing our experiences brings people together and helps to soothe the soul through connection. Much of why I wrote this book, and will candidly share my story, is because I want my truth to become a sacred bond between us. I want what I share to help you now in your journey, and give you the strength to one day share your story with someone who needs to hear it. I want you to feel seen, heard, and understood by opening up to your truth.

From sharing your story, a transformation will happen. You will begin to feel that what once burdened you beyond comprehension has been lifted, and you will find a new perspective that will allow peace and grace to return to your life. Until that happens, I'm going to share many stories throughout this book of the lives lost by suicide, and the love that continues beyond physical boundaries, so that you don't feel so alone. Once you release the notion that you're not alone, you can begin to feel more comfortable speaking your truth. The darkness can no longer consume you and restrict you when you give it a voice. Light lives on the other side of sharing, and I encourage you to share when you are ready. In doing so, you can also become a part of the solution to erase the stigma of suicide and heal in a new way.

It is my desire that you find yourself able to rise from the ashes like a Phoenix, and in your re-emergence find solace in sharing your story in a way that inspires healing in you. Of course, this will take time. You may say, *I'll never share my story*, especially if you are early in your grief journey, and that's okay. I never envisioned I'd be sharing stories of suicide and loss within the early years of my journey, but when I was brave enough to share the first time I couldn't believe the response I received and how many people opened up and told me how they had lost a brother, a mother, or a friend. People I had known for a short time would walk up to me and thank me for sharing, and proceed to pour out their own suicide stories. As I continued to share that impact kept growing, and I started to see the ripple effect of my bravery. So I say, keep the door slightly open to the possibility of your story healing both you and someone else.

As you begin to develop your strength and *own your story*, you will find an unbelievable release of shame and guilt by sharing it.

You'll be surprised at how you will create a safe space for others to open up and share their own experience. In the beginning, you may find it easier to tell other people my story, or one of the stories in this book before you can tell your own, the same way I was able to tell Morgan and Christine's story before sharing mine. This book is filled with stories, and one may resonate with you enough to become the catalyst that will break your silence.

My hope is, along the journey you'll find the strength to stand in your story. That as time passes and you begin to heal, parts of your story will emerge like a determined and unstoppable flower pushing its way through a dry, concrete-hard ground, and climbing toward the light, growing with implausible strength.

Healing Moment

To get started on your healing path, this is the perfect moment for you to reflect and envision yourself sharing your story. I understand this may feel scary to you now, and you can't begin to find the words to express what has happened. I remember not knowing how to articulate what I was feeling in the aftermath, but what I found was that the more I put words on paper and spoke to people I felt comfortable sharing my feelings with, the more I began to grow my confidence. I realized that my story was worthy and one that needed to be shared– this is a baby step in that direction. You may find you need to come back to this healing moment more than once to add to your story, including more thoughts and feelings as your story evolves, and that is perfectly fine. What's most important is the process of writing your thoughts about the events unfolding and feeling all the emotions pour onto the page. Take your time with this first Healing Moment, and be kind to yourself as this is your first attempt.

What would be the title of your story? Thinking about your loved one, choose a title that describes your relationship with them, or how they made you feel when they were still alive.

Are there people in your story you want to include like family and friends? What is their connection to you and your loved one? Explain why their relationship is a significant part of your story. Add as many or as few people to your story as you like. If you want the story to be only about you and your relationship with your loved one, that is fine too.

What have the people in your story endured and how would you depict the events that led up to your loved one's death?

What is something you want others to learn from your story? If you think about someone listening to your story, it can help you to decide what you want them to know. For instance, the background of the person, their relationship to your loved one, or if you choose a complete stranger, how would you explain what happened to your loved one?

Now close your eyes, take a deep breath, and imagine yourself telling this story to someone you feel safe sharing it with. By doing this visual process, you will begin to unleash some of the emotional burdens you are carrying, and it will empower you to speak your truth from a place of peace. Eventually, over time, and through practice, you will feel more and more at ease with your story. The story which created who you are as a person, a spouse, a parent, a sibling, and a friend, is waiting to be told. You are this beautiful complex human being all because of that story you've lived and fully experienced. When you feel fear bubble up, remember you are not alone. I'm here with you and so are the loved ones of every suicide death. We know your trepidation, we've experienced it ourselves, but we also know that living in silence is no way to live freely and fully. It's time for you to own your story and love the beauty of its diverse experiences including the ugliness you currently may be feeling. Realize it's your life journey that has uniquely made you who you are. Remember, no one gets through life unscathed and without bumps in the road. Those bumps are what mold us, shape us, and transform us, especially the ones that feel more like a crevasse than a pothole.

Now that you've visualized yourself telling your story to someone, how do you feel? Take some time to write the feelings, thoughts, and fears you released in the process. Does your story feel a bit

lighter? As you continue to visualize yourself telling your story you'll become more comfortable and less fearful.

However much you completed this exercise, and were able to release some of the burden, I want to congratulate you for the courage you have shown by making this a part of your healing. Many people never get to the point of sharing their experience, and this first step you have made by answering these questions and then visualizing yourself sharing your story has made it more of a reality for you.

If you found this difficult, that's okay. Just be willing to come back and try again when you have made more progress through the book.

As you begin to do the healing steps in this book, answers to questions you are pondering will come directly to you, and through the intimate details of the stories of the lives lost too soon, that I share in the upcoming chapters, you will discover a deeper under-standing of the commonalities we each share. By reading those stories you will connect with the struggles and the perseverance, just like I did with Christine and Morgan's story, and gain insight into your own experiences which will allow you to release some of the negative emotions that may be preventing your ability to heal. I believe that by sharing personal stories with others, you will find the answers you have been searching for, and ultimately discover some sense of peace.

This is not to say one story is the same as another, just as no two people grieve the same, or live the same experiences, yet I do hope there will be a common thread you can pull that will help you unwind your deep exploration for answers to help dissolve your pain. I know you feel like you need to know it all now, but please be patient with yourself. Accept that some answers are not for you to know immediately; some things *are better* learned over time and you'll also discover that some answers will never be confirmed and are best to be left unknown. When you feel like you're done seeking, searching, and the yearning subsides, the healing will begin.

Remember, this is a *Healing Book designed to lead you on your path of self-discovery.* As you work your way through it, you will begin to find joy and harmony through connection again. The best part is, we are a community of survivors. We will always have a huge hole in our hearts, but together we can share our stories and find some sense of peace knowing that our stories are *not shameful, or ugly.* They are beautiful stories of life and love, and through them we gain the greatest Strength.

2

TOKENS

"My greatest strength is my vulnerability to share my story
so that others feel brave enough to share theirs."

- CINDY TANK-MURPHY

I've been in and out of therapy throughout my life. Therapy is an integral part of the healing process, and I strongly recommend you find a good grief counselor, spiritual leader, or support group to begin your healing work as soon as possible. Surround yourself with people who support you and acknowledge what you are going through. This isn't the time to retreat or fill the void with unhealthy, self-sabotaging, debilitating behaviors. Therapy is designed to help you navigate the feelings and emotions you are experiencing, and learn coping strategies to help you deal with tough days in a healthier manner.

One type of grief therapy comes in the form of creating a keepsake, such as a memory box with photos, objects, and stories of the bereaved. Placing personal items into a box or memory book, which represents feelings, emotions, and personal thoughts of your loved one will help to put a physical connection with those intangible feelings and provide a personal token of the love shared between two people.

Tokens can help bring forth appreciation for the time you had with your loved one and provide a sense of admiration by memorializing treasured gifts that honor them. I became genuinely connected to the impact and importance of tokens on my second visit with my new therapist, Wendy, when I did something I'd never done before. I told her I had a vision during a recent meditation that I was meant to write this book. *Oops! Did that just slip out of my mouth?* In my excitement, I shared when I first had the epiphany to divulge my story, but now a few days later, the fear had consumed me, all that excitement vanished, and I was frozen in fear again. It felt absolutely paralyzing to be exposed, naked, and sharing my story. I've had this fear of being watched and judged ever since I was a teenager and I caught some boys sneaking around my bedroom window one night, wondering how many times they may have peered into my private room without my knowledge. I grew up on an acreage, where our surroundings were more inaccessible to others. Even when I got older, and lived in the city, I never got used to exposed windows. My husband still thinks I'm crazy when I complain about people looking right into our windows at night. I recently felt exposed when our neighbors cut down their trees that used to cloak my back patio door. If I shower at night, I will keep the lights off, or only dimly lit, even though the windows are completely opaque. From a young age, feeling watched and judged has accumulated a strong mix of anxiety and a fear that my private space is unprotected. I shared this fear with my therapist.

Upon my admission that I suffered from a perceived fear that I'd be negatively judged, embarrassed, and even rejected if I were to share my vulnerable thoughts in a book, my therapist gave me some sound advice which made me rethink this defensive response I've been holding onto since a very young age. Wendy's feedback to me was one I hadn't expected and I was curious why I hadn't considered it myself.

Our conversation went something like this:

Wendy: *"Why do you put so much pressure on this being a book that you have to publish before you have even begun to write it?"*

Me: *"What do you mean?"*

38

Wendy: "It's as if the minute you write something on paper, you fear everyone will see it. What if you considered your book a 'token' for the person, and the family you're writing about? You know, a gift; something to remember their loved one by, something you could give to them and they could hold dear forever."

Me: "Hmmm...that's an interesting concept...You mean, if I just write these stories and then give them to the people I researched and talked to as a gift, I don't have to worry about whether or not I decide sometime down the road to print it or share it with anyone else?"

That got me thinking... *Maybe I don't have to completely expose everything about myself all at once.* Perhaps, I could slowly allow people to enter my private space and peer into my personal thoughts. Over time, I could decide whether or not to show anyone my writing and reveal some of the inner feelings I have. Maybe I could see how overcoming my fears and limiting ideas would in fact benefit others more than my own personal apprehension. Wow. I liked that idea.

With that in mind, I ended my therapy session feeling energized and ready to step into my calling once again. I realized I needed to listen and trust this undeniable desire to share my story. It was the catalyst for the format of this book and inspiration to practice what I knew to be true: my strength lies within my vulnerability.

As the months went on and my book began to evolve, I knew my story was not the only one that needed to be told. Thousands of stories could be in this book because there are thousands of accounts of families dealing with the devasting loss of loved ones to suicide. However, I have chosen the ones that I feel will teach you an approach to help overcome your grief and benefit your desire to heal. I share these additional stories as 'tokens' of hope and connection. They will provide a form of solidarity, similar to a candlelight vigil that brings people together in the midst of a tragedy and unites us as a community of survivors.

I believe tokens are a necessary part of surviving grief and mending the wounds that are deep and difficult to heal without attention and care. Creating your own token is the beginning of easing the trauma and allowing your mind and body to emotionally and physically breathe and relax. It will help you feel more connected to the person you loved and give you positive memories to hold onto forever.

Healing Moment

Find a box or scrapbook and create a sacred keepsake of items that remind you of your loved one. You may have photos, movie tickets, love letters, or gifts that have significant meaning to you. It could be any symbol that represents the affection you had for this person. Anything that reminds you in a positive way, or makes you feel more connected to the one you have lost. Tokens can be big and small, expensive and rare, or simple and random. There is no right or wrong kind of token. It just has to mean something to you.

What tokens do you want to place inside your box?

_____

_____

_____

_____

What do those tokens mean to you?

_____

_____

_____

_____

Those tokens are now for you to cherish and revisit whenever you feel disconnected from your loved one. They will help ground you in love, remind you of the good times you spent together, and assist you in times you find yourself regressing in your healing journey. Hold the tokens in your hand, feel their touch, essence, and the love they possess, and allow them to help return that love to you.

Since tokens are a large part of the healing process, I wanted to add some very special tokens of love in this book in the form of a caring tribute to foster love and understanding for you and those you have lost. I have done this by including some token chapters dedicated to LeRoy, Morgan, Jay, Lourdes, and Tyrone. Telling their story is my heart-felt token to their family whom I met with and interviewed so I could share their loved one's story with you. I hope they cherish the gift of my token as much as I cherish writing it, and, in turn, you gain a deeper understanding of a token of love and the gift within each and every person's story. You will find these tokens amidst the chapters, highlighted and showcased in their own unique and beautiful way. I share them as a way to remind us that we all have a story and that a story can heal.

3

OBITUARIES

"That it will never come again is what makes life so sweet."

– EMILY DICKINSON

Honoring your Loved One

Death, and Life. The two co-exist and are not the opposite of one another. Author Kahlil Gibran once said, "For life and death are one, even as the river and the sea are one." American culture memorializes our loved ones with funerals, eulogies, and obituaries. They are all an essential part of the healing process. An obituary is unique in that it honors both the deceased and the living survivors. While usually written by the family, obituaries memorialize the life story of the deceased, and can provide a loving remembrance that will live on indefinitely.

My husband is obsessed with obituaries. I say this lovingly. I believe he finds solace in reading them. He regularly checks the funeral home websites to see who has passed. I believe it's a way for him to connect with his hometown roots and feel a sense of peace with the ending of life.

Maybe there is something about seeing the summaries of life on paper that makes a person feel better about their own mortality. Knowing that people were loved and respected based on the words written in a newspaper or funeral home website provides a sense of acceptance, and peace of mind that one day his own life will be memorialized in a similar loving manner.

I myself feel that obituaries signify an important part of the grieving process. While many believe that an obituary's sole purpose is to inform the public about someone's death, I believe there is a far more powerful purpose. The act of writing the obituary, or life summary of someone, whether solo or with the help of family, helps to solidify a written acknowledgement of the death. Many grief counselors will say that the first stage of grief is denial, so by acknowledging the death in this way you are taking the first step toward acceptance and healing.

You may have not thought about obituaries in either of these ways, but I am sure that you can understand why it is an important part of life and death. We might not even appreciate the healing benefits of the obituary writing process, however, it plays a significant role.

Changing the Narrative

When a loved one dies by suicide, it's often quite rare that their obituary will state the cause of their death. In our family, we didn't share my father's cause of death in his obituary. At the time, we weren't aware of how impactful it could have been to do so. We were in shock and going through the emotions of disbelief and denial.

I recently spoke to a friend who mentioned she often wonders about the cause of death for someone who dies unexpectedly so young. She said that statistically, it's more common for a young person to die in an accident or by suicide than any other cause. According to the Centers for Disease Control and Prevention (CDC), and quoted on America's Health Rankings, 'In 2018, suicide was the second-leading cause of death among 10- to 24 year-olds.' The World Health Organization (WHO) statistics ranked suicide as the 'fourth-leading cause of death among 15- to 19 year-olds,' globally in 2019.

My friend went on to say that she felt sadness for the families who feel ashamed to list the cause of death when it's due to suicide. I found her perspective interesting, however, I understand why people don't want to say their loved one died that way, especially in the early phase of their loss. They are still trying to comprehend it themselves, and it's just too difficult to talk about, let alone ingrain on paper when the wounds are so fresh and deep. They may feel ashamed, filled with guilt, and overwhelmed by the blame and confusion. I know that's how I felt.

Yet, my friend's comment intrigued me and I started to wonder, *what if every death by suicide was honored in the same respectful way as a death of a terminally-ill person who is honored after their hard-fought battle is lost to their disease? Or, possibly similar to the respect of a soldier passing in battle or the admiration of a first responder who succumbed in an unforeseen disaster?* Suicide can sometimes be the outcome of an illness, we've just chosen to call it something other than a passing or death the way we do with other illnesses. Mental illness **is** an illness. What if we started to look at it no differently than cancer, diabetes, a stroke or heart disease? Wouldn't we write an obituary that factually stated how hard our loved ones fought their mental illness to the end?

Representative Jamie Raskin, of Maryland, lost his 25-year-old son to suicide on New Year's Eve, 2020. The family spoke openly about Tommy's battle with depression and the cause of his death as suicide. A tribute from his family included Tommy's final message to them. It read:

"Please forgive me. My illness won today. Please look after each other, the animals, and the global poor for me. All my love, Tommy."

How personal, yet so honest, and profoundly beautiful that they felt compelled to share his final goodbye with the world. It certainly made an impact on many friends and family at the time, including me. It made me wonder, *what if everyone who lost a loved one to suicide was so brave? What if we had listed my father's cause of death in his obituary?*

44

It may have read something like this;

"LeRoy, a devoted husband, and father, lost his lifelong battle with depression on July 22, 2014, and decided his own exit from this lifetime."

I sometimes ask myself, what if everyone's obituary who died by suicide was written with the same honesty, fortitude, and honor as Tommy Raskin's family chose to share in their darkest days following their loss? Would stating his cause of death help change the narrative of his life? Would people start to realize the breadth and magnitude of his mental illness?

What type of change could such devotion to telling the truth have on the general population and would it make suicide less taboo? I believe it would create a significant paradigm shift. One in which the world would start to listen to the cries for help, the devastation of mental illness, and the need for massive changes in our healthcare system in regard to treatment for behavioral health patients. I believe lifting the stigma would give permission and allow those currently suffering in silence to voice their pain safely and get the help they desperately need.

I envision a world in which depression and suicidal ideation are taken more seriously from a healthcare perspective, especially if it was studied with the same financial backing as cancer research. We would have better outcomes for the millions of people struggling every day with their will to survive. Suicide can be preventable with treatments such as therapy and medication, so perhaps we could save even more lives by increasing awareness of how prolific suicide is becoming? These are some of the many thoughts and questions that flood my mind because I know that the only way things will change is through awareness, openness to change, and dedication to *making* the change happen.

When families gather to write the obituary of their loved one, together they are creating a memory, and a story of their devotion and connection with the deceased to be shared with the world. What they may not realize is that the obituary writing process helps them heal. That's why writing an honest account of your loved one's life and nature of death can be an extremely beneficial part of mending the distress. There is a level of reassurance that your loved one, in that moment, was 'seen' in the world, just as the Raskins wanted to make it known that their son, Tommy, was a victim of his disease and seen for the full spectrum of his life.

Writing an obituary for your loved one may help you shift your mindset and relieve any negative emotion you have attached to their death. It may lift the shame of secrecy that you've held within and give you the ability to write your honest emotions and personal truth. Take some time to recall the things you enjoyed most about them and how those memories make you feel. Recount their life and how you want to remember them. Be genuine about how you want the obituary to read and what it shares.

Healing Moment

Read or Write an Obituary for your loved one.

Find your loved one's obituary and read it out loud to remember their accomplishments, hobbies, livelihood, life moments, and family. Save it in a place where you can read it whenever you feel like honoring them. You may want to frame the obituary as a keepsake or laminate it as a token for a memory box.

If your loved one never had an obituary written after their death, this is your opportunity to write one. In the space below, write about your loved one. It doesn't have to be formal or follow any particular template. Instead, focus on writing about your loved one's hobbies, life interests, accomplishments, family, and what made them special to you. And, if you are ready, write the true cause of their death.

OBITUARIES

It is wonderful that you took the time to honor yourself and your loved one with an obituary of this nature. When we take the time to write our thoughts and feelings we allow them to move through us and dissipate, bringing forth healing and understanding. This may have been the first time you have shared in this way, and, if so, I honor your effort. If things are still too raw or unsettling, come back to this exercise when you are ready.

In the spirit of both tokens and obituaries, I'd like to share with you the obituary of my father; the one that was published upon his death, and the token I wrote through my healing.

LeRoy Tank was a beloved father, husband, and friend to many and in sharing both of these renditions, I hope you get a better understanding of his life and our loss. I also hope that you can see that both versions of his story are here to help you know that true healing comes in being honest with ourselves and with the one that passed.

A Token Sharing of

LEROY

September 9, 1948 - July 22, 2014

LeRoy A. Tank, age 65 of New Hampton, Iowa, passed away on Tuesday, July 22, 2014 at his home in New Hampton.

LeRoy Arthur Tank was born on September 9, 1948 to Harold and Mabel (Lewig) Tank in New Hampton, IA. He was raised in Lawler until the sixth grade when his family moved to New Hampton. LeRoy was a 1966 graduate of New Hampton High School. Upon graduating, LeRoy began his career in the masonry business working for Tank and Sons Masonry. In 1968, LeRoy was drafted into the United States Army and later received his honorable discharge. On August 23, 1969, LeRoy was united in marriage to Sandra K. Zmoos, of Waucoma, at Trinity Lutheran Church in New Hampton. To that union four children were born: Cindy, Jenny, Krisy and Jason. Soon after their marriage, LeRoy began Tank Brothers Masonry with his brother, Alan. Later, he started Tank Masonry. LeRoy always took great pride in his family. He especially enjoyed taking his grand-children for rides in the golf cart. LeRoy's hobbies included fishing, working in his shop, attending auctions, and collecting antiques. He also restored vintage automobiles and tractors. He loved the Arts and enjoyed creating music, ceramics, drawing and architecture. LeRoy had a love for animals, always supporting humane societies. He was a member of Trinity Lutheran Church and the Iowa Barn Foundation.

LeRoy is survived by his wife, Sandy of New Hampton; daughters, Cindy (Kevin Murphy) Tank-Murphy of Naperville, IL, Jenny (Paul Freeborn) Tank of Naperville, IL, Krisy (Joel Godfryt) Tank-Godfryt of Sahuarita, AZ; son, Jason Tank of Chicago, IL; grandchildren, Avery, Addison, Paxton, Lydia and Brayden; sister, Lois Hackman of Waterloo, IA; brothers, Wendell (LaVonne) Tank and Alan (Karen) Tank both of New Hampton, IA; sisters-in-law, Lurlean Tank and Jean Tank, both of New Hampton; brother-in-law Clarence Haupt, Jr. of Sumner, IA, as well as numerous nieces and nephews.

He was preceded in death by his parents; siblings; LaVerne Tank, Helen Haupt, Arnold Tank, Ruth Tank and Walter Tank.

This is my father's obituary. It was written by our family with the help of our funeral director a day after his death. When I first read it, I felt like it encapsulated his life beautifully based on the amount of time we collectively put into writing it and considering the intense grief and shock we were dealing with at the time of its origination.

As I've explained previously, I will be telling stories to help us connect in solidarity and in order for you to gain an understanding that you are not alone. By reading these stories you will see similarities and ties between you and your loved ones. There is a commonality that all of our loved ones have, and that is they endured a pain so deep, so emotional, and so complex, that they knew no other way to rid themselves of it. **It took all their strength to live.**

After my father passed, I found some peace in knowing my story wasn't all that unique and that what I was going through was something many people who had lost a loved one to suicide had experienced before me. I made connections with my story by reading memoirs of suicide survivors, talking to other survivors in group settings, and most recently by reading the stories shared on social media group sites specifically for suicide survivors. What is most notable about reading stories of others' loss, is that for a split second, you forget about your own loss. It gives you a small, mini pause to associate the loss you've just read about and how it impacted someone other than yourself. In that pause, we can feel empathy for another human being going through a similar situation, and when we can empathize with someone else's pain, we can begin to find empathy for ourselves and see more clearly that holding onto negative emotions like blame, guilt, shame, and anger against ourselves is not helping us heal.

The Story of LeRoy, Father. Told by his Daughter, Me.

Since this entire book was written based on the gifts my father gave me, I wanted you to know a bit more about the man and his life. I feel sharing his story and the many layers of him will shine a light on his illness, and also on how amazing he was as my dad. I'm proud of his strength, his perseverance, his hard work ethic, his dedication to his family, and how much he taught me in more ways than one. There is so much positive goodness to share about his genuine love of life and the love he had for his family.

I suppose my father's story should be the easiest token for me to write, but sometimes the one closest to us is the most difficult. In writing this story I began to uncover more about this man who used to encourage me, prepared me with valuable life skills, like changing a flat tire, and sharing his philosophy with me, "do the things you love, and get rid of burdens in your life," although he didn't feel comfortable enough to share his darkest burdens with me. It helped me to understand that his life was filled with more ups than downs, and I wanted to once again honor his life and my life in it.

My father was a workaholic, rising in the morning by 3 am on work days and coming home late in the evening. His work was hard and labor intensive. He was a masonry contractor and his scarred, sandpaper-calloused hands proved to me as a little girl that Daddy's work was not easy. His touch felt more like a prickly cactus than the soft caress I craved as he'd hold me on his lap. It's safe to say that he knew all too well the truth in the saying, "An idle mind is the devil's workshop." He kept his mind and body busy, with work being his way of keeping the devil at bay.

I called him an alcoholic many times throughout his life, even though he technically could stop drinking. Alcohol just happened to be his drug of choice to self-medicate and quiet the constant chatter of thoughts that possessed his mind. He was a loving man, caring deeply for animals. We always had pets around the house, not just cats and dogs. We had rabbits, chickens, pigs, and miniature horses throughout the years. Dad sometimes went to a farm auction and bought the animals no one else wanted. He couldn't bear to see them slaughtered for no other reason than rejection. I remember the first and last time my dad ever hunted. When he brought home his wild animals he had killed to feast on for our meal, we must have made it clear we disapproved. I know I cried. Knowing him, he cried along with me and vowed never to hunt again if it made his "first love" so sad. From that day on, he rarely, if ever, pulled the trigger on a gun, with the exception of his last day on earth.

As much as he cared deeply and loved his family, he wasn't the dad who wanted to be around for the parent-teacher conferences, dance and music recitals, or basketball games. Those social activities would have caused anxiety, and the bleacher seats were not conducive to a man whose back lifted heavy concrete blocks every day. He needed to work hard, provide for his family, and if there was time to squeeze in anything else, it was to keep busy with a hobby that would either relax him or engage him in reckless behavior that could potentially get him into trouble. He ran at two opposing speeds. Either fast like a Chevrolet Camaro on the race track, or at a dead stop like a Chevy truck sitting on cinder blocks. Looking back now, I can see patterns of potential bipolar disorder, but he was never diagnosed.

His complex story begins with an upbringing by parents who I didn't get to know that well. Unfortunately, we didn't participate in as many family gatherings with them as we did on my mom's side of the family. Perhaps, it was partially due to the age gap between some of his siblings, or the bad blood over the family business. My grandfather was a contractor, and my dad and his older brothers began working for their father at the early age of fourteen. Some of the brothers left school altogether to work solely for my grandfather's business. Dad had always wanted to attend college to become an architect. It was his dream, but unfortunately that was not his father's dream. My dad felt like his older brothers never forgave him when he left the family business to start his own competing business. I think he always felt like the black sheep of his family.

I've heard rumors, which I don't know to be true, that my grandmother struggled with depression and may have left her children, at varying ages, to get away from it all for small lengths of time. I can envision her storming out of the little pink house on Chestnut Street, with a suitcase in hand, and driving off in her burgundy station wagon to the next town to stay a night or two in a motel, but I have no idea if there's any truth to my imagination. What I do know for fact is that she dealt with some heavy life struggles, losing two young children to diphtheria the same year, in 1944. Knowing these difficulties she and my grandfather endured helps to understand the complexity of the family and perhaps some of the secrets that haunted it for generations long before I came to be.

My father met my mother shortly after his grandfather died. My great-grandfather, Charles, had died suddenly of a heart attack. He and my great-grandmother, Louise, lived on a farm not far from the farmhouse my mother grew up in and lived at the time with her parents. My great-grandmother was afraid to sleep in the house alone after her husband passed, so she asked my mother, who was a teenager at the time, to come and stay the night with her. My father came to visit his grandmother on one of those nights my mom was there. From all accounts, it was love at first sight. My mother says she had never seen a more handsome young man.

Soon after meeting, they began dating. This was 1965 in the midst of Vietnam. Dad was drafted in 1968 and honorably discharged not long after basic training due to an apparent mental breakdown. I find it hard to envision him being drafted to a war he believed he would never return from as many of those young men believed. He never spoke of that time in his life. He wouldn't even allow us to watch the television show M.A.S.H. I think he despised how anyone could find humor in the midst of a war. It definitely made a lasting impact on him, and one that changed the trajectory of his life forever.

I came along in the summer of 1971. I was the first child and his "first love," as he fondly called me. One of my favorite photos is of me at the age of one, sitting on the tanned bare back of my father who appears to be completely exhausted from a day of hard work. The hand-written caption on the back of the photo reads, "Cindy just woke Daddy." I look like a very happy baby in the photo, but my father looks like a scared twenty-four-year-old wondering how he is going to provide for his young family. However, he was always a great provider and worked harder than anyone I have known.

He poured himself into his work and probably felt the most at ease when he was working hard in the sun. He was handsome with his dark skin, baby blue eyes, and tall, thin frame. His skin was sun-kissed, golden brown and to me he looked a lot like a young Elvis Presley, his hair slicked back and always in place. He had the most jovial laugh of anyone I knew. I hear his laugh to this day as if he's standing right next to me. When things weren't so stable, he sunk into the deepest, darkest hole of depression. I swear I could see directly down that hole just by looking into his eyes.

My memories of my childhood years aren't as vivid as my husband's memories of his childhood, at least the memories I want to remember. My husband can tell stories of family trips as early as four or five years old. Me? I have the great memories etched in my mind from flipping through massive family photo albums. We have plenty of images of us living a perfectly normal happy life, I just don't seem to recall them like my husband does from memory. There were always smiles and lots of laughter in our house from the photo album. I know we had tons of love around us growing up. I remember hiding under the bedsheets with my dad and sister as he would pretend that cowboys were looking for us. They'd ride up on their horses – clip-clop, clip-clop, clip-clop. In his low cowboy voice, he'd act out the conversations as we all hid in silence so as not to be found. We'd giggle and laugh until his cowboys would find us, and then we'd scream! I sometimes wonder if memories like that are only a movie I play over in my head because I pieced them together from the photos in those albums or if they were as real as they seem in my mind's eye. It's a bit foggy, like much of my childhood years.

Where the fog of recollection seems to lift are those late nights staying up with my mom, keeping her company until my father would come home, and then I remember the fights. Those nights, unfortunately, come through more vividly than the happy times. I know this because there aren't any photos of the fist-shaped hole in the wall, the spittle coming from his mouth in rage, or the crying and pleading my mother would do. Those photos never made it into our albums and yet I can recall them vividly.

The oldest of four children, I felt a certain responsibility at a young age to protect. I was just turning 16 when my father had his second known mental breakdown. I don't know if he was actually diagnosed at the time, as I was still a child, but I did know he was sent away to a hospital to recover for weeks. The stress left on my mother was too much for her to bear, and she ended up joining him at the same hospital. It was a very dark time in all of our lives.

Like our family photo albums, time passed, everyone persevered, and I went to college. By then, my father had accumulated a couple of DUIs and spent a few nights in jail for driving under the influence. His business collapsed, and he slowly crept into an even darker place. I felt guilty and responsible for my siblings, who were still home and dealing with a new kind of chaos. A dad swinging back and forth through depression and the lack of a steady income added an extra layer of pressure.

We made several attempts to get him help throughout the years.

This is probably the most frustrating and saddening thing about having a loved one struggling with mental illness. As an adult child, I had no recourse to help him. If he didn't pose a threat to himself or anyone else, our hands were tied. The shortage of assistance wasn't due to a lack of trying. Everywhere we turned for help, we were told the same thing. "If he doesn't want help, we can't do anything. Call us when he's about to hurt someone or himself, then we can step in."

I lived more than five hours away, and it was impossible to know his mental state at any given moment. My husband and our children would make trips to visit and see the signs of struggle and chaos but didn't know what to do. Just when things would seem hopeless, it would turn around as if nothing was ever wrong. We'd have family visits that were filled with water parks and lovely family dinners. We played the part of a middle-class, cohesive family, but each of us had a little piece of security and normalcy taken from us. A small chip that most people couldn't see unless they looked closely.

It was the year my nephew was born when I got the call that would change our loving cohesive family unit. I picked up the phone and was greeted on the other end by my mother panting, "He's going to kill me, Cindy!" That night I was paralyzed in fear. I could hear my father pull the phone away from my mother and throw it across the room. I sat helpless, listening to thumping and yelling in the background, not able to comprehend the situation or respond to it. I braced for a sound I was frightened I might hear, the loud discharge of a gun. I remember lying in a curled position on the beige carpet in my home office, with the phone tightly pressed against my ear, just listening, while tears streamed from my eyes. I couldn't pick my limp body off the floor. I've heard of people frozen in terror, but this was the first time I had experienced anything like it. Having no way to fight or flee the situation, my overwhelmed mind shut down, unable to process what was going on inside my childhood home, so all I could do was lie curled up on the floor like a child, helpless. Finally, after what felt like time standing still, I got the nerve to react and called the police. That was the last night my mom and dad lived together in the same house.

As the years went on, he checked out of family gatherings, mostly out of choice. His depression was at a critical point where self-isolation and dissociation took over. He was in constant pain, both physically and mentally. I remember when I realized just how much pain he was in as he'd groaned at the simplest movements like slipping on his shoes or getting up from his chair. I'd call and beg him to come to visit us, but his excuse was always about how his back would not hold up for the five-hour car ride. The masonry work had taken a significant toll on him, and I understood his unwillingness to come even though he yearned to see his family. He adored his grandkids. So much so, he would push through his constant pain to take them for rides on his dilapidated golf cart – he never touched a golf club – but he picked up an old cart from a farm auction. Probably the best purchase he ever made. Oh, how he loved the freedom he got in that cart and time with his grandkids. In those moments, you could see a sparkle in his eyes; they weren't so bottomless in those brief moments. He also enjoyed giving others small random acts of kindness, often anonymously, with little or no desire to be thanked. He just wanted to spread kindness, joy, and love. One story shared by a neighbor after his death makes me proud to call him my father.

> "Very sorry to hear about LeRoy. I lived in two houses to the east of him. One year before Halloween, I came home from work to find 3 pumpkins on my picnic table. I knew they came from LeRoy, so my daughter and I carved them, and we took one back over to his house. He wasn't home when we took it over, so we hope he enjoyed it. He will be missed as a neighbor."

He was a gentle, kind, and giving person. Many people were lucky to have him as a friend and a son, and I was lucky to have him as my father. He fought dauntlessly with those damn demons his entire life.

Life can beat you down one too many times. During a phone call with him in the spring of his final year with us, he said to me, "Cindy, I don't think I can go on much longer." I started to cry. I knew exactly what this meant, yet I couldn't comprehend that he was serious. He said, "I know, I can't do that to you all." We never spoke of it again.

Mom and Dad had been living in separate places for several years, and Dad was lonely. He wanted nothing more than for Mom to move back home with him. The opportunity would present itself as a possibility in the summer of 2014. Mom, who had been living with her father, needed to find a new home. Her brother was buying the farm and would soon be moving into the home with his family, and we needed to find Mom a new place to live. My grandfather was months shy of turning 90. She had been a great companion to him, but it was time for her younger brother and his wife to care for him. We discussed buying her a home in town, but ultimately, she decided to move back to where she raised her four children. She and Dad had formed a friendship in recent years and the two were able to spend long periods of time together without anger or resentment over the past. Even though they hadn't lived in the same house for six years, Mom would stop over multiple times each week to talk, drop off some groceries, help with his laundry, and visit their home, which she had put so much of her life into.

As long as Mom felt safe around him, we were willing to give the situation a try. It was reassuring to think that two people who still had a love for one another could put aside the past and become good companions. Besides, they both leaned on each other for support even with all that had happened in the past. We began to decorate the spare bedroom into a cozy room for Mom. My sister and I made trips back to our hometown and helped clean the house and prep it for her return. We felt like this was a good compromise for both of them. Dad would have companionship and Mom would be able to live in the home which she had taken such care to ensure was cheerful, warm and comfortable for her family. The move was planned for late July that summer.

As we prepared for her move back home, our entire family, including my sister who lived in Tucson with her husband, gathered for the 4th of July weekend in Illinois. It would be the first time we would all be meeting my nephew, the youngest grandchild. My dad even agreed to come. It was lovely to hear that he was willing to make the five-hour car ride, despite the pain he would endure with his back. However, he loved his grandkids and wasn't going to miss meeting his youngest for the first time. He and Mom drove out together that weekend.

I will never forget that weekend. The minute they arrived at my house, I asked Dad how his back was from the long trip. Expecting to hear him groan and say how stiff and sore he was, his reply was a sign I missed. "Feeling fine. No problems here." We spent a wonderful weekend together. It was as if my parents were a happily married couple and I recall thinking that weekend about how much in love they looked and acted. He sat with his arm around her as the two of them laughed and listened to music together. What was happening? Were all our previous concerns total nonsense? Maybe after a certain amount of time, two people can put all their pain and anger aside, and be able to live the rest of their lives together as a couple.

That weekend he talked more than I'd heard him talk in years. He was sharing all sorts of wisdom to his grandkids. We took a beautiful family photo, one in which he even gave us a half-smile. I wish I would have paid closer attention to what he had to share.

When the time came for everyone to leave. I had a strange feeling. I hugged my father for what seemed to be longer than an average hug goodbye. I certainly didn't mind. He seemed to be in a great place, one he hadn't been in years. I told him I'd see him soon. My sister, who was returning to Tucson, felt something odd too. "Did Dad tremble when he hugged you goodbye? What was that?" she questioned. It wouldn't be until a few weeks later that we'd know the answer.

Dad took his life on July 22, 2014, from a shotgun wound. My mom found him hunched over a chair in the backyard. He didn't leave a note. He left us with his final goodbye weeks earlier, and we will never be the same.

I believe my father had made his decision to end his life before he came to visit us one final time. His visit was filled with calmness, affection, and a false reassurance that he was well, when in reality, I believe he had come to peace with the idea of ending his life, ending his pain, and leaving his lasting impression with us. I share this story with you so you can grasp the idea that there are things that we can not always understand about our loved ones or see coming. You may be wondering why someone would have calmness before the end. This subtle warning sign of a person suddenly becoming calm after a period of depression or moodiness is well documented. After a period of depression or agitation, a person may suddenly become peaceful and seem as if they aren't struggling anymore. The calmness that comes over them can be deceiving to people around them. They may also prepare their personal affairs or give away prized possessions, things my dad did prior to his death.

I didn't know these subtle warning signs before losing my dad, but I'm glad to be aware of them now. Knowing these signs after the fact, makes me feel more empowered to help ensure I will see them if I'm ever in the position to help save someone else's life. I can't help my dad anymore, but knowing I can potentially help save someone else, gives me purpose. I know that in sharing my story I can help educate you so you can also feel empowered and one day allows your story to serve a similar purpose.

Get rid of the things that burden your life and
do the things you have a passion for.
-LEROY A. TANK

YEARN

"Where you used to be, there is a hole in the world, which I find myself constantly walking around in the daytime, and falling in at night. I miss you like hell."

~ EDNA ST. VINCENT MILLAY

Stage One - The Yearning Phase

In the weeks following Dad's death, I felt like I was living in a fog. My husband and I had bought a new house and the move was already planned, a week after his funeral. There was so much to do. Besides showing our home to prospective buyers and packing for the move, one of the important things to accomplish was school registration for my daughters in a new district. I remember sitting in the registration office, filling out paperwork, and feeling my eyes begin to tear up. I thought to myself, *No one here knows what I've been through in the past two weeks.* They were all going about their lives, while I was sitting there destroyed by massive grief and feeling like an 800-lb gorilla was sitting on top of me crushing me to my core. Everywhere I went I felt disconnected and invisible to everyone around me. I couldn't complete a simple task without being distracted, forgetting what I was about to do, or completely losing my composure. In a split second, I'd be brought to tears from a song playing in the grocery store or seeing a dad holding his daughter's hand.

I began to ask myself all sorts of questions. *Why didn't he leave a note? Why did he act so happy just a few weeks earlier? Why didn't I do more for him? Did he suffer? What was he thinking at that moment? Was he scared or relieved in those final seconds? Why did he refuse to seek help? Why, why, why?* I yearned to know why my father took his life. I searched for answers about his life that would make me proud of him, not the disappointment and shame I was feeling. I tried to process and comprehend how he could leave us this way. All I felt was alone and isolated begging to know, *what could I have done differently? When he gave me signs he was struggling, why hadn't I done more?* I even longed for the ugly details of his past, which I didn't really want to know, but they kept creeping into my head. *How could I stop these intrusive thoughts?*

What I began to notice in the early stages of my grief was that the yearning kept me from processing the situation and moving forward—seeking answers I would never find kept me in a place of being *stuck*. When all I could do was think about the *what*, the *why*, and the *how*, I couldn't see the future. I couldn't fathom how I might be able to live my life without him and without the heavy grief weighing me down. It wasn't until I stopped questioning everything that I began to see through the fog.

I have come to realize our human need for acceptance and understanding causes us to ruminate about things unknown. Even though we consciously acknowledge that the search for answers is futile, we still find ourselves rummaging through every thought, moment, and exchange of words to find the answers that are not always there. What we don't recognize is that when we let go of the hunger to know, we are usually fed the answer intuitively. Through a deeper realization and at a point of knowing and surrender, we can come to a place of realization that we've held the answer the entire time.

If you find you are currently stuck asking all sorts of questions, it's a natural part of the process. Everyone I talk to who's lost someone they love to suicide has been through the yearning phase, wondering why it happened or if the answer is out there. There is no time limit for the yearning phase, and I'm sorry that I can't tell you how long it will last for you. It may never entirely go away, but those who are years removed from their loss also often say they've come to some sort of acceptance in order to move forward and the yearning subsides.

Desiring answers to questions is innate, however, I will let you in on a little secret; I, like many people I've talked to, began to heal only *after* I stopped aching for the answers. I found that once I released my insatiable need and accepted there were no answers to the vast questions I held, I began to come to terms with what Dad was feeling and thinking, and those thoughts would come to me naturally in my quiet time. When I accepted that some things are not for me to know in this lifetime, the healing started and I began to feel more at ease. I could feel and sense what I needed to accept in order for me to have peace of mind. Peace and calmness came to me more easily when I stopped questioning everything constantly. Over time, my yearning shifted from feeling like there was a void I couldn't fill, to remembering the priceless memories with my dad, and I began to smile, chuckle, and beam from those cherished gifted remnants of the man I loved.

Neither grief nor yearning is a linear path, as I found out the hard way. I thought everything was behind me after eight years since his death, but in all honesty, I've had moments where I've cursed my father for *passing this terrible disease onto my daughter* as if he somehow is pulling puppet strings from above. There are similarities in his life that have started to unfold for my daughter. Genetic history is often a key to unlocking not only the disorder but also acquiring the correct treatment. While I won't punish myself for what I couldn't do for my father, I will never stop fighting to find a treatment that works for my child. I will do my utmost best to ensure that she lives a much better life than my father was able to achieve.

Do I live with the fear of losing her to suicide? Of course I do, but I have come to reconcile the fact that I can't live my life on *what-if* scenarios. None of us are promised tomorrow. A tragic event, such as a car accident, could just as easily take her from me. It's not in my control. When I finally recognized how finite and fragile life is, no matter how attentive and deliberate we may be, I could release the worry of the unknown. I have no authority to predict any particular death. It is inevitable that I will experience more loss in this lifetime, and I must have faith that I can survive whatever life cultivates for me.

Perhaps things were spiraling out of control in your life with your loved one, or you may have been in the dark and had no awareness that something was wrong. It doesn't matter what you witnessed or didn't see coming. If your loved one didn't want you to know what was going on, there was a reason they chose not to tell you. For the same reasons you can't blame a toddler for touching a burning stove if they've never been burned by one, you can not blame yourself for not knowing your loved one was struggling. You couldn't know what suicidal thoughts were percolating to the surface. You can only be responsible for what you know at any given time, and punishing yourself for the things you didn't recognize or consider to be of concern isn't helpful to you or anyone at this point.

For someone experiencing suicidal ideation, the terms the medical profession uses, the self-loathing thought patterns, and the tricks the mind plays on its victims become all-consuming and leave no room for rational thinking. For me, I knew things were bad with my father. I was aware that he was in a lot of pain, both physically and mentally. I was conscious of the fact that he was potentially suicidal, or at least ready to give up. He told me a few months before his death when he stated, "I don't think I can go on much longer, Cindy." Having this knowledge was terrifying, and I didn't know what to say or do at that moment. No one had taught me how to respond to such a situation, so I shouldn't blame myself for not having the knowledge to react differently. Even if I had reacted more proactively, I am not sure it would have changed the outcome. He had refused to accept help so many times before that I was led to believe that there was nothing more I could do for him.

After his passing, I couldn't stop thinking about my lack of acknowledging his need for professional help. *What could I have done differently? Why didn't I force him to seek medical treatment one more time? If only I'd pushed harder. I wasn't the only one who knew he was suffering. Why didn't someone else step in to get him help?* He told me he could never do that to us, so I believed him.

I have accepted that I couldn't have changed the outcome. I could have chosen to live with that guilt believing if I tried harder to save him, he'd still be alive. But ultimately, there is no way of knowing whether my efforts would have been successful. So instead, I choose to release all the guilt as it serves no one. I choose to release any responsibility for his choices. His life was his. He decided what was best for him.

Moving Through The Yeaning.

During a recent suicide grief meeting I attended, a mom spoke about how she was searching for answers to why her son took his life. She had every reason to have a strong yearning to know what was going on in the last minutes of his life. The day he died, she had driven him to his therapy session in a downtown highrise. She couldn't understand what had happened during that session to have caused him to leave the therapist's office and jump to his death in the street below, while she sat waiting in the car for his appointment to end.

This grieving mother spoke of how he used to tell her that he felt something was physically wrong with him. She was a nurse and she wanted to solve the mystery of what was ailing her son and would cause him to take his life. Her husband sat quietly next to her listening to her talk about how if she could just determine what his health problems were, it would give her some sort of answer and perhaps some peace. When she finished, he turned to her and said, "Why do you care to know what was physically wrong with him? It doesn't matter. It won't bring him back."

She was still in the yearning phase of her grief. She was still seeking answers to questions that no one could answer. She was stuck on wanting to know the *reason*. Her husband had started to make amends with the yearning period, realizing that no matter what he may or may not find out, it wouldn't impact anything in their current reality. Having the knowledge wouldn't change the outcome.

Our timeline for healing is often unique and doesn't match our spouses, children, siblings, or other family members' journey. This can cause significant stress on a marriage or family relationship. The one still yearning wants to know why and the one who has accepted that there isn't always an answer, struggles to communicate, and this is because two people are at different points in the grief cycle. What is important is to honor and support each other no matter where they are in their grief.

In my personal process, journaling my feelings has been transformational and helped me to achieve clarity and cope with the grief that often lingers. The process of expressing the thoughts and stress I was harboring gave me a sense of closure and enabled me to release some tension. You may be holding onto similar emotions, and I can guarantee you that it's not serving you. In fact, I may be so bold as to say they may be indirectly hurting you. Yearning for things you can't obtain closure for and wanting to understand the inexplicable can only lead to angst.

One way to help alleviate the negative thought pattern and feelings is to write a letter to your loved one who passed. Some research, including that of Harvard Health, suggests that writing out your deepest emotions can help you improve your mood, immune system, and well-being. You might benefit greatly by picking up a pen and writing to your loved one. Write down how you feel about them leaving you and why you feel that way. You might be triggered into a powerful release of emotions, and it's okay to let each emotion flow. Let the tears roll down your cheeks, and write as each and every thought comes to you. Often the most effective writing comes in the form of a stream of consciousness; an unstructured, inner monologue that is uninterrupted as your feelings and thoughts come to you and as you write them on the page. Use this unfiltered form of sharing to release any pent-up emotions, putting words onto the paper without judgment; you are writing only for yourself. The process will feel easy once you get started.

Find a quiet place and avoid any distractions. Allow yourself all the time you need to answer the following questions. There are no right and wrong answers and only you will see what you write, so let yourself open up in ways you may not have allowed before. When we let the emotions flow, we activate the healing process.

What questions do you yearn to know about your loved one in their final weeks or days?

What are you still struggling with and searching to understand?

_____

_____

_____

_____

What questions can you accept not finding answers to and allow yourself to release?

_____

_____

_____

_____

Now that you have a flow of answering the kind of questions that perpetuate more profound healing, continue asking yourself some of your own questions to seek even greater understanding. _What are some of the things you yearn to know? What questions have you dared not ask, or what questions run rampant in your head?_ Use the area below to continue this introspection. Anything you write here will be vastly helpful and healing and may unlock some answers to help move you out of yearning.

_____

_____

_____

_____

You will find that I use a lot of writing exercises to help you shift from one focus to a new one and redefine new pathways that will help your healing process. Writing has the capability to grow and change our view of negative experiences. Studies have shown that when we write with meaning about a tragic memory and feel the emotion associated with that event, we can reap positive benefits. Writing helps us release bottled-up emotions which can lead to distress and by placing those feelings and thoughts down on paper, it provides us a safe place to confidentially disclose them, and in return, it helps improve our mental health. Perhaps even more beneficial to releasing those emotions from being captive inside us is the way in which writing increases our self-awareness. Writing presents us with an opportunity to turn our attention inward, giving us a deeper understanding of our behaviors, motivations, values, and beliefs. When we are more self-aware, we are better able to cope with outside influences with better self-control, more confident, and we become more accepting of others.

There are over 200 research studies conducted in the past 35 years that confirm the valuable impact of expressive writing and its positive health benefits, including lowering blood pressure, building immunity, increasing resilience, decreasing anxiety, depression, and the ruminating thoughts by those who report having experienced trauma. A Harvard Business Review article shared a recent study that stated, "Narrating the story of a past negative event or an ongoing anxiety 'frees up' cognitive resources." The research suggested that "trauma damages brain tissue, but that when people translate their emotional experience into words, they may be changing the way it is organized in the brain." To me, the research supports what I've known to be true for myself. When I write with the intention of finding clarity and focus from a place of inward reflection, I gain a whole new perspective I might not have had before I began my writing. My mind calms, and my body feels lighter and more at peace. This is why I believe in the positive benefits you will receive from these writing exercises throughout the book.

Healing Moment

Releasing the burden writing assignment

- ❖ Write a letter to your loved one.
- ❖ Think about the questions you wrote down. Decide whether you want to ask your loved one some of the questions or if you are ready to accept that there are no answers to them.
- ❖ Read the questions aloud. Do they serve you in a meaningful way? If they don't, then it's probably best to let them go.
- ❖ When you have completed writing the letter, it's time to release the burden and the questions.
- ❖ Burn it, tear it into a million pieces, and bury it in your backyard. Dispose of it in a way that feels right to you.

Example of a letter:

Dear Dad,

You've always been my hero. I looked up to you. I emulated your hard-work ethic in my career. You taught me the value of giving to others. You were such a strong man. Why did you have to leave me? What were you thinking the day you decided to end it all? Did you ever think how much your actions would affect me? It shattered my life. What did you expect Mom to do when she found you? I'm left to help pick up the pieces you left behind. I want you to know I still love you and miss you every day.

Love,

Cindy

Now it is your turn. Use this space to write your own letter. Fill it with all the questions you have kept bottled up in your head and heart. My letter may seem relatively benign to what you may be thinking, feeling, and wanting to express to your loved one right now. I don't want you to write something that isn't authentic for you. You must write what feels right in your current state of grief. I'm several years removed from my father's loss, so my letter isn't the same as what I would have written to him a week, a month, or a year after he passed—but I did not keep those writings because this process is about releasing the burden. The more times you write this letter and release it, you will begin to see a pattern. Your questions will become fewer, your temperament will shift, and you will begin to change old patterns into new ones. You must allow your writing to be meaningful and emotional in order to gain true benefit from this exercise.

Well done on taking the time to do this work. Writing a letter and asking these questions can cause you to reflect on those feelings and thoughts you may have been harboring for a long time, and by doing this work, it brings forth the ability to release those unwanted thoughts. Each time you do this exercise, work to relinquish more thoughts that may be holding you back.

Journaling can be therapeutic and a valuable avenue for releasing stress and pain even years after your loss. If you find writing helpful, make a plan to write for a few minutes every day. Keep a journal next to your bed because you may find that your thoughts start to circulate when you lie down at night or even keep you awake in the middle of the night. I found that having a journal next to my bed to write down what I was thinking allowed me to let it go and helped me to drift off to sleep once it was out of my head and onto paper.

As much as writing has been a proven method for improving mental clarity and health, other self-care modalities can assist with your inner work and healing process. An article in USA Today shared how suicide survivors use self-care techniques to stay healthy and well, including embracing the simple things in life, being kind to yourself, and talking to yourself like your best friend would. A fellow colleague, Dr. Yasmine Saad, a clinical licensed psychologist, shares that self-care techniques can greatly improve your health and connect you with your life force. "When you experience a loss, especially to suicide, you are consumed by the violence of the death, so it is important to connect to the force within that pushes life forward. Holistic healing modalities like Qigong, Yoga, and Reiki help to reconnect you to that life force. It is also crucial to work on your mindset and allow yourself to heal at the body, mind, and spirit level with spirit referring to the essence of you. It is very common to lose one's own sense of purpose after a loved one's suicide. These holistic modalities reconnect you with your purpose in life."

It's important to not only make self-care a priority but also set goals which after time will become habits. Be sure to use specific goals, such as agreeing to play cards with friends twice a month or walking for 30 minutes every night after dinner. Just like exercising one time won't make you physically fit, using self-care needs to be consistent to see results. Choose activities that you can do often and that you will stick with. Remind yourself that a few minutes of self-care is better than no self-care, so even if it's a promise to read for 10 minutes every night before bed, that time you set aside will add up over time.

There is a tendency for some people to think self-care equals self-indulgence. Let's clear up any misconceptions because self-care has nothing to do with being selfish. It's about taking time to do things that fill you up with positive energy and ensure your needs are being met so that you can be healthy, take care of others, do your job more productively, and better cope with stressors throughout your day.

I've found ways to do this through meditation, reading messages in the form of symbols or gifts from my angels, and working with energy healing techniques. I've traveled outside the United States to explore different cultures, perform humanitarian work, and learn how to grow my mindset. These are things I may never have explored before losing my father, and they have helped me build my confidence in my innate wisdom, provided self-reflection, and reconnection to my spiritual self, all of which have proved to balance my mind, body, and soul. These practices help me see the universal and unconditional love and support all around me.

Find your favorite self-care techniques and practice them daily. Be open to expanding and learning new concepts that will enhance your way of thinking and open your senses to self-compassion, even those which make you uncomfortable. If I didn't find these healing modalities, I could easily be stuck in the yearning phase. They grounded me, and I discovered a sense of peace.

Finding self-care modalities that work for you

There is no one-size-fits-all when it comes to expressing self-care, so it's important to think about things you've enjoyed in the past. A good place to start is asking yourself, *What did I love to do as a child?* *What types of self-healing activities would you like to explore?* Check the boxes of any modalities and self-care methods you'd be interested in trying or that you already do on a regular basis. The key is doing something consistently and finding joy in the practice.

- ✤ Mediation
- ✤ Riding a bike
- ✤ Soaking in a bathtub
- ✤ Hugging your loved ones multiple times a day
- ✤ Volunteering at an animal rescue
- ✤ Reiki Healing
- ✤ Gardening
- ✤ Journaling
- ✤ Psychotherapy/Talk Therapy
- ✤ Paddle Boarding or Kayaking on water
- ✤ Using Essential Oils
- ✤ Yoga
- ✤ Take a class to learn something new that interests you
- ✤ Play or listen to music
- ✤ Chiropractic Care
- ✤ Cuddling with a pet
- ✤ Acupuncture
- ✤ Healthy Diet & Exercise
- ✤ Equine Therapy
- ✤ Qigong
- ✤ Massage Therapy
- ✤ Spiritual Counseling
- ✤ Take a scenic drive
- ✤ Zero Gravity Floating
- ✤ Forest Bathing/Nature Walking
- ✤ Sitting in sunlight to boost serotonin

- ✤ Travel or read books about other cultures
- ✤ Find a hobby that provides pleasure and calmness

What other self-care options can you think of that would give you enjoyment and a sense of relief from your day-to-day stress? Add those ideas below in the notes section. After you've thought about the ideas above and any additional ideas you've included below, take some time to research what options are available where you live or plan a trip to a place that offers what your body needs, whether it's to a forest preserve, a lake, or a yoga class.

Consistency is the key to creating healthy patterns and habits. Self-care is one of the most important things you can do in this entire process to help you cope with the changes and challenges you're facing. Self-care is proven to reduce or even eliminate anxiety, stress, depression and improve concentration, happiness, and energy. When you treat yourself as you would your best friend, you are practicing good self-care techniques. However you find balance, it needs to be something that feels right for you, and you'll want to practice it regularly.

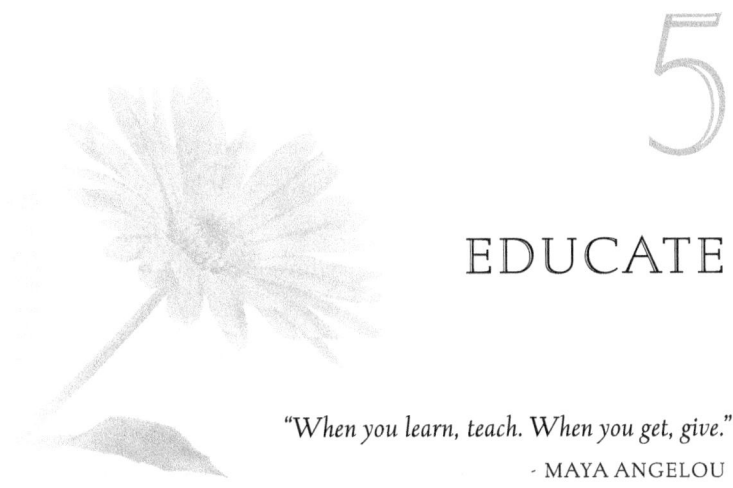

5

EDUCATE

"When you learn, teach. When you get, give."
- MAYA ANGELOU

Stage Two - The Educating Phase

Along my journey of self-discovery, I decided that educating myself on anything and everything that dealt with suicide and my father's mental illness would help me to become a better advocate for mental health. I knew this was a positive next step in my healing process and felt that if I could understand the clinical explanation behind his illness and the actions of his death, it could help me comprehend the actions he took that were caused by his illness. I decided to learn as much as I could to make accepting his death a little easier, and more importantly, I thought that by educating myself I could be an advocate and support those who had gone through or were going through what I had. Deep down, I hoped I could use what I learned to bring some sort of relief and guidance to someone else experiencing the same agony as myself.

I had some preconceived ideas about what 'helpful education' I might find when I began opening up books, reading websites, and learning from experts on the topic. I was skeptical that I wouldn't find answers because my past experiences with hospitals and mental health institutions were not favorable in providing me with the tools and resources when I needed them.

What I surprisingly found was that my past skepticism actually allowed me to see the stark *contrast* between what was not acceptable to me previously and the *clarity* to discover what I believed to be the more positive outcome. I found articles online that, in fact, addressed similar fears I had with the mental health community and in my own inability to comfortably and confidently reach out for help, and I also found resources that addressed my concerns and provided me with helpful steps to move past those fears.

Let me share some of the steps I took in my process to help you understand how I began to put pieces of my past dissatisfaction with the medical system together with my current situation and how those experiences shaped my inquisitiveness and exploration of my father's suicide. I'll admit it has been a journey, but one that has allowed me to take what I have learned through my process and use it to educate and assist you.

The first time I vividly recall visiting someone I loved in a hospital was when I was fifteen years old. That summer, both my mom and dad were admitted just a few days apart to a mental health unit—my dad for depression and suicidal ideation, my mom for psychosis. I was old enough to understand what they were experiencing, plus I had seen with my own eyes what both these diagnoses looked like up close and personal. It is a scary situation for anyone to witness but painfully impressionable for a fifteen-year-old trying to understand the world while at the same time witnessing her parents battling unseen, but entirely real, diseases. I remember calling my grand-parents to come to help me because I didn't know what to do when Mom drifted into her psychosis.

It took time for the doctors to stabilize their health with medica-tion, but eventually they both returned home, and things went back to normal. In fact, by the time summer ended and school began in the fall, we all had forgotten the events from June, and it was as if it never happened.

This was an education well before I even knew the future it was preparing me for. Still, I used this past knowledge to fuel my desire to learn more about my father's illness, and I now can see patterns that weren't as visible to me before his passing.

As I got older and went off to college, I began having heart palpitations regularly in my junior year. I started to worry that I had a severe heart condition. The fluttering was so intense that it felt like my heart was doing summersaults inside of my chest. After talking to my mom on the phone and a few friends at school, they convinced me I should go to the emergency room to have it checked out immediately.

My friend drove me to the hospital, where I remember the fear of the unknown while sitting and waiting through the intake process. I sat in the sterile, curtained 'holding cell' for what felt like hours while nurses periodically checked on me. They put electrodes on my chest and began monitoring my heart which was pounding uncontrollably.

The doctor finally emerged looking perturbed, as if I was wasting his time that evening or he had more important patients to see. He took one look at me and said, "You know what's causing this." I was stunned and responded, "No, what is it?" He then began a berating, belittling tirade, which I finally understood to be his way of accusing me of doing drugs, and as a result, it was his diagnosis that the cause of my irregular heartbeat was my own doing. When it finally sunk in that he believed I had taken drugs, I broke down in a full-fledged panic attack sobbing uncontrollably and gasping for air. When I finally started to calm down, the nurse explained that if it wasn't drugs causing my heart palpitations, then it was stress-induced anxiety, and the symptoms were my body's reaction to that stress.

That experience left me distrusting the medical profession

when it came to anxiety disorders and panic attacks, judgment, and empathy, and the encounter gravely affected my future trust in a doctor discerning a mental health crisis. How could he make such an accusation when I had come in so scared and concerned that I had a serious medical condition? The irony is my medical condition of stress and anxiety went from bad to worse when I walked in the door of that ER. If the medical professionals had started with compassion rather than speculation, what escalated into a panic attack never had to happen.

When my daughter, at the tender age of nine, had her first panic attack, I was already carrying major trust issues with doctors and mental health. Her first panic attack had begun over the lack of response from her teacher to a bullying situation. She was terrified of her teacher and the terror she felt at that young age set her into a panic attack that lasted several hours long. My first reaction was, *How is this normal for a nine-year-old to hyperventilate to a point where her limbs go completely numb?* I drove her to the hospital, and by the time we arrived her extremities were lacking oxygen, and her legs were too numb for her to walk on her own. I carried her into the ER, where they sent us immediately to a room and placed her on oxygen. Several hours later, and after administering a benzodiazepine medication, we were sent home. With no instructions other than to give her the medication for a few days. That was it.

Where was the education when I needed it most? I had lost an opportunity to understand what was causing my nine-year-old to experience an acute physical reaction to what seemed to be an emotional situation. I still was trying to connect the dots in my own rationale. The next panic attack happened a few weeks later. "Sh*t, here we go again," was my instinctive reaction. The school nurse called because she began having an asthmatic coughing attack, which was quite common for her, when running around and playing outside. When the nurse and I were unable to control her breathing, and she began hyperventilating, 9-1-1 was called, and the school went on lockdown. This caused her to become even more distressed because she thought everyone in school knew the lockdown and ambulance arrival was because of her. This panic attack episode lasted as long as the first, but this time the ER doctor gave me stern advice, "Nip this in the bud, now."

What the hell does that mean? Once again, no education, just some cryptic and concerning advice. I was clueless about what a panic attack was, let alone how to 'nip it in the bud.' Wasn't there some additional medical advice the doctor could have provided me with? Could the doctor not have explained to me what a panic attack was and how to control it in the future?

Over fifteen years ago, my sister was living with me. She started to have chest pains similar to my college experience in the ER, and it continued to the point that we felt it was essential to get her checked out immediately. We arrived at the emergency room, and they began the routine exams and tests. Luckily, we didn't have a serious issue to deal with... once again, symptoms from stress-induced anxiety. But while we waited in an emergency bay, a loud alarm announced an incoming trauma. Most of the staff began to react accordingly and told us we'd need to wait as they had to deal with a truly urgent matter. Yet, I'll never forget the comment of one ER staff member who ideally shared her lack of compassion for the incoming suicide patient, "We don't like to help people who don't want to live." WTF?! Once again, I was mortified at how callously a medical professional could push a mental health crisis aside.

Those callous words came crashing back every time I brought my daughter to that same ER. I returned to those words, "We don't like to help people who don't want to live." My young daughter couldn't control the physical symptoms of her panic attacks, just like the suicidal person coming into that ER fifteen years ago couldn't control their physical impulses of wanting to end their pain. If I could understand this, why didn't a medical professional who trained for years understand that suicidal thoughts and actions are a physical outcome of a serious medical condition?

Each of these events has shaped my ideals and impacted how I view the medical system. And, they have also encouraged me to begin a diligent journey of self-discovery and in-depth learning so that I could educate myself in the hopes of helping others through the ups and downs that the system creates. I'll admit I was self-learning, evaluating my own knowledge as it was happening to me in real time. Training I didn't necessarily ask for, but one just as important as if I were studying professional ethics in medical school. It was immediate and intense, as the knowledge began flooding into me, the more I read, the more I wanted to understand.

I found it encouraging as this newfound knowledge I was gaining started to quell my yearning. I began to attend a few survivors of suicide group sessions and learned I wasn't alone. I started to understand what those who had been attending survivor sessions longer than I had found in their educational growth: healing takes time. I gained an important new perspective through my exploration and began to see deeper into the underlying issues. As a survivor, I mentioned I felt guilty for not doing more for my dad when he showed serious depressive symptoms, but what I didn't know at the time was how those symptoms could lead to suicide. Even though I was exposed to some of the typical symptoms, I still hadn't connected the dots between the consistency of the symptoms over time in combination with the lack of any medical intervention. I didn't thoroughly understand his symptoms were generated due to his illness and not just a shift in his personality, disposition, or temperament. I now realize his lack of accepting medical treatment was a significant detriment to his health outcome. Had he taken an active role in his mental health, treatments could have been significantly beneficial.

I know now that I can't take responsibility for his lack of seeking assistance. But I can help reduce the stigma which caused him to not reach out for help. This slight distinction has helped me reconcile the guilt I felt for a very long time, allowing me to release any responsibility for his lack of medical intervention and pushing me to become an advocate in erasing the stigma so individuals like my father could take responsibility for their mental health just like they do their physical health.

That awareness has also encouraged me to expand my research and gain new insight into the current behavioral healthcare system. I know that we are in crisis when I look at the rising rates of suicide in our society today, and for that reason we can't afford to have only some success. We must have greater positive outcomes for people seeking mental health crisis intervention because confidence in our healthcare systems will encourage more people to seek help. I know there are plenty of health professionals who treat their mental health patients with great care, but my experience led me to believe that the people who choose occupations in mental health get burned out quickly. They are often overworked, understaffed, and have no other choice but to push patients in and out through a bureaucratic revolving door. It's totally understandable when the system they work in is overwhelmed and broken in many ways.

However, despite my grievances, I admire anyone who enters the mental health profession. Many mental health providers have entered the field because they have been personally impacted or have loved ones affected by mental illness. I believe that for our children and ourselves, we MUST do better when it comes to diagnosing, treating, and providing good health outcomes. We need to educate the masses about the truth of mental health and stop the stigma that keeps people from educating and advancing the professional field because more people need to feel confident in seeking treatment and getting relief from their symptoms. Medical intervention doesn't mean medication only. I have witnessed many non-medication, scientifically-backed treatments to relieve symptoms, including therapy, yoga, brain stimulation, and self-care techniques which all can effectively reduce symptoms for certain conditions. It may not be the entire answer, but it is a start.

We can all help debunk the myths around suicide with our own education. Healthcare workers' misperceptions about mental health and those associated stigmas prevent us from reaching better outcomes for mental health crises. Our police and first responders are a secondary group of professionals who absolutely need to be equipped and trained in Mental Health First Aid to the same degree that they are trained in CPR. If we don't improve the system, we risk losing good healthcare professionals to the inevitable cycles of cynicism and burnout.

We have a long way to go, but educating the general public is one way to help the crisis. Survivors of suicide loss are in a unique position to help in this area, and the more we can lean into our situations, and the key lessons learned, we can create something positive from our grief, and the more the system will improve overall.

The shift has started, and now more than ever, we are in a position to help the momentum of changing the narrative around mental wellness. I imagine a time in the near future when everyone routinely seeks a mental well-being check-up with a doctor just like they currently do for our physical health. With statistics that show 1 in 4 adults will experience a mental health issue at some point in their lifetime, it is imperative that we move from thinking this is a disease that only impacts 'other people' *and* 'won't impact me' to knowing and educating ourselves on the key factors and symptoms so we can intelligently and confidently assess it when it impacts us or those closest to us.

We've made strides in reducing the stigma of mental health and suicidal ideation. However, when medical personnel make statements about not wanting to help suicidal patients, we obviously still lack knowledge and understanding. NAMI (National Alliance on Mental Illness) made this statement which was initially run in a blog by Luna Greenstein, on June 23rd, 2017:

"You wouldn't blame a loved one for having cancer symptoms that might spill into everyday life, so don't blame someone for having a mental illness with active symptoms."

In your own journey through the medical system, you may have heard disparaging sentiments from doctors or people in your life. Or you may have felt like I did when confronted with a psychological crisis and were given little to no explanation on your next steps to get more information or assistance. While wanting to help, you may have felt confused, fearful, and uncertain of where to turn when someone you knew was in crisis. I want you to know you are not alone.

I want you to understand that no matter how you've felt in the past about the process, lack of compassion, or challenges in getting the right treatments, when you take initiative and responsibility to seek the information you need for your health and to heal from your grief, you'll find you become empowered. The truth is, you've already begun this phase by purchasing this book and reading it! Congratulations!

Every word shared here is designed to give you the clarity and healing you need to overcome and gain the resilience you have within you to persevere. As we go forward, you will find chapters that share an even deeper knowledge about how mental health impacts suicide ideation. There are additional examples where you will learn how important our language is around suicide and how having that knowledge gives you a voice in collective healing. Other examples will dive into the symptoms of the illness and are where I share valuable lessons about forgiveness. While you might not recognize how this correlates to your healing process at first, I believe your healing comes from your strength to acknowledge the things you know from your personal experience with suicide and accept the things you have yet to learn. As survivors, we have an obligation to heal not only for ourselves but also to help those around us who might be on the verge of crisis. The lessons we gain from this tragic experience and the healing we provide ourselves along our journey are what will heal our hearts and the planets collectively.

Your educational phase may look similar to mine or entirely different, but it doesn't matter because what you search for will be exactly what you need to comprehend and implement for your particular situation. You just need to begin your exploration. It will lead you to discover what questions you need to be answered.

While in this discovery phase, I challenge you to think about your emotional and mental well-being with at least as much vigilance as you do your physical health. If you visit a doctor for routine check-ups to ensure you're healthy, then do the same for your mental health. Seek professional help as you would for any physical condition that arises. Your mental state and well-being are paramount in your healing process and should not be overlooked.

If I asked you to rank your physical health on a scale of 1 to 10, 10 being top-notch fitness and health, you could probably fairly quickly select a number and then tell me why you selected it. For instance, you might say, "I'm a 6 right now because I was just told I have high cholesterol, I haven't been getting good sleep, work has been stressful, and I could easily stand to lose a few pounds of excess weight." If you have a more serious health condition, such as heart disease, diabetes, hypertension, or cancer, you probably would rank your physical health lower than a 6. My point is we all have standard benchmarks which we are comfortable referring to when it comes to our physical health. But what if I asked you to rank your mental health similarly? Would you have the same confidence to say, "I'm a 6 today, or maybe even lower," and what are the benchmarks you'd use to define your ranking? I believe many of us would admit ranking our mental health is a whole lot harder than it is ranking our physical well-being, yet one is not more important than the other. In fact, chronic emotional stress causes many diseases in the first place.

Much of your healing will unfold as you work through your own education exploration. As you discover and uncover much of the learning around the symptoms, causes, and conditions that forewarn suicide, you'll gain a greater understanding of it not as just an action taken by your loved one but a condition they needed treatment for, just as I did with my father, learning that he didn't have control over the symptoms and conditions of his illness. By exploring this deeply, I began to forgive myself for the feelings of resentment I was holding onto. I know you, too, can begin that forgiveness which will move you to the next step in your healing. Letting go of things outside of your control helps you see more clearly that you are not responsible for them. I encourage you to begin your education exploration and seek to find the answers you need to repair yourself and be a light to others in similar need of repair. You will be surprised at how you can make an impact and become an advocate.

Healing Moment

When I experienced these less-than-favorable hospital situations, I asked myself, *what can I do to improve our mental health care system?* I'm not a medical clinician, but I need to take responsibility for my health and my family's health. I decided it was important to advance my education; I needed to be trained in Mental Health First Aid and QPR, an emergency response technique to assist someone in crisis, which stands for 'Question, Persuade, Refer.' I completed the training and have since successfully used it to save my daughter in many dire situations that have unfolded.

I have encountered situations in which my training has helped strangers. Once, I was traveling for work when I overheard a young woman, emotionally distraught, crying on her cell phone. She was talking to her mother in an airport restroom, trying to figure out how to get out of an abusive relationship with the father of her children who was traveling with her. I offered to take her to get some help, not only because I had the tools but because I know if I were her mother, I would have wanted someone to provide help to my daughter. Everyone can take a moment to help de-escalate an emotional situation by offering help and support. It could mean the difference between life and death in a crisis situation.

To drive this point home, if I came across a person having an apparent heart attack in the airport, I'd react by offering CPR, or if someone were choking, I'd administer the Heimlich maneuver, both of which are life-saving techniques to help the person. Anyone can be trained in mental health crisis intervention, learning when to offer support, how to react, and what to say to help de-escalate the situation.

When we actively take on a role to improve something that has impacted us significantly, we begin to feel more in control and prepared for future situations that may arise of a similar nature. We may even save a life.

Suggestions or Ideas:

+ Take a Mental Health First Aid course.
+ Donate to an organization that creates awareness for suicide.
+ Read a book on mental health awareness and crisis management. (You've already started by getting to this book chapter!)
+ Join a Survivors of Suicide group and participate in their 'walk for life,' and other outreach programs to raise awareness.
+ Volunteer for a suicide crisis line. I've met survivors who find this work very rewarding and healing because they feel like they can help prevent another loss.

- Start a local organization if you don't have a survivors group in your community.
- Become a youth mentor to help teens struggling with suicidal ideation.
- Google 'Mental Health Awareness Volunteer Opportunities,' and you will find a long list of ways to get involved.

Take a minute now to decide on one thing you can do to make a difference and make it your goal. What are some steps you can take to begin to achieve this goal? Write down your action plans.

By moving in the direction of a solution and educating yourself, you go from being a bystander or victim to becoming an active participant and advocate. Your new knowledge can help someone in need, change a person's perspective about mental health, or even intervene someone in a crisis situation from harming themself. Having knowledge is a powerful tool for yourself, as well. You will feel more secure and confident when you are educated and informed.

6

HELP

"It's a great day to be alive!"

- A DAD

A chalkboard hangs in my basement storage area with this quote handwritten in white chalk. It's just as I found it eight years ago in my father's workshop. It used to hang on the wall beside his partially restored 1929 Ford Model A. It symbolizes to me his ability to make the most out of his difficult situation each and every day he graced this earth.

My dad loved country music, so it's quite probable he stole this line from the uplifting tune Travis Tritt recorded in 2000 with the same title, 'It's a Great Day to Be Alive.' Dad would have connected with and appreciated the song's lyrics, *"...the sun's still shining when I close my eyes. There's some hard times in the neighborhood, but why can't every day be just this good."* When I hear this song, I can picture him piddling around in his workshop, singing and brimming with joy, as he unearths his treasures and proudly displays them after pulling them from the worn boxes of collectibles he's brought home from an auction. It truly is a great day for him to be alive.

My father taught me that steady perseverance and a consistent work ethic were important but that finding a hobby you enjoyed was just as valuable for your soul. There are times I wish I could muster more of his same enthusiasm and gift in finding joy in the simpler things in life, but it's sometimes hard to get to a place of happiness since losing him.

When I went to college, he always reminded me to do something I loved and not settle for something that didn't fulfill me. No amount of money was worth doing something you hated or made you feel inauthentic, he would share. I miss his wisdom and willingness to teach me the value of knowing my authentic self, even though he wasn't forthright in sharing all of himself with me or the rest of us.

I could have used his strength and encouragement on the occasions I've had to walk into the hospital with my daughter to address her own inability to cope when her mental condition reached crisis levels. Each time I remember myself feeling scared and uncertain, yet hopeful that this time we'd get the help she deserved, and relieved that she was in a safe place where she couldn't harm herself and I wouldn't have to be responsible for her safety – a complete ball of nerves and every emotion in between, all happening simultaneously. On one particular visit, my daughter had agreed to voluntarily admit herself to the behavioral health hospital after a crisis situation and a four-hour assessment process. She had been having strong urges to harm herself and, thankfully, let me know she needed help to control those urges and a safe place where she couldn't act upon them. A hospital with psychiatrists and therapists on staff around the clock is the safest place for someone experiencing active suicidal thoughts, and my daughter was able to identify when her urges got to a breaking point. The piece of paper explaining the intake process, which the receptionist handed to me upon our arrival, said it would take approximately two hours and could be more, as "wait times may vary based on the volume of patients present and their acuity."

We've unfortunately had multiple visits to this hospital, and some are more acute than others, but every time I'm saddened by how many young people come through those doors on any given evening. On that occasion, I noticed the demeanor of the patients and their families as they entered the building and realized how similar we must appear. Another mother and her daughter were behind us in line. As the daughter pulled at the frayed strings of her bulky sweater, I could sense the fear and uncertainty of what was to come. A few minutes later, a young couple in their early twenties entered. He had bleached blond hair, and she was thin with candy apple red dyed hair, and both of them never looked up from their phones or made eye contact with anyone. I could sense they were just as fearful as the rest of us in not knowing what would happen, but also strong enough to acknowledge the situation was one they couldn't handle on their own. The waiting room was silent. The television was secured tightly against the wall with a plexiglass shield overtop and no sound, and there was an aquarium in full view, but even the fish were hiding.

Finally, they called my daughter's name, and we were ushered behind locked doors to a second waiting room. A sort of holding room for the long process ahead. Here we were joined by a mother and her son, he was wearing an oversized hoodie with the hood pulled securely over his head while his mom filled out some additional insurance paperwork. Fifteen minutes later, that mother and son left for the formal interview evaluation with a professional. Another distraught mother entered the room showing the same signs of concern and worry that I felt. Together we watched as the clock ticked slowly, the sound of the hand moving echoed in the deafening silence; it felt as though time stood still. My daughter leaned over, and in a whisper, she asked me if we could leave. I whispered back and explained that she was now 19 and the decision was hers to make, but she would need to speak to someone who will help her make that determination. I would have never said that the first two times we came to this same facility. I would have said, "Absolutely not. You're going to stay here until we see someone." However, this time, I'm comfortable saying that to her because I know they will not allow her to leave until she is assessed, and I want to keep peace and trust flowing between us. She promises that if another half hour goes by, she will find someone and ask them to let her leave. I knew she was in a lot of discomfort. Her leg wouldn't stop twitching, and she struggled to get comfortable in the leather chair. Her skin was crawling, and she had been having such high anxiety, her heart was beating out of her chest. The medication changes that occurred four weeks prior caused these severe side effects, and she was ready to jump out of her skin, or worse...

Almost two hours in, they called her name, and we finally made our way to the next holding room; this one is for the interrogation. I'm allowed to come for the first part to help provide her diagnosis and our family's mental health history. I'm thankful she is willing to allow me to accompany her. First, we get the physical assessment out of the way and then the questions about medications. The family history is tough. Yes, we have a long line of family history, and every time I talk about it, I speak very matter-of-fact, yet inside I feel the room shake beneath me. I can only imagine how my daughter feels whenever I share this information. It's like a constant reminder of her diagnosis, and I fear she believes she's defective. Nothing could be further from the truth, my daughter is the most brilliant and creative person I have ever met!

I am then politely asked to step back to the waiting room so that the mental health assessor can ask her personal questions without me there, and wait another half hour. When I'm allowed to return, the assessment is complete. It is determined that the best situation for my 19-year-old daughter is for her to voluntarily admit herself for inpatient treatment. I'm not surprised; this was the expected outcome, but it still took my breath away. I recall the last time she was hospitalized for inpatient treatment and the promise I made to myself that I'd never let her spend another night in a place like that again. However, I'm a rational person, and I knew that was the best place for her that night. It was the place she needed to keep her safe. I encouraged my daughter that this would be the best place to make medication changes and if she chose not to admit herself, a week was a long time to wait while experiencing active suicidal thoughts for her next appointment with her psychiatrist. She agreed. Thank you, angels.

A sense of relief overcame me. I was relieved that I wouldn't need to be vigilant that night, staying awake while she slept rustling next to me in bed. I wouldn't need to hide the keys, double-check that all the medicine in our house was locked away, or scan the room for anything that could be used as a noose. As I left the parking lot at midnight, I texted my husband to say, "I'm on my way home, alone."

Soon enough, days went by and things were improving. She was ready to have her family session to discuss short and long-term plans, and go over her safety plan for coming home. Due to Covid, we weren't allowed to visit her, which was extremely hard on all of us. As I sat in the waiting room to see her for the first time—two and a half days ago, I started to watch people again. Another mother-daughter duo fills out the initial paperwork. The daughter is wearing a sweatshirt that ironically reads, 'Today is a brilliant day to save a life.' I overheard another mom ask the intake clinician, "What is going to happen next?" They got up from their seats and I quickly realized this is what they call a triage moment. The daughter stands, and I couldn't help but wonder when she ate her last meal or kept any food down. Her long hair looked distressed from the lack of nutrition and her frail body gave no room for misinterpreting her dire situation. I had waited for less than ten minutes, witnessing all of this and in walked yet another mom. This mom was alone but she clutched a notebook and pen; she was prepared to take copious notes. She stepped to the front desk and I could hear her say her son was brought here this morning and she's looking for information. She was determined to find answers, just as I was when I began my quest years ago.

I wanted to reach out and hug each of these moms. I wanted to tell them I knew how they felt and give them some words of encouragement and comfort. But in that place, no one looks at each other, let alone talks to one another. This is a silent place. I have the unfortunate knowledge and appearance of what it's like to be a 'repeat visitor,' and I feel a slight level of confidence when I am there that I didn't have the first time I stepped foot into the building three years ago when inpatient treatment was completely new and terrifying. I had a flashback to our first time and how perplexed I was that some parents looked less terrified. I didn't realize until now that they had been repeat visitors and I was the newbie.

If you've been through the intake process at a behavioral health hospital, you may understand what I'm talking about when I say *I had earned my repeat visitor badge.* However, this chapter is crucial for those who may be afraid right now, and are paralyzed and unaware of what steps to take to move forward. I've been in your shoes, in that place where you are too afraid to react. If you are in crisis, or you suspect a family member is in need of urgent care, please act now. It is okay to ask for help. If you don't know where to go, go to your nearest emergency room. Don't convince yourself it's not an emergency.

My intention for this chapter is to share what it's like to admit a patient to a behavioral health hospital or to the ward that treats psychiatric patients within your local hospital in order for you to feel more comfortable taking the steps to walk through those doors. I know how scared I was, and I want to relieve your fears and let you know it doesn't have to be any more difficult than any other trip to the emergency room. If you feel someone is in crisis or you are in crisis, go to the nearest emergency room like you would if you had a physical injury that needed immediate attention. If you don't know what to say when you arrive at the ER, tell them you are having a psychological emergency. If you are lucky enough to have a hospital designated for inpatient treatment for mental health, you are at an advantage over many. I learned how lucky I was to have a behavioral health inpatient treatment center just two miles from our home. With less than 2000 behavioral health facilities that offer 24/7 inpatient treatment in the U.S., my situation is not the norm. If you live in an area that doesn't have a specialized mental health hospital, you may have to drive hundreds of miles, like my father would have had to drive to get similar treatment, but this can't be a reason not to seek help. When we had exhausted all of our resources locally, we resorted to other options. We drove my daughter to a facility 130 miles across state lines to seek another treatment center with many recommendations to see if they could provide her with new treatments. I make this point because most people would do this if their child needed specialized treatment for a rare disease or they wanted a doctor who specialized in that disease in order to get the best outcome. Therefore it shouldn't be unreasonable to go to these lengths if you can't find the mental health treatment needed at the closest place offered to you.

You may be asking why I'm spending so much time talking about getting treatment when you've already lost someone. Here's what I want you to understand. You may think you'll never find yourself in a situation where you'll need to react to a mental health crisis again, and I hope you never do, but I challenge you to think about that rationale based on the facts. 1 in 4 adults will develop a mental health condition this year, according to the National Institute of Mental Health. The Centers for Disease Control and Prevention, CDC, reports that almost 10 million Americans suffer from suicidal ideation every year. What we also know to be true is that if you have a family member who suffers from a mental disorder, you and your relatives have a much greater risk of developing one as well. With those facts, I would bet that you will come across a time when this information you gain today will help you in the future. Many of us know someone suffering in silence today, we just may not know what to do. I hope to give you the tools to start conversations and the resources to help you react.

I met Keri through another survivor while doing research for this book. She is a licensed therapist who also personally knows the devastating pain of suicide. Keri has lost three close family members in her life to suicide. Her first loss came at the tender age of 15 when her aunt died from a self-inflicted gunshot wound. Keri recalled how at that young age, she feared she could end up like her aunt someday, and due to the fact that she was personally dealing with depression, this was terrifying. Keri has since lost her father and her brother. It is hard to imagine and comprehend the devastation in her family, but unfortunately, it is not that uncommon.

For some time, the psychiatric community has known that mental illness can be genetically passed on through families. While it does not mean that mental illness or suicide is inevitable in families with a history, recent studies have made it clear that the genetic link to suicide could be as much as 45-50%. I believe this is critical to understand. The remaining risk factors are a combination of psychological, sociocultural, and environmental causes, such as unemployment, financial loss, physical or sexual abuse, witnessing domestic violence, and easy access to lethal means to name a few.

Knowing your risks makes it easier to acknowledge that you, a family member, or a friend may be struggling. I want you to be extra vigilant about potential mental health symptoms you or someone close to you might be experiencing right now. Unfortunately, there is an additional risk besides the genetic link within families who have lost a loved one to suicide. Statistically speaking, anyone reading this book because they are grieving may be at greater risk and in need of help. Friends and family members who have lost a loved one to suicide are at high risk of attempting suicide themselves. You may be vulnerable to feelings of emptiness, experiencing insomnia, or being fixated on self-blame and extreme guilt. These are all symptoms that need attention and intervention by a health professional. One study by the division of psychiatry at University College London said people who had lost a relative or friend by suicide were 65% more likely to attempt suicide than if their loved one died from natural causes. I feel compelled to share my concern for you at this point in the book. I care about you and want you to know you are not alone. I also know you want help and to heal because you chose to read this book, but I realize some of you may be hanging on by a thread. I ask you to be honest with yourself. If you are in crisis, please know it's safe to ask for help. Here are actions you can take right now.

- Call or text the National Suicide Prevention Hotline/Suicide and Crisis Lifeline at 988.
- Drive to the nearest ER or Behavior Treatment facility
- Dial 9-1-1 or your local emergency center.
- At the very least, please tell someone you trust right now.

I want you to also understand that you don't have to be suicidal to need help and ask for it. If you feel hopeless, are not eating or sleeping, or are not able to do basic personal care, such as brush your teeth and take a shower, you may be in crisis mode. This is very common in the early stages of your grief and you shouldn't feel ashamed for having these emotions. Please reach out to a healthcare professional immediately. If you don't know where to start, schedule an appointment with your primary doctor. They will refer you to the right treatment based on your visit and their assessment of what level of care you need.

No matter how you feel today as you read this chapter, I want you to have the resources readily available in case you need them tomorrow or a week from now. Write the Suicide and Crisis Lifeline, 988, (formerly known as the National Suicide Prevention Hotline) number down on a sheet of paper, and place it in your wallet, purse, or in a location that you visit regularly. On July 16, 2022, the former ten-digit number was replaced nationally with the easy to remember three digit number, 988.

Call or Text 988

Keep this number somewhere safe, so if a day comes when you, a family member, or a friend is in a crisis, it's readily available.

Resources to keep on hand:

- ✤ **Suicide and Crisis Lifeline (formerly known as National Suicide Prevention Hotline)**: 988
- ✤ **For International crisis numbers**: https://findahelpline.com/i/iasp
- ✤ **Crisis Text Line:** Text HOME to 741741
- ✤ **The Trevor Project:** 866-488-7386
- ✤ **Trans Lifeline:** 877-565-8860 Canada: 877-330-6366
- ✤ **Veterans Crisis Line:** 899 press 1

Reaching out for help before someone is in an emergency situation is helpful, but whether someone is able to get treatment before a crisis or not, it's important to realize there are resources at any and every stage. Seeking help should never be seen as a weakness. In fact, it takes significant strength to admit something isn't right and to take action. Even if you don't receive the help you need the first time, never allow that to stop you from continuing your education and exploration of finding something that does help. If I had stopped searching after those failed attempts of finding medical intervention in the beginning, I would not be sitting here as someone who finally found success and be sharing it with you. Keep asking for help until you feel satisfied with the answers you receive and the treatment that provides you and your family with relief.

The Sharing of

MORGAN

Bettendorf, Iowa

Jul 30, 2001 – Apr 6, 2014

Morgan Laurayne Schmidt, 12, Bettendorf, Iowa, formerly of Jasper, died Sunday, April 6, 2014, in Iowa.

She and her twin sister were born in Buffalo, N.Y., on July 30, 2001, to Derek and Christine Schmidt.

Surviving are her parents, Derek and Christine Schmidt, her two sisters Allyson and Morgan's twin Mackenzie Schmidt, Bettendorf; a brother, Andrew Schmidt, Bettendorf; and her grandparents, Karen and Daniel Dunn and Charles and Sandra Schmidt, all of La Crosse, Wis.

She was preceded in death by grandfather, Robert Duncan.

Morgan was in the seventh grade at Pleasant Valley Junior High School, and was a state qualifier in cross country.

The funeral will be at 11 a.m. CDT Saturday in Our Lady of Lourdes Catholic Church, 1506 Brown St., Bettendorf, Iowa. Burial will be in Mount Calvary Cemetery, Davenport, Iowa. Memorial contributions may be made to the Morgan Schmidt Memorial Fund.

The Story of Morgan, Daughter. Told by Christine Schmidt, Mom.

"It's All Love, Only Love."
- MORGAN SCHMIDT

Morgan is a special angel to me. She's made a profound impact on my life since I learned of her story on May 10, 2016, after I googled, *"Why have so many people died by suicide in New Hampton Iowa."* She represents everything I feared in my daughter, though I didn't realize it at the time. I was seeking wisdom to prepare for my personal events which were about to unfold. I was frozen in disbelief and unsure of how to prevent my daughter from becoming an angel like Morgan. I believe Morgan and her mother, Christine, helped me save my daughter's life.

I'd been in touch with Christine through email up to that point, but I was about to speak to her live for the first time. Christine was the first interview I would have with a survivor of suicide. I was not sure what to expect. I wasn't sure I would be capable of wrapping my head around why a 12-year-old child would want to die. All I knew for certain was that I was supposed to connect with Christine, learn as much as possible, and share it during a talk I was giving in San Diego a few weeks later. I felt guided by a higher power as I picked up the phone to call a stranger and interview her about her daughter's death. I was thankful to have angels supporting me, giving me strength beyond my imagination. My palms were sweaty and my heart was racing as I waited to hear someone answer the ring on the other end of the phone.

"Hello?" Christine's voice instantly gave me a slight sense of relief from the anxiety brewing inside me. She had a calm, confident demeanor, she didn't seem like a fragile woman who was about to break down at any moment, although I would not have held it against her if she had. I was doing all I could to hold back my tears as we talked.

Christine and her husband have been married for over 26 years. She shared with me how they met in 1992 and began their family with the birth of their first daughter. Christine reminisced on the early days of her marriage, sharing how much she always wanted to be a mom. It was a dream come true for Christine when she became pregnant with their first child, but when the couple struggled to get pregnant with their second, it took a toll on her maternal dreams. She and her husband spent seven difficult years before they finally welcomed their 'miracle babies,' Morgan, and her twin sister. The family felt almost complete and soon would be when they welcomed their only son a few years later.

Christine, a stay-at-home mom and devout Catholic was always attentive to her children's needs. The more I've gotten to know her over the years, the more amazing she has become to me as a mother, wife, and Christian. In 2010, she wrote a book, 'Strengthening Our Faith One Moment at a Time,' which highlighted stories of how she *found her love of God in cherished moments with her children, friends, and family*. The book description says, *Her faith was tested and strengthened, one moment at a time*. I am in awe at how accurately that description represents Christine's personal character and how she has always leaned into her faith for her strength. She wrote this book several years before Morgan passed, and it's just as relevant to how she shows up in life today, as it was over a decade ago.

Christine enjoys sharing how Morgan was a content, happy baby, who met all of her growth milestones. As a toddler, she played the 'good twin' role, always wanting to please. She had a sweet nature about her, which was something that never changed throughout her childhood.

By the seventh grade, Morgan was maturing into a lovely young lady. Her big brown eyes and contagious smile made her instantly popular in her Iowa junior high school. On top of her attractive-ness and kind demeanor, she excelled in academics, athletics, and friendships. Morgan was strong-willed and a fierce competitor. She ran cross country and had recently achieved the status of a state qualifier in Iowa. She was an honor student with perfect attendance and was extremely responsible. She possessed all the right cues that parents typically look for to ensure their child is thriving. Everything appeared to be well above the normal benchmarks with Morgan. "She had an electric personality," said Christine. But with popularity at such a young age comes the horrible reality and downside of being targeted by bullies wanting to knock girls like Morgan off the top. Morgan was starting to feel those pressures and friendship troubles began. This all seemed pretty typical stuff to Christine, girls being selective about who would be invited to a party and who they pur-posely wanted to exclude. Morgan was sensitive to these exclusions as most 12-year-olds would be; she couldn't understand why she wasn't invited to the parties. Why did they all of the sudden want to exclude her, and what were those kids saying behind her back? The insecurities and lack of self-confidence were taking their toll on her.

Christine recalls knowing she was having a few issues with her friends, but Morgan was a private person and didn't divulge all the details to her mom. Morgan would have been appalled if her mom had talked to another parent about the bullying concerns and it was that fear that probably kept her silent about the pain and shame she was experiencing.

In 2014, there were several news articles about teen suicides attributed to the social media app called Ask.FM. Children would post anonymously, which allowed cruel comments and false accu-sations to spread viciously. Many of the comments were of a sexual nature meant to hurt the victim's reputation and shame them. I remember this time vividly because my daughter was in junior high and a friend of hers was targeted on this same site. I called the girl's mother to let her know it was happening. She thanked me because, like most of us parents, she was still trying to navigate the early social media treacherous waters for our young children. We didn't have any tools or resources to help us back in the early years as apps were being developed on smartphones with little understanding of their effects on children's and teens' emotional well-being. It took parents reaching out to each other to help monitor these types of activities. Even my daughter's junior high school administration refused to intervene. When I tried to bring attention to the hateful messages being spread amongst their students, I was told it wasn't a school-sanctioned activity, so they wiped their hands from it.

Unbeknownst to Christine, Morgan was a victim of online bullying on one of those anonymous apps. By March of seventh grade, Morgan was consumed with friendship struggles and being victimized. Vicious posts directed at Morgan for everyone to see spread like wildfire. "You aren't as pretty as you think you are."

These words cut through Morgan's heart and deep into her core with a pain so intense she began having physical symptoms such as stomachaches and headaches. Christine recounts a day in late March when Morgan called her from school and asked if she could come home because she was feeling ill. Christine picked her up from school and took her to lunch, and when they got home, Morgan fell asleep on the sofa.

As Christine began making dinner for their family a few hours later, Morgan got up from the sofa, crying. She said she felt sick, didn't want to eat, and had a headache. Christine gave Morgan an ice pack, some soda, and some headache medicine. She told Morgan to lie down and that she'd be up to check on her later. She continued making dinner, believing Morgan just needed to rest upstairs in her bedroom.

As she was clearing the dinner table that evening, she got a text message from one of Morgan's friends. The message read, "You need to check on Morgan." The text startled Christine. What could be wrong? She looked at her husband and said, I just got this text message. She couldn't fathom why she received it.

Christine and her husband ran upstairs to check on her. When they entered the room, Morgan seemed listless and appeared asleep. "Morgan, are you alright? I just got this text message to check on you. What is going on?" After arousing Morgan a bit, she stuttered, "I'm fine, I'm fine." Christine could tell that Morgan wasn't quite right; her speech was slow and a bit off. Finally, Morgan tearfully confessed, "I took too many pills."

According to Christine, Morgan had ingested the entire bottle of headache medicine she had taken from the kitchen drawer when she went upstairs along with an additional bottle of medication she had found upstairs.

Christine and her husband rushed her to the emergency room in their hometown, where Morgan was admitted to the ICU for potential liver and kidney failure. They felt a small sense of relief that they had caught it in time as Morgan was responsive and communicating. Through her shock and disbelief Christine recalls asking her daughter, "Morgan, why did you do this?"

Morgan replied, "I'm done. I'm so done with this life, my friends, and the things going on at school."

What kind of pressure causes an otherwise high-achieving, young 12-year-old girl to say she was done with life? Christine needed help figuring out what had caused her little girl to take such drastic measures to end her life over what she saw as typical school-aged drama. She knew she couldn't figure this out on her own.

Once out of the immediate danger, Morgan was medically released to come home, but Christine knew she wasn't out of the woods yet and requested that Morgan be admitted to the University of Iowa Hospital's psychiatric unit. Morgan spent seven days there.

During that week in the hospital, Morgan attended group

sessions, met with a psychiatrist, and was diagnosed with clinical depression. Christine still felt there was a lack of concern for the severity of Morgan's suicide attempt. She didn't feel like seven days was enough time to get to the root cause, nor enough time for the low dosage of antidepressant medication to reach efficacy. It became apparent to Christine that Morgan was going to say and do whatever it took in order to be released.

Being completely disconnected from everything outside of the hospital most likely created anxiety for Morgan about what was to come once she was released. What were people saying about her absence and would their attacks, whispers behind her back, and exclusion from friend groups continue once she returned? I'm sure this added to the pressure she felt and the intense desire to leave the hospital.

During Morgan's final family meeting, a session in which the hospital therapist, parents, and patient meet to go over an exit strategy or safety plan, her therapist made it known that Morgan was being released to the best possible situation. Christine still felt scared and didn't have the confidence that anyone had really prepared her for what to do for her child in the days following her release.

Upon Morgan's release, her family rallied around her doing everything they could to help acclimate her return home and her return to school. She came home on a Wednesday and attended a partial day of school on Thursday, but by Friday things began to unravel. Some kids had found out why Morgan wasn't in school the past week and Morgan emptied out her entire locker that day, never planning to go back the following Monday. Looking back, had she known Morgan's actions, Christine would have responded differently, but once again Morgan kept everything to herself. She didn't even share her darkest secrets with her twin sister.

That Friday evening, Morgan had a friend spend the night and on Saturday the entire Schmidt family went hiking. Nothing seemed too out of character to Christine and her husband; Morgan seemed to be settling back into a routine. Fear still filled Christine, but she was doing her best to give Morgan some space, at least not letting her know she was watching over her shoulder. It was a delicate balancing act between allowing Morgan to feel respected at home and keeping a vigilant eye on any potential red flags.

Sunday morning came and the family began to routinely prepare for church service that morning. Morgan wasn't feeling well again. To ease her stomach, Christine made her some toast and thought she'd be okay by the time they left, but Morgan still insisted that she didn't want to go to church and asked if she could stay at home.

For a split second, Christine shuttered and thought "I can't let her stay home alone," so she offered to stay home with Morgan, but Morgan was convincing, "Mom, I'm really okay, this is just a stomach ache and I'll be alright here alone." Morgan's father also offered to stay home with her but Morgan's persuasive reassurance that she wasn't going to hurt herself, was enough to encourage her mom and dad that they were just overthinking the situation.

Christine put both hands on the sides of Morgan's little face and looked directly into her big brown eyes and said, "Morgan, I love you and I will be back in an hour. We're going to go hiking, so rest up for our picnic later today." Morgan nodded and replied, "Okay." She gave her mom a hug and said "I love you too." Then walked over to her dad and hugged him and said, "I love you, Dad."

When the family arrived home from church, Morgan didn't respond to the family calling for her, but that didn't cause alarm right away. Christine thought to herself, *I'm a calm person, but something doesn't feel quite right.* Morgan hadn't responded to texts on their way home from church and now she wasn't responding to them calling for her. The family split up to search the house for Morgan. A scream filled the entire house. Morgan's twin sister found her. She had hung herself in the family basement. Christine and her husband immediately began CPR while the police and paramedics were called and began arriving.

The chaos that ensued that Sunday morning would forever scar this close-knit family. Paramedics ascended to their home and took over the efforts in trying to revive Morgan for what seemed like forever, but also not long enough. Christine climbed to the top of the stairs and felt a visceral release of agony course through her body as she fell to her knees and let out an excruciating wail. She had never felt such pain before in her life, nor had she experienced such an emotional and physical reaction as she did that day.

The medical team continued to work to revive Morgan upon arriving at the hospital but in the end, they told Christine and her husband that Morgan had been without air for a long period of time. They would have to make the difficult call to stop the resuscitation efforts.

Standing in Morgan's room the evening after her death, Christine examined all the Christian reminders she had instilled in her daughter. The Serenity Prayer inscribed on a plaque, along with her Bible and rosary from her first communion lay on the nightstand and dresser. A recent craft project of the letter 'M' along with stickers Morgan used to describe herself; smart, funny, good friend, sister, baker, runner, sat still and lonely, and two bracelets in a small dish curled together, one Christine's and the other Morgan's. As she touched Morgan's treasures, she made a pact with her. *I'll work from here, and you'll work from heaven, and somehow we're going to save lives and make sure this doesn't happen to anyone else. I don't know what I'm going to do, but I'm going to do something.*

It was Christine's faith, connection with God, and devotion to Morgan that would put her on the path to educating children about the impact of bullying and why it's so important to always be kind. She kept the promise she made to Morgan that night when she stood in her room just hours after she was gone.

Not long after Morgan passed, Christine had a dream. As she gazed into Morgan's eyes, and Morgan smiled back, she told Christine, "Mom, It's all love, only love." Morgan repeated it three times and on the third time, Christine jolted out of her sleep. It was Morgan's message to Christine that she was safe. *There's no reason for you to worry, Mom, because where I am now, is all love, only love.*

7

SURRENDER

*"Surrendering is not about giving up. Surrendering is
to accept life's path with the faith that when things
don't go as planned, you will emerge in a
new and transformed way."*

- CINDY TANK-MURPHY

Stage Three - The Surrendering Phase

A year into my grief, I was struggling to find balance with aspects
of my life, such as my family, work, purpose and spirituality. I had
lost my identity in some ways, feeling as though my life no longer had
significance. The things that I had wanted to achieve prior to losing
my dad no longer excited me, and it was hard to find pleasure in any
area of my life. I had to make a choice. If I wanted to move forward
and find my way back to a joyful, passionate, and purposeful life, I
knew that I needed to break the cycle of these intense feelings of
disbelief and bewilderment that I kept feeling. I needed to surrender
and accept that this was my situation. Once I accepted that this was
the card I was dealt, I could see past the tragedy with faith that I
could transform and emerge a better person.

According to the research by Barle Wortman, and Latack (2015),
there is such a thing as traumatic bereavement. *A death is considered
traumatic if it occurs without warning; if it is untimely; if it involves violence;
if there is damage to the loved one's body; if it was caused by a perpetrator
with the intent to harm; if the survivor regards the death as preventable; if*

the survivor believes that the loved one suffered; or if the survivor regards the death, or manner of death, as unfair and unjust.

When I think about this definition and how suicide fits perfectly within it, I start to contemplate why we, as suicide survivors, tend to bereave differently than what would be considered typical grief from death. The nature of death itself isn't what is traumatizing, but rather how we interpret and process the death. It's the recurring thoughts of suicide and the gruesome images of our loved ones in horrific circumstances that cause us to feel differently about the death versus someone who died from natural causes. It's our perception that causes that trauma inside of us.

If our loved one died peacefully in bed, we might not experience the same trauma as someone who died a violent death because the manner of this type of death is one we can accept more easily. Thus, it makes sense that we need to get past the 'perceived trauma' to grieve and heal in a healthy way, similar to someone who isn't experiencing traumatic bereavement. But more importantly, it's not healthy for us to recall the act of death repeatedly; our loved one would not want us to continue to ruminate on their death.

There are reasons why the act of surrendering can help with what healthcare professionals call complicated grief or complex grief. These terms are used to describe someone who is unable to function due to the severity of their grief. If you are experiencing what I personally experienced in my grief process, you may benefit from seeking professional help. And, as I discovered, a therapist can assist you with the surrender phase.

Wendy Hayum-Gross, an LCPC and MS.ED, shares why therapy is so critical to the healing process. "When you meet with a profes-sional, they will listen, validate, and empathize with your current situation, and also provide you with effective tools." This process of validation and empathy for our feelings is important because it allows us to accept our feelings and emotions without judgment.

Once our feelings are validated, we no longer feel as threatened or overwhelmed by them. We start to feel accepted, understood, heard. We can move through the emotion more easily, as well as have a better ability to regulate our own emotions and self-soothe more appropriately. By normalizing our feelings, we lessen the grip they hold upon us. Once we succumb to the fact that these are appropriate emotions to have in this situation and allow ourselves to release them, they can no longer control us.

Typically when someone passes, we get this sort of care from our family and friends. They provide a layer of comfort that supports our healing in this manner. Unfortunately, when the death is a suicide, we don't always get that same validation from family and friends. Sometimes family and friends disappear amid our tragedy because they are scared or don't know what to say or do to acknowledge our feelings. This is why seeking professional counseling is important to aid your healing journey. Wendy suggests we also seek support groups and work to reframe a new narrative that works for us, so we don't get stuck replaying an unhealthy story to ourselves. Holding onto beliefs that don't serve us can't change the outcome, or bring back our loved ones; they only serve to hold us back in progressing forward.

There is a tendency to believe that by surrendering, we give up control of any outcome of our loss. We tend to crave control for various reasons, so, understandably, surrendering can sound scary, ridiculous, or even weak, as if we are giving up somehow, but that's just not true. In fact, the act of surrendering has the opposite effect and can actually provide us with more control. Surrendering is about accepting uncertainty and believing that we have more to experience and live through in order to embrace our life journey fully. We can't predict what happens next in our lifetime, whether good or bad, and we certainly can't avoid future grief from a loss, as that is inevitable. Still, we can have a sense of knowing that whatever happens next in our life, we can prevail and move forward.

Once I realized that allowing myself to surrender was what I needed to do, I felt a burden lifted. It was refreshing to realize that my ability to accept my situation gave me back my power. Power in knowing that no matter what happens in life, I can handle it because I have faith and I believe that everything is a part of my journey. We don't hold that kind of power or control in seeing the future, but we can control how we respond to our future. Letting go of future expectations and focusing on the present is all within our control. Trying to control the situation of our trauma only builds anxiety, depression, resentment toward others, and undeniable fear. These are not positive control strategies. If we surrender to the devastation and allow faith to feed our appetite rather than fear, we can shift from trauma to transformation.

Let me share with you about a mother that I'll call Beverly, who lost her 15-year-old daughter. Her daughter, Erica, was a bright, gifted surfer and writer. Beverly's motherly intuition knew Erica was struggling, yet Beverly felt helpless and as if everyone around her had failed Erica. Beverly had been doing everything she could to get her daughter the help she needed and was even willing to send Erica to the opposite coast if it meant her daughter could find herself and get away from the tumultuous relationship with her father, Beverly's ex. Sadly, she took her own life before Erica could take the next step to seek refuge in a new place. There were signs that Erica wanted to take her own life, such as when she had written on her bathroom mirror, *I want to die.* but her father, who refused to seek help for his daughter, had erased it and never told Beverly. Her ex's lack of response haunted Beverly. It's unfathomable to me that anyone, let alone a parent, would not take such a handwritten note with the utmost seriousness. My heart aches for Beverly because I know if she had been aware of Erica's note on her bathroom mirror, she would have reacted immediately.

It's taken Beverly years to get to the point where she can accept what happened to Erica, and she told me that she credits her current outlook and perspective to several things. First, she found a psychologist who helped her talk through her pain. Second, she found coping mechanisms such as meditation and spinning classes. Finally, she turned to God. She read "The Prayer of Jabez," by Dr. Bruce Wilkinson, and found a spiritual 'knowing.' When the tension and anger would bubble over, she found techniques that helped her release the trauma that would build up within her body.

But it wasn't until Beverly surrendered that she felt a fundamental shift and began to put the pieces of her life back together. "I wanted to drown myself. I wanted to die. I got on my knees and turned it over to God. I cried, Take this from me!"

Beverly's story of healing is filled with moments of blissful climbs only to be followed by free falls back into complete agony, as many of us experience after suicide. The road of hope, healing, and survival is never linear. We all heal at our own pace and no one can tell you when you will begin to have days of feeling more joy than pain, but I promise, if you follow the techniques and healing moments within this book, you too will begin to pull yourself slowly out of the darkness. It takes effort and the desire to change and transform yourself. It will be unpleasant sometimes, but it will be worth all the self-discovery.

"We have free will," Beverly shares. "I realized I still have a life, and God gave me this life." That realization helped Beverly see that she had a choice to make. Once she began to surrender and truly believe that she had done everything she could to help save Erica, the healing was easier to accept. "I put myself on the battlefield for my daughter, but we do not have control over anyone." It was this type of knowing that allowed Beverly to heal. The unknown was much worse. She needed to find her 'straight rudder,' to steer her ship and stay on course.

Beverly is just like you, me, and all of us who have lost a loved one. We are just trying to navigate our way to a path that allows us to surrender. Once she did that, she gained a deeper understanding of the struggles and what was transpiring in her daughter's life. Beverly's purpose shifted once Erica died, and she began to find ways to share with others what Erica's life had taught her. Surrendering is a gift we give ourselves, for it allows us a profound shift in perspective from one of *why did this happen to me?* to a mindset of *how can this experience I have gained help someone else?*

Have you had a moment of surrender since losing your loved one? Have you been able to let go of your disbelief and confusion to allow your burdens to be lifted? If surrendering seems impossible right now, this next healing moment will help change your perspective. Once you surrender, you will appreciate a view beyond the wreckage. A bright, beautiful, joyful view awaits.

Healing Moment

I want to take you through a series of open-ended questions to help you discover what surrendering might look and feel like to you personally. The questions are meant to prompt you in your current state and help you shift and come to a place of surrender. The questions may bring up strong emotions for you, so it's important that you feel safe and protected. Part of surrendering is allowing yourself to sit with these uncomfortable feelings and let them flow. During this exercise, I want you to release what emotions are holding you captive. Write what naturally comes to you after each prompt and take time to reflect on your responses.

Take a deep breath and say aloud, "I am ready to surrender. Take this from me," then answer the following questions with honesty and clarity.

The emotions I am holding onto that are not serving me right now are...

I'm afraid to surrender these feelings because...

It feels impossible to let go of my anger or guilt because...

I'm ashamed because...

Instead of fear, anger, and shame, I want to feel...

What is the worst case scenario if I let go of control and surrender...

I surrender feelings of...

I accept love because...

Now that you've answered these questions, think of what a surrender moment would be or look like to you. What could you do in order to symbolize your willingness to surrender? How would it feel to fully surrender and allow yourself to believe you are worthy of a positive, fulfilling future?

Some ideas of what a surrender moment could look and feel like:

- Recording how you are feeling in the present moment in a journal.
- Creating a memory book of your loved one.
- Connecting with or attending a support group.
- Praying to a higher being and asking for burdens to be lifted.
- Getting involved with a passion project in which you feel fully engaged.
- Starting a gratitude practice daily.
- Sitting quietly and feeling all the sensations within your body.
- Dropping to your knees and asking for forgiveness and any shame, guilt or anger to be lifted.
- Allowing yourself to cry whenever you feel the emotion surface to release the pain.

These are just some ideas for you to consider. You may have your own idea of what your surrender moment looks and feels like. Maybe you'll decide to go skydiving and surrender to the fall, or practice yoga and find your inner calmness. No matter what you decide to do in order to solidify your surrender moment, allow it to shift you a step closer to the transformation that awaits you. You can begin to realign yourself with positive and strengthening beliefs that can inspire greatness for yourself and for those around you. I believe in you.

8

TRUTH

"The truth is often painful, but lying to hide the pain only postpones the inevitable."

- CINDY TANK-MURPHY

There is no greater bond than the love between a parent and child. Besides the love they give, parents provide protection, validation, and safety which fosters mutual trust with their children. If you have children who have been impacted by a suicide loss, you know that it is critical you address their emotional well-being and support them in a manner that continues to foster that bond. This chapter will help you address how to talk to them about suicide in a language that is age appropriate. A few common questions parents ask after a death are: *should I tell my child what happened? Will this be too much for them to handle, and how do I find the words to talk about suicide with them?*

My daughters were just ten and twelve when my father died. I knew I should be honest about his death, but I couldn't fathom how I would tell my two innocent children that their grandpa had taken his life. *Would this news destroy them in some way? Could hearing about suicide so young somehow endanger their emotional development?* I was still battling with myself about how to talk to my girls about his death. *How do I share this horrific news?* My husband was not so sure we should tell them at all. He couldn't bear to see their innocence shattered. I too feared this would be too damaging for them to understand.

I asked for help. I spoke with the funeral director, looked online for resources, and confided in my sisters. In hindsight, I can't believe I questioned whether honesty was the right thing to do. It finally dawned on me that if I kept this a secret from my daughters, I'd be teaching them it wasn't okay to discuss suicide or anything else that is uncomfortable and scary. They would certainly learn the truth at some point. Worse yet, they might overhear someone's conversation at the wake or funeral. I realized that my fear of wanting to protect them would eventually teach them indirectly that suicide was shameful and that they couldn't even talk to me about it. This was not something I would want to instill in my children. Instead, I wanted them to remember their loving grandfather as someone who fought hard to stay alive but unfortunately lost his battle. I wanted them to know it wasn't shameful and that we were a family that would talk about hard things together. I needed to be the one to tell them the truth.

Both of my daughters had heard my loud, eruptive outburst upon hearing the news. They knew he was gone, and they immediately questioned how he died. In fact, my oldest and more intuitive child sensed right away that this was different from the death of her great-grandparents, who lived to old age and died of natural causes. Within minutes of her hearing and seeing my reaction to the news of her grandfather's death, my daughter wrote a two-page letter to him. She told him stories she wanted to remember, how much she missed him already, and what he had taught her in her short twelve years of life. It was as if he had visited her and wrapped his arms around her as she wrote, "No one will forget you, Grandpa, I never will. I know you hear me; the Holy Spirit inside of me is too strong to say you can't. I feel like I felt you hug me. And suddenly, I relaxed. My prayer goes to you tonight. May God forgive you, love you, and take care of you. Amen. Love you, Grandpa!"

The morning after we got the news, my oldest began asking what had happened. I knew she sensed it was something awful. She begged her dad to tell her what had happened, but he only shared the necessary details; we needed to be together as a family to discuss Grandpa's death, and I was already on my way to Iowa with my siblings. He and the girls would drive over separately the following morning.

When we decided that we needed to speak with them honestly, the grief was extremely raw, since we had less than 24 hours to process our emotions. We sat them down at the kitchen table of my in-law's home. I don't remember everything I said, but I remember how calmly and honestly I spoke to my sweet innocent daughters. I told them that Grandpa had been sick for a long time. I spoke to them as if I knew they were strong enough to hear the news, allowing them to ask any questions, and only sharing the cause of his death and not any details. If they wanted to know more, I knew there would be time to delve deeper, but I needed to discuss their grandpa's illness honestly. I made sure that I spoke about his depression as a disease, so they would understand that there was nothing that they could have done differently and that no one caused grandpa's death. I used the word suicide and explained what that meant, even though neither of them needed any explanation. I told them they could always talk to me and their dad about Grandpa. I assured them that if they had any questions, we were there to answer them and support their concerns.

Telling my daughters was one of the hardest things I've ever had to do, but I have no regrets about how we managed that moment. The most important thing you can do with children is to be their rock. Show them that you are there to listen and allow them to ask questions.

According to Wendy Hayum-Gross, LCPC and MS.ED, telling children the truth is important when it comes to a death by suicide, but she says it is also important to use age-appropriate terminology. A child under the age of five doesn't understand permanence. A child between six and eight understands that death means they will no

THE STRENGTH TO LIVE

longer see that person, but they still believe they can talk to them and will be connected to them, which is very therapeutic for their age. A child nine or older deserves a frank, honest discussion that they can understand. Be honest with your terminology and don't say things like "they've gone to sleep." Using words like that can scare a child into thinking they could go to sleep and not wake up. Children take things very literally, so the words you select are important. It's fine to speak in terms of your faith-based beliefs. Saying that the person is now in heaven is appropriate if that's something the child can relate to.

Wendy says the best approach to speaking to a child about death is to begin by asking them open-ended questions. She cautions adults not to expect children to react as parents do. Children may not be sad in the same way we grieve as adults. They may express their feelings through anger, disappointment, and fear.

How are you feeling? What do you know about death? Have you heard anyone talking about grandpa's death? These questions will not only ease the child into sharing what they already know but also help ease you into the discussion. I believe we sometimes underestimate what children can comprehend and what they already interpret from watching our reactions and responses, so it's important to ease their minds and find out what they already know. Wendy recommends you do something with the child while talking, such as cooking together or playing a game that involves using your hands, like playdough. Allowing them to focus on another activity helps you and the child feel less intimidated and scared.

Lastly, it's always important to reinforce that the death was not their fault. If the suicide is a parent or sibling, a child will sometimes feel like they were the cause of the death or were the reason the deceased was troubled. Continue to reassure the child this is not the case long after the initial conversation, as children will feel they are to be blamed for why their mother or father left them.

Tiny Ears

There are good resources available on how to talk to a child about suicide death. Here is a list of some helpful tips, which I personally used when talking with my girls. I found these tips on the National Alliance on Mental Illness (NAMI) website.

- Don't lie, trivialize or pretend it didn't happen.
- Talk about mental health and mental illness with care and dignity.
- Reassure them that this will not happen to them.
- Comfort them and answer their questions honestly.
- Reassure them that even though a suicide occurred, it doesn't mean the person they have lost didn't care about or love them.
- Avoid sharing graphic details.
- Allow them to have questions about God, faith, and religion.
- Engage their efforts to work out what they are going through in a spiritual way if they are inclined to do so.
- Seek professional counseling.

The way we say things is often just as important, if not more, than what is being said, which is why it's helpful to think about what you want to say before talking to children. Taking a bit of time to process what needs to be shared can make all the difference in the delivery of the information. Our tone, steady voice, and using words that instill our confidence that together we will share our grief openly and honestly will make a difference in how the child receives the information and processes it. We sometimes believe we are sparing people when in truth a lie is much more damaging. Is there someone who deserves to hear the truth? What is an age-appropriate way to tell them? Use this space to put your thoughts together, if there is someone young you need to tell.

I know from my experience how devasting and challenging it is to talk to your children about a loss by suicide. It took every ounce of my strength to hold it together for them throughout that unforeseen conversation. But, I promise the truth shall set you free, and it is so important to keep an honest, open dialogue with your children, because you want them to find their solace with you, and to feel comfortable talking to you about any mental health challenges that may surface for them in their lifetime.

9

WORDS

In 2017, I went on a humanitarian trip to New Zealand, as a way to expand and enrich myself. Having witnessed how previous trips I had taken with people focused on a higher purpose had shifted my mindset and broadened my consciousness, I knew this trip would continue to heal me. One of the many amazing experiences I encountered there was living among the Waitaha indigenous nation. The Waitaha are believed to have been the earliest Māori inhabitants and hold ancestral traditions dating back thousands of years ago. I won't pretend to have great knowledge of their traditions as my stay was only a few days, but I will share how impressed I was with the traditions I did learn in that short time.

Upon being greeted in the most loving and ceremonious way—I was mesmerized by one simple rule we were given. "Do no harm." That was the *only* rule. We were told we could do anything we wanted while we visited, as long as we didn't harm anyone else. Those simple three words stuck with me and had a profound influence. You'll understand why I bring this up later in this chapter, but first, let me share my early experiences trying to navigate my daughter's illness.

I felt alone in my concerns and awareness of my child's mental health. No one else seemed to share my same concern when my daughter worried about wildfires and hurricanes, things that would never affect us since we lived in the Midwest. I knew my daughter was an overly anxious child, and from a very young age there was angst that she couldn't quell. In my opinion, neither her pediatrician nor her therapist took my concerns for her mental health seriously, even with the family history I'd shared with them.

She had deep empathy for things outside of her control from a young age. She would worry for days or weeks, to the point of giving herself stomach aches and headaches. She worried about the planet becoming polluted because trash was lining an area of land near our home. The worry consumed her to the point that I finally suggested she write a letter to the energy company, which owned the land because I thought maybe that would help release her worry. She wrote to them and asked if she could help them pick up the trash, and then she took the initiative to write to President Obama and inquire about what she could do to help save the planet. She was only 10 years old.

Around that same time, I noticed that she was feeling disconnected from her body. Her drawings pointed to some very ominous images – guns, knives, death, and people floating above the ground, as if they were suspended in the air, with large blacked-out eyes that appeared to be blankly staring into space. Her therapist was concerned and had her drawings analyzed by another professional. In the end, the professionals determined the emotional trauma she was experiencing was brought on because my daughter didn't feel safe at school. Unbeknownst to me and my husband, she was being emotionally bullied by a girl in her class, and when she tried to advocate for herself and get help, her teacher had told her to stop complaining about being bullied because she didn't believe her. She had no adult to protect her at school, which is a very frightening thing to go through at 10 years old.

Adults hold so much power over young developing minds, without even realizing it. Just as they can make a huge impact positively, they can crush a child's security in a split second. One adult erased my daughter's entire perception of safety because words and actions have a profound effect when a child is feeling insecure and unsafe. We sometimes only think of physical abuse of children as being detrimental, but emotional abuse can be just as damaging. Whoever came up with the saying, "sticks and stones may break my bones, but words will never hurt me," had it backward. Broken bones will heal, but words can become ingrained into a child's psyche which can last a lifetime. Because words can be damaging, I believe it is important that we talk to our children about how they *feel* on a regular basis. Children need to learn that it's okay and normal to feel sad, lonely, mad, and disappointed. Likewise, it's normal to feel all the positive emotions. By improving our communication and how we express and regulate our emotions, children will learn how to react and self-regulate their challenging feelings. I've learned that although I didn't realize it at the time, I wasn't asking my children the right questions when they were hurting. I asked them how their day was, when instead I should have asked, *What made you happy today? What made you mad or scared? Was that experience a good one? Tell me how you felt after that situation.* If I had asked the right questions, I might have realized how miserable my daughter was at school much sooner. Children need to know they can express their emotions in a safe space without judgment so they don't learn to keep those feelings hidden.

I am certain that this teacher was not the sole reason for my daughter's mental and emotional instability at that time, but she did create trauma within my child, which is why I feel the need to share this story and help to shed light on how impressionable adults can be when they interact with children. We all make mistakes. I certainly have made more than enough, but knowledge of our mistakes can lead us to do a better job next time.

One day, my daughter came home from school and I could sense that she was upset. After hours of trying to figure out what had happened, she finally told me that her teacher, the same one who told her she was *not being bullied even though she was*, had been walking to class on the upper hallway at school, which overlooked the lower level. Her teacher was apparently having a bad day and made an inappropriate gesture to another teacher amidst feeling overwhelmed. She placed two fingers pointed at her temple and virtually pulled a trigger with her thumb, leaving a traumatic imprint on my daughter.

I'm emotionally triggered every time someone makes that gesture. It's never appropriate, especially in an elementary school in front of fourth graders. *Have I made that gesture?* Maybe, before my father's death. I do know I have jokingly asked someone to "talk me off the ledge" after enduring an excruciatingly long business meeting in which I was assigned enormous amounts of follow-up work. I realize now how not only ridiculous that sounds, but how hurtful it sounds. After losing my father, I have never uttered those words and vow to never make that mistake again. For those who have never experienced a loss by suicide, it's understandable that they don't think anything of the phrases and gestures that mimic killing oneself over something trivial. They don't mean to cause harm and their intentions are not to hurt others.

This is important. It's something I feel very strongly about. I want us all to change the narrative of how we talk about difficult things. Let's imagine a similar gesture or phrase used in a situation where someone wanted to make the same emphatic notion they were *so* upset or embarrassed that they wanted to die, but replace suicide as the cause of death with cancer. "OMG, tell me I only have a few weeks to live! Cancer, kill me now!" Sounds ridiculous, right? Yet, our society constantly abuses and mocks the severity of suicide without any regard for how it impacts those of us who have lived through such a devasting loss.

One of my fellow survivors, Beverly, knows firsthand how callous and insensitive people can be about suicide death. People will say things they wouldn't ever dream of saying if the person died of natural causes, but for some reason, suicide is seen as a crime.

Beverly got a frantic call from her ex-husband stating that she needed to come to his house immediately, which wasn't a typical occurrence, so she immediately sensed something terrible had happened. She arrived to discover a full emergency team had taken over the front yard. Beverly soon learned that her 15-year-old daughter had braided a noose from strings she found in her father's garage. I can feel the agony Beverly still bears over the idea of her daughter sitting in her bedroom, fingers moving back and forth in a rhythmic braiding pattern while contemplating her final moments on this earth.

"I had to watch my daughter come out in a body bag." My throat was tight as Beverly tells me this horrific detail. Police canvass the front yard as Beverly is left sobbing uncontrollably in the driveway, and unbelievably, an officer approaches her and has the nerve to say, "I hope you won't make any trouble." I have no idea what the officer meant by those remarks, but what an insensitive thing to say to a mother who has just found out her daughter has died. What purpose did that comment serve? It served no purpose but to cut a deep wound in the already severed heart of a grieving mother. It's hard to imagine why people would be cruel in such a time of devastation, but I believe it has something to do with their misunderstanding of suicide. Often people are unaware that their words have a hurtful meaning and that words can be abrasive, abusive, and unkind when used in poor judgment to the context of the situation.

Because words matter so much, it's important we discuss how they impact our conscious and subconscious interpretation of them. One of the first things I learned from the support group I attended after my father's death was how important our use of language can be in helping us to heal. I still cringe when someone says, "committed suicide." The definition of commit (verb) according to Merriam-Webster is "to carry into action deliberately: PERPETRATE *commit* a crime; *commit* a sin." It's no wonder the word commit and committed insinuates that the deceased is a criminal. The adjective definition of committed has a negative connotation as well. Merriam-Webster's definition of committed is "placed in confinement (as in a mental institution) *committed* patients."

While I understand the use of 'committed' comes from the verb definition of commit, it's hard to come up with any other time the past tense of commit is used for anything other than a 'sinful act,' such as, 'committed murder, committed adultery, committed sin.' I've never heard the word committed used in conjunction with a positive noun, at least not one I can readily recall. Let's give it a try. She 'committed love, committed happiness, committed joy.' *Nope.* None of those nouns are used to create the action of falling in love, feeling happiness, or experiencing joy deliberately. It's no wonder that the words *committed suicide* directly insinuates that the deceased is a criminal or, at minimum, because of how they died, the deceased is deemed not as valuable to society.

We use the correct wording when we explain the cause of death for any other reason. He 'died by natural causes, died of an overdose, died by a heart attack.' We have a responsibility to change the narrative. It has become better in recent years, more media outlets and television announcers have acknowledged the more respectable language of 'died by suicide.' I have no issue with helping to correct this language when I hear it. Until I learned the nuance of the meaning, I didn't think twice about using 'committed,' but now that I do understand it, I politely inform people that the proper way to discuss the topic is to say someone 'died by suicide.' I've never met anyone who didn't appreciate me pointing out what wasn't obvious to me at first either. My conversations usually go something like this:

Friend: I still can't believe Anthony Bourdain committed suicide.

Me: Yes, it's hard to understand mental illness and the complexity of death by suicide.

Friend: What was he thinking? He had so much to live for.

Me: We'll never know the pain he was carrying around, but as someone who has lost a loved one to suicide, I can work to try to understand their pain. Prior to my father's death, I used to say committed suicide, but after experiencing it firsthand, I've changed my language. I now say he 'died by suicide' because I don't believe my father committed any crime. He just lost his will to carry that pain any longer.

I go back to that simple rule spoken by the Waitaha – *Do no harm.* It's hard to know if we harm, whether it's a gesture or a phrase that is so commonly used in casual conversation. We think nothing about the meaning and power we give it until we experience the real-life version of it. We survivors know the harm it causes, the gut-wrenching trigger that makes our heart race and re-experiences the trauma.

A few years ago I saw a post on Twitter by Glennon Doyle, an American author and activist. She was addressing youth coaches and my heart sank and warmed at the same time when I read her post.

"Dear coaches of the sports: thanks for all you do. Please, please stop calling those running drills 'suicides.' It silently pains at least one player on your team every time, guaranteed. Thank you."

During a recent group workout at my local fitness center, I had the opportunity to use my Glennon Doyle-like courage. A young, encouraging, female athletic trainer named Nikki began to explain the exercises we were about to perform which would challenge our bodies and build endurance. One particular move was called a 'suicide burpee.' As soon as Nikki said those words, I could tell she felt almost as horrible to be using the terminology as I did in hearing it repeated over and over during our high-intensity training session. She said, "I don't make these names..." I immediately felt my body tighten each time she repeated the move, but I decided this was my chance to practice using my voice for change. With each move, I was building the courage to address a national fitness chain's choice of names for a workout move that was making me more uncomfortable by the minute for reasons besides the soreness in my body.

After cooling down, I walked over to thank Nikki for kicking my butt with the workout, and I asked her if I could make a suggestion. I started by telling her I knew she didn't make up the names for the workouts, but I wanted to make it known that the word 'suicide' used in a workout can be very triggering to survivors of suicide. She was completely understanding and thanked me for letting her know and said she would bring it up with the national headquarters. I was pleasantly surprised to find out the following day that Nikki had followed up on her promise. She was excited to share with me that headquarters had appreciated my comments and would be eliminating the name across the country going forward! My voice made a difference. One drop at a time, we can create a ripple of change.

I'm grateful that I continue to gain courage from others, like Glennon, who inspired me to use my voice for good in the world. She said what we survivors think and feel when we hear those triggering phrases or see the gestures that weren't necessarily intended to harm us, but do in a very traumatic way.

Do no harm. It seems easy, yet so complicated when it comes to how we use language without thinking about the implications and the impact our words and gestures have on people who have experienced suicide loss firsthand.

Healing Moment

At my father's wake, we had a greeting line for friends and family to share their condolences with my family. I was the first one in line, with my mom and siblings aligned to my right. I shook hands and thanked guests for coming and for their condolences. A gentleman, who was a high school classmate of my father, approached. This gentleman had a severe learning disability. He stepped forward and declared, "I heard he blew his head off." His searing words caused me to break down on the spot. I started shaking and couldn't speak for several minutes. Thankfully, I was surrounded by my family who immediately noticed how upset I was and comforted me. I have forgiven his remark because I knew that he did not have the ability to understand that his words were hurtful, but for those who do understand, it's time we address this issue.

Whether someone says something inappropriate, unknowingly or not, many of us feel triggered instantly by their hurtful words. Let's take some time to recall those hurtful moments, and let's take it a step further and explore the possible reasons someone might say something hurtful; then we can release the pain of these words so that we can begin to heal.

What hurtful things did someone say to you after your loss? List as many things as you can recall.

_____

_____

_____

_____

Describe where you were when you heard them.

_____

_____

_____

_____

Was this person someone you knew or a stranger to you, and why do you think they said those words? Were they scared or unable to express their thoughts?

_____

_____

_____

_____

Do you want to release it and forgive the person who said it? Yes, I release the hurtful words and forgive this person. Here is what I'd say to them.

_____

_____

_____

_____

No, I'm not ready to forgive this person. Here's what I need to feel safe.

_____

_____

_____

_____

One final action that you can do to solidify your disconnection from these negative feelings and release the hurtful words is to scratch them out with your pen. By scribbling over the words you are consciously signifying and releasing them for good.

THE SHARING OF

JAY

1950-1976

Jay, age 26, of 1153 Churchill Street, St. Paul. Survived by wife, Meg; parents, Dr. & Mrs. J. E. Habegger, of Geneva, Ill.; sister, Mrs. Dr. James A. Weigel of Centralia, Ill.; brother, Jon Habegger, Student of St. Olaf College; grandmother, Mrs. Frank Habegger of Berne, Ind., Memorial Services, Thurs. 8 pm at Trinity Lutheran Church, Corner of 21st Av. S. & 5th St.

Jay Habegger is remembered as a loving husband and son, a gentle and good friend. Jay's life was marked by a drive for excellence and the pursuit of happiness, qualities that inspired those close to him, but qualities which also created an unresolved tension in his life. Jay's struggles and death have left a painful silence in those touched by him. So many questions are unanswered.

The Story of James Jr. (Jay), Brother. Told by Jon, Brother.

I met Jon at a suicide survivor's support group. I decided I should attend a group session because it had been several years since I stepped foot in the church where the group gathered every month. I remember the first time I attended this support group, I was nervous, afraid to admit why I was there, yet I felt drawn to the group as a way to gain some answers to what I was going through. For me, the group setting offered a therapeutic benefit, especially in the very beginning of my grief. The first meeting I attended was just weeks after my father passed, and I had no idea what to expect. I was surprised to see so many people in the room, many of whom had been attending the meetings for years.

I took a seat next to Jon. He began by saying that it was the anniversary of the story he was about to share, and that is the reason he came tonight. Although he hasn't been to a group meeting in years, like me, he felt compelled to come tonight to share how he found his brother Jay's remains after many years of not knowing where he was buried. It was this group that years earlier had encouraged Jon to search for his brother's ashes before his mother died. I was inclined to believe he was summoned by the angels to come tonight so I could hear his story.

Jon lost his older brother Jay, over 45 years ago. Jon has lived two decades longer on this earth, yet I can still sense the pain in his voice and the solace in his eyes as he tells his story. Time starts to wear down the rough edges of the hard, sharp rocks we carry on our backs, but the load remains heavy for a lifetime. Jon has been carrying those rocks longer than the rest of us in the room. I envision him sitting in these meetings many times before and talking about his brother Jay and how he left far too soon. Jay was 26 years old when he passed. This evening is different though; Jon chooses to share a story of redemption, and I'm glad he did.

Jon started coming to the group early in its inception while studying for his Social Work degree. One of his class assignments was to attend a support group to gain a better understanding of what group therapy offered. He shared that he couldn't relate to alcohol or drug abuse groups that were suggested by his professor because he'd never known anyone who suffered from a substance dependency or addiction, so he struggled to find a group he felt he could benefit from. After he reviewed a list of support group suggestions, the one that immediately jumped off the page was a suicide support group. He had lost his brother years earlier to suicide and had no idea such a group even existed but knew it was a sign that he needed to join the group, and this decision gave him a lifeline and helped him gain further understanding of his brother's death. Since joining the group, Jon's involvement grew quickly. He held a former board president title from 2008-2010 on the non-profit arm of S.O.S (Survivors of Suicide). This organization was formed by a woman who lost her mother to suicide and knew that she needed to provide a safe place for others like herself, struggling to comprehend their loss.

Jon, along with some of the other loyal members of the group, are a stark contrast to the new members, who have lost sons, a daughter, and a mom in the past few months; all freshly opened wounds. The tears flow freely in these sessions, but there is also love being shared amongst the pain. We share a common bond which is quickly evident when the stories begin, though we'd gladly give up that connection in exchange for never experiencing this loss.

As with many suicide deaths, the family is unsure of how to proceed with funeral arrangements, memorial services, and whether they should even host friends and family during this devastating event. *Will people whisper about your loved one's death? Is it worth celebrating life when it's purposefully ended by the deceased? How do you answer questions about what was "wrong" with your loved one, which will inevitably come up in conversation?* There are so many unanswered questions that it's hard to identify closure around death by suicide. Jon's family had some of those challenges. His brother Jay was married at the time of his death, so many of the decisions were made by Jay's wife rather than his parents or brother. When the decision to not have a formal burial was made, Jay's immediate family was never told what had been done with his ashes.

Jon recalls how coming to these meetings after Jay's passing was a blessing to him and his recovery. During one particular occasion, he told the group how he had no idea where his brother was. It pained him to not have a place he could go visit his brother. He envied people who spoke of going to a gravesite on an anniversary, or a birthday or whenever they were close by to visit. It was that evening with the support of his caring group members that someone gave him some sound advice. That advice led him on a journey of locating his brother. Jon went on to detail the phone calls he began to make, the trek he took across state lines, and finally the discovery that his brother's ashes had been scattered in a cemetery in Minnesota.

His quest to find Jay was initiated by this group and he felt so passionate, he chose to come back this evening to share it with all of us. I could feel his devotion and why he knew it was important to share his story with those in attendance. It's moments like the one Jon endured that as survivors we feel compelled to share our story with others healing from a loss. We share what helped us as a means of paying it forward.

I asked to meet Jon a few weeks after our initial introduction at the support group to learn more about his story. We sat down at a restaurant. Jon ordered a salad and I had a soda. As we began to reconnect, I told Jon more about my goal for this book. He was extremely gracious with his time and willing to contribute to helping the cause.

By the time Jon had found his brother Jay, his mother was 87 years old and his father, several years prior, had passed away. It was the closure he and his mother both needed. Jon was able to drive to Minneapolis with his mother and visit Jay's resting place for the first time in over three decades. The lake at the cemetery was exactly the place Jon believed Jay would have wanted his ashes scattered. Jon also made a commitment the following year to his mother, in her final months, that he would spread some of her ashes in the same place as Jay. Finding Jay was healing in so many ways.

Death was no stranger in the Habegger household. Jon grew up with his brother and sister and recalled having dinner conversations about the autopsies his father performed that day. Their father, a doctor and pathologist, spoke about death in a very clinical and scientific way. This would seem to help Jon in his healing over the loss of his brother and perhaps give him a very direct approach to death that many might find odd, but I understood.

Jay was a great brother by all accounts. Even though he was six years older, he loved spending time with his younger brother, Jon, and took good care of him. Jon recalls a time when Jay cut his hair, but Jon didn't like how it looked and Jay felt extremely bad. Not a typical remorse a brother might feel over such an insignificant disappointment. Jay took little things to extremes when it came to his concerns for his younger brother.

When most big brothers might have been more selfish as a teen-ager, Jay was overly sensitive to Jon's needs. He didn't like that his brother would miss ice cream with the little league team after the game. He not only appreciated his little brother's love of trains, but he also made sure his brother got to experience his passion, personally taking him on excursions. Jay always ensured Jon never felt left out, perhaps signaling just how intense his own pain and emotions were over feeling alone or left behind.

Jay's faith had led him to St. Olaf College, where he met his wife. After finishing undergrad, Jay married her in 1973. Together they moved to Minneapolis to begin seminary school to become ministers. But something changed in Jay; he no longer wanted to fulfill the calling he had previously desired and set off to work as a waiter, quickly rising to Maitre d', leading the waitstaff. Jay was never content with being mediocre. He desired perfection, no matter what his current focus was. He was in constant search of his life purpose, so he decided on another career shift and began to attend law school. Ultimately, Jay just wanted to help people.

Nine months into their marriage, Jay made a suicide attempt. He had taken a large number of pills but woke his wife in the midst of the overdose to let her know he needed to get to the hospital quickly. It was his initial cry for help.

Jay completed his death a few years later by taking a bottle of aspirin, turning on the gas, and performing the act of 'Hara-kiri.' In Eastern culture, it is called 'Seppuku.' It is a ritual type of suicide that originated in Japan amongst samurai warriors in the 12th century. The act typically involves stabbing oneself in the stomach. It was considered an act of bravery and an honor to die in this way.

His wife found him in the basement when she came home from seminary school. The trauma of this finding was most certainly one that she has had to relive over and over again. Jay had shared with her that he wanted a cremation and not a traditional burial when he died, not something many 26-year-olds discuss within their third year of marriage, perhaps a sign Jay had been making plans.

At the time of Jay's death, Jon was 20 and studying abroad in Hong Kong, teaching American English to students at a Lutheran rural middle school. A knock at his door at around 10 pm came with the concerning news that Mr. Ma, the school principal where Jon taught, was coming to visit him immediately. "That can't be good. Someone has died," Jon responded. He could sense the looming bad news, although he had no idea the news would be of his brother's death.

As the car approached, Jon could see that Mr. Ma was not alone.

He had brought with him two American teachers, a husband, and wife, and Jon could see the wife was crying in the backseat. Mr. Ma and the male teacher stepped out of the car.

"Okay, who died?" Jon insisted on getting straight to the point which surprised the older men. Stunned, they replied, "Your brother," followed by, "It was a suicide." Jon was expecting to hear his father had a heart attack, not to hear his 26-year-old brother was gone and that he had *chosen* to die. With those words, Jon's life came crashing down. 7800 miles away, his mother, father, and sister were dealing with the loss. The following morning, he boarded a plane back to the U.S. and arrived on the day of Jay's memorial service. Jon arrived just prior to the service. For Jon, it was the only recognition of Jay's death, and as I hear Jon explain this, I can't help but wonder, how was he able to process all of this in just 24 hours?

Honoring Jay's wishes, his wife arranged for his cremation and told the funeral home to "dispose of his ashes." There would be no burial ceremony for Jay, only the monumental memorial service held in St. Paul, MN. I suppose it's hard to understand what was going through the mind of a newlywed wife, but her actions and words speak volumes about the devastation she wanted to erase completely. It was as if she wanted no memory of Jay to exist. If it didn't happen, she wouldn't have to relive that horrific scene every day for the rest of her life. Jay's departure was the ultimate abandonment for her.

Jay was an exceptional student and an outwardly successful person. Jon wrote this about his brother in a Chapel Talk at St. Olaf College one year after his death.

He was number one or near the top in all the things that he attempted. Jay was an Eagle Scout. He had earned his Pro Deo et Patria award in scouting. He had been valedictorian of his high school class. Jay graduated from St. Olaf in 1972 Magna cum Laude and Phi Beta Kappa. Jay received high praise for his work as Maitre d' at the Radisson South Hotel. Jay was loved and respected by all who knew him. If anyone had a problem, they came to Jay for assistance since they knew he was willing to help. But looking back, I see that the continual successes took a toll on Jay. Jay believed that his love came from his work. In Jay's mind, he had to continue to succeed if this love and respect were to continue. Jay could not accept another person's love and respect for just being himself. Jay began to take on challenges that offered little or no chance of failure. He had to continue to succeed rather than put any doubt in anyone's mind that he was less than perfect. If he were not perfect, how could people still love him? He was undoubtedly pained whenever he asked himself that question. However on the 28th of September (1976), he did answer that question. Jay answered in the negative. He believed that people would not love and respect him anymore if he were less than perfect. Jay could not accept that he was loved not for his successes, but rather for himself.

Jay wrote a letter to Jon a few days before his death. Jon did not receive the letter until a few weeks after Jay's passing because it was mailed to his Hong Kong address. This is an excerpt from a letter Jay wrote to Jon. Jay had just begun law school at the University of Minnesota two weeks earlier.

Law school is challenging me in more ways than academic ones. One doesn't plow through intellectually unstimulated -- the workload is too great. It's many hours of hard work, especially the first year, to get the basics. My entirely new milieu is teaching me things about myself, some of which are rather painful. However, this is what personal growth and living in the ambiguities of our world are all about. In many ways, I stagnated personally during my real-world job years. Here's my chance to get into the growth cycle again.

Jay was a perpetual seeker of perfection, and when he realized he could not live up to his expectations of himself, he lost his will to go on living because who could ever love him? I know from my research that perfectionism is linked to an array of mental health issues, including depression, anxiety, self-harm, eating disorders, and compulsive disorders. The self-loathing that comes with striving to be perfect and to do everything without failing is overwhelming, yet our American culture is indoctrinated with *win at all costs, never accept defeat, and never let them see you fail.* We seem to be a society that is instilling mental disorders in our youth. It's no wonder we continue to see mental health plaguing our children, and then those children proceed to grow up and be adults who may or may not find a suitable treatment, or develop coping skills.

When I learned of Jay's perfectionistic tendencies I began to understand him as someone who suffered silently. I learned a great deal about how perfectionism is linked to depression, something I had not contemplated before I began my research. There feels like a correlation between the method of death he chose and his obsession with perfection. Hara-kiri is seen as an honorable way for a Samurai warrior to die after a battle; an atonement for being captured by the enemy, and one that takes tremendous courage. The Samurai culture is one of honor, bravery, and selflessness, which I sense were all very important to Jay. I read an article about the 'way of the warrior,' on a travel site called *Inside Japan.* I found the following excerpt interesting.

Not only were the samurai skilful warriors but they were also expected to be highly cultured and literate; to be skilled in the harmony of fighting and learning. An ancient saying aspired to by warriors was bun bu ryo do: 'the pen and sword in accord', and it was common for samurai to enjoy calligraphy, tea ceremony, poetry and music, and to study.

To me, Jay was a Samurai; he lived like a warrior in every sense of the word. To Jon, he was his older brother and someone he looked up to for all of his accomplishments. I was touched by Jon's willingness to share his personal letters and tribute to his brother. Reading Jay's own words helped me understand the depths of his insecurities and how hard he worked to prove himself worthy of love. If only he could have seen what everyone else saw in him—a brave, honorable, intelligent, Renaissance man.

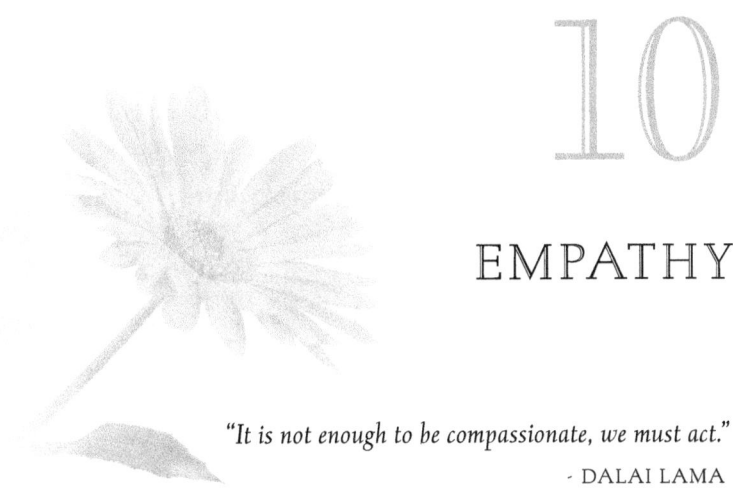

10

EMPATHY

"It is not enough to be compassionate, we must act."

- DALAI LAMA

Stage Four - The Empathizing Phase

I believe empathy is the response to being compassionate for someone's situation through the act of kindness and understanding. Empathy is the ability to put yourself in someone else's shoes and view their feelings in a situation from their point of view without judging or interpreting how you think they should feel. When you can put yourself in someone else's shoes and act upon that feeling, you exhibit something more than just feeling sorry for them. It differs from sympathy, where you may be moved by the thoughts and feelings of another, but you don't truly acknowledge or understand the person's pain and you may even try to minimize or look for a solution to their situation. It's easy to confuse sympathy with empathy, but the difference is that empathy involves sitting with that person and sharing their pain alongside them. Compassionate empathy goes even deeper and enables you to know when to act in a manner that helps another person.

A sign that you are beginning to heal is when you feel the nudge to pay it forward through compassionate empathy. This nudge may come as an offer of support to console someone in need, share a story, or perform a kind gesture to another person who's going through their own loss. It can be as simple as listening without judgment to someone sharing their experience of losing their loved one.

I remember my first time having this strong urge to pay it forward after my dad died. I was sitting in a coffee shop a few weeks after his funeral, and my husband and I were talking about our car when I felt instinctively drawn to the table next to us.

I glanced over at a twenty-something-year-old man sitting with a blank stare across his face. There was an aura about him that made me instinctively feel concerned for his well-being. I had no reason to believe he was hurting, but I sensed that something was troubling him. I couldn't help myself, I stopped the conversation with my husband mid-sentence and turned to the young man.

"Are you alright? I hope you are okay."

He turned his head slowly and responded, "Yeah."

"I'm sorry to bother you, but I felt the need to ask if you were alright and let you know if you need help, I'm a good listener. I just lost my father a few weeks ago, so perhaps I have a heightened awareness of grief. I just wanted you to know someone cares."

I have no idea if this man was troubled, or worse yet, contemplating whether his life was worthy at that moment, but it didn't matter to me whether he was or not. I sensed that at that moment I needed to say something, that it was important to send a message of hope to him. It was a very small, simple gesture and I will never know whether or not it had any impact. I just allowed myself to be open to sharing what I felt and sensed.

As a survivor of suicide, my awareness of those around me has increased in a profound way that has benefited my emotional intelligence. I believe that survivors have a fresh set of eyes, our senses are heightened in ways others aren't. We hold an amplified responsibility along with this enhanced skill, to globally change the narrative on mental health. *Who better than the wounded and grieving inhabitants of the earth to transform the way cultures across the globe view suicide and mental illness?* One thing we all can agree upon is we never want anyone else to go through the tragedy we have endured. This newfound lens on life is what makes our position one of power, and that power can be used in polar opposite directions; for good or bad.

We have one of two choices we can make. We can become bitter, or we can choose to become better. The choice is ours.

Once I got past the Yearning and Surrender Phases, I made a choice to lean into the loss and work to find inner peace by accepting that there was nothing I could do to change the situation. Because of what we've gone through, we hold a 'knowing' that people who have not survived a suicide loss don't have. We know that people can be intensely hurting, but they mask and conceal it so well that no one ever realizes the severity of their pain. I've tried to be aware of those around me with a new set of eyes and ears. If I see any sign of pain on someone's face, I try to share a glimmer of hope with them. It may be a simple "hello," and "take care of yourself," or more in-depth, similar to the service I do for my daughter's well-being.

A few years ago, my family was heading to grab a sandwich before our Saturday activities which usually included a few soccer games and errands. We decided to stop at one of our favorite sandwich shops. As we entered the strip mall, I noticed a man sitting on the curb just behind the trash dumpster, slightly hidden from the bustling of life happening around him. His face was looking down, his clothes were worn and dirty, and he hadn't shaved in months. Beside him sat a bag of blankets and what personal items he owned. My heart sank and I immediately told my husband to stop the car, "Drop me off here, go inside to order and I'll be there shortly." My family knew what I was up to, as this wasn't the first time I was drawn to a homeless person who needed some human interaction and connection. I spent the next several minutes learning his name, where he grew up, where he slept at night, and why he was sitting on the curb that day.

I bought him a sandwich and we continued our conversation about his next adventure. He was planning to hitchhike to the Carolinas to find winter work. He would do odd jobs whenever he could find them until the weather back here in Illinois got warmer. This was his life; one day, one hour, one minute at a time. I came back several times to see my new friend to give him a bit of spending money and asked if he needed a new blanket. Unfortunately, I've not seen him in years. I wonder how he's doing, if he's found a permanent home, or if he's still sleeping in the cold and longing for companionship. My interactions may not have been much, but I believe that every act of kindness can have some impact. I've read stories of a restaurant manager who helped a homeless man get a job by purchasing him a pair of shoes and a suit after sharing interview techniques with him, and a waitress who paid the check of a grieving couple after they lost their 9-month-old daughter. The impact of these acts of kindness is profound. We may never know the true effect of our actions with a stranger, but I'm certain we touch more people than we realize when we take the time to recognize their struggles and acknowledge that we are all fighting silent battles in our lives.

Studies show there is a high prevalence of mental health disorders amongst the homeless population, but I didn't need to read articles to comprehend that. When I look into a homeless person's eyes, I see the depression, despair, and inability to care for their own basic needs, something I've seen in many people suffering from mental health-related issues. Because of this, I look at the homeless with greater empathy than I did prior to losing my dad. I can see the pain and suffering in them now more vividly and with a new understanding. We all crave connection because it is necessary for our survival. Before I was afraid to approach someone I didn't know, but now I feel compelled to provide a small sense of validation and kindness because I know I may come across someone who is hanging on by a thread and my simple interaction may get them to tomorrow, or to next week.

I receive joy from seeing the gratitude on their faces, and I know they feel dignified being acknowledged even just for a few short moments. Sometimes just the recognition of our existence provides a day worth of encouragement. I see this as a gift that my father's passing has provided to me.

You too can begin to use your 'empathy lens' to help others and in doing so, you will find it distracts you from your personal strife when you focus on someone else and genuinely want to help another human being. When you have that first nudge to offer a caring hand, I encourage you to act. Act boldly and bravely because you have a new gift of 'knowing.' You can be a beacon of light in the darkness for others struggling, just like Jon was when he decided to come to the *Survivors of Suicide* meeting and share his story with the group. Now, I appreciate it when someone shares a story that helps me. It didn't begin that way, but as I worked through my healing, I came to realize our entire existence on this earth is simple; *It is to help one another.*

Paying it forward gives purpose to your grief and helps your healing process. There are scientific reasons behind why sharing what you've learned with someone else makes us feel better. When we lend a hand to someone in need, we release *feel-good* chemicals in our brain giving us what studies refer to as a 'helper's high.' Helping others is also known to reduce stress and increase our self-worth, which is a positive way to heal during grief.

You may find empathy and compassion for the homeless like I have, or you may have the desire to volunteer and assist the elderly, or even participate in a community youth organization. It doesn't matter where you focus your time and energy, but instead, all that matters is that you find a path that is right for you in offering your innate ability to help others. You decide how you feel called to help others with your newfound attunement. I want you to begin thinking about what you might be feeling called to do in the service of others.

How have you used your new heightened senses and awareness

of those suffering around you? Think of a time you have felt compassion toward a person or were drawn to help others around you. How did you respond to that desire to help?

Healing Moment

Write down something you've learned from your loss. Did someone share some guidance with you or did you read an article that provided you with a new perspective? Reflecting on an example of something you have learned can help you dismiss or regulate some of your unproductive thoughts. I want you to turn your focus to what you've gained so far during your healing process.

Since losing _____, I've learned...

_____

_____

_____

_____

_____

_____

Think about a time when you sensed your new 'empathy lens' and how it showed up in ways it didn't before losing your loved one. Write down an example of a time you felt called to show compassion for another person. How did that make you feel? Did you feel that 'helper's high' after you assisted the person?

Think of ways you could show compassion for others with your knowledge. What kind of impact do you envision your concern for someone else's well-being could instill in them? How do you feel when you picture yourself providing a caring hand to another in need? You can benefit from this experience as much as the person you're giving care toward. Your compassion in action will release feel-good endorphins in your brain.

Others could benefit from my compassion because...

If you have children in your life, you can use your power of compassion in an important manner that can encourage social and emotional development. One way to do this is to ask your children how they feel about situations and encourage them to share and discuss their emotions on a regular basis. Rather than asking them *how their day was*, ask them questions about the emotions they felt throughout the day. *How did you feel before taking your test? Were you scared, and why do you think you felt that way? What made you sad or angry today? Tell me something that made you feel grateful today.* This is just an example of how your knowledge and compassion combined can have a lasting impact.

Compassion Meditation

In this next exercise, I'm going to ask you to follow a guided meditation to help strengthen your empathy, compassion, and caring self. Empathy is a skill that can be learned and enhanced with practice. As you read this book, you will be automatically enhancing your natural empathy because I am helping you to build curiosity, explore new ideas and concepts, and encourage you to place yourself in other people's shoes, all of which are ways to develop your empathy.

Read the guided meditation and then close your eyes and envision the story, and picture a person who fits the description of each person you meet along your journey.

Sit in a chair with your feet flat on the ground. Relax your arms in your lap or to your side. Close your eyes. Take a deep breath in and hold it for a few seconds, slowly releasing the breath in a long exhale. Do this for three inhales and exhales.

I want you to picture yourself walking along the beach. The sun is glistening off the ocean and the waves are gently flowing over your bare feet. You feel the sand collapsing beneath your feet as it wraps between your toes. You look up and see a person sitting on the beach with their head lowered, and you can tell they are crying. You wonder if the person has lost something or someone. As you approach the person, you realize you *know* this person. This is someone you care deeply about. You extend your hand to them and ask if they need your help. They respond, "Yes," so you sit down next to them. You hold the space at that moment with them, feeling, sensing, and honoring their emotions. You say nothing, as you don't need to communicate that you are there in support of them. They just know, and after some time passes they thank you for stopping to see if they were ok. You stand up and smile at them as you continue on your wander along the beach. As you stroll along the beach, you notice the most beautiful shells, and you reach down to pick a few up and put

156

them in your pocket. You know they will come in handy, but don't quite understand how or why right now. A few more yards down the beach, you see a child no more than six years old sitting with their feet in the water. They also have their head lowered, and you can sense they are scared. You approach the child and ask, "Are you lost?" The child replies, "Yes, will you please help me?" You reach out your hand and say, "Yes, of course, I will help." Together you and the child walk holding hands. You remember the shells you have in your pocket, and you give them to the child, who looks at you and smiles.

Soon the two of you approach a path that leads up to a home. At the top of the steps leading to the house, you see a woman who appears distraught and frantic as she paces back and forth. You can't help but wonder if she's lost something or someone. You and the child climb the steps, and as you get to the top, the woman realizes you are there, and she runs toward you and swoops up, and embraces the child in her arms. You now know that this is the child's mother. You've brought the two of them together.

You are now free to leave them together and continue on your journey. You continue to walk as the sun begins to set over the ocean, and pink and yellow shades of color fill the sky.

You have one more person to meet on this walk. The last person you come upon is someone you have had difficulty with in your life. You are frustrated, irritated, and maybe even angry with this person. You are tempted to walk past this person and not acknowledge them until you see they are also suffering like your friend and like the child and the mother you've already met along your journey. Feeling compassion, you extend your hand one more time and ask this person if they need help. "Yes," they reply, and surprisingly, they reach up to you to grab your hand and say, "Thank you for caring enough to offer me help, even though I've not always been good to you." You smile back at them and reply, "I am a caring, compassionate person, and it gives me pleasure to help you."

Take a few more deep breaths before you open your eyes.

Now take a few minutes to write down what you felt as you approached each of the people you met along the beach.

How did you feel when you helped your friend/person you care for deeply?

_____

_____

_____

How did you feel when you handed the beautiful shells to the child and took hold of their hand?

_____

_____

_____

How did it make you feel when you realized you connected a lost child with their mother?

_____

_____

_____

How did it feel when the person who has wronged you in the past reached out to grab your hand and thank you for stopping to help them?

_____

_____

_____

Now that you've taken the time to share a lesson you've learned, and experienced how you've felt compelled to show compassion for other people, do you see how focusing your time, energy, and understanding on someone else's concerns can help you feel better? The act of selfless service to others is a powerful tool for you to tap into when you start to feel yourself sliding back into the self-pity zone.

Paying it forward can be as simple as posting a story about your loved one on a Facebook Survivor's Group to help another along their journey or providing lessons and guidance to someone who is grieving like you. It is profound progress on your journey of healing when you're able to offer some beneficial advice that will help another survivor of suicide along their own healing journey. This is a beautiful gift we can give to honor our loved ones and enhance our own empathy for others.

AIRPLANES

"Those we love never truly leave us, Harry.
There are things that death cannot touch."
~ JACK THORNE

It's been said that **love** never ends, even after death; this I believe is not only true, but I would add love can even be felt after death. I've talked to so many people who have felt the presence of their loved ones as if they were still right beside them, giving guidance and reassurance from the other side. I personally have had far too many similar experiences to question or take for granted that these encounters are not real. I am a believer in the ability of our loved ones to connect with us on the other side and offer signs of their love. Many times they will want to reach out to us to let us know they are close and alright. They may also have stronger messages to share with us of guidance, reassurance, and support. If we are open and accepting of their beautiful messages, we can receive them as they are intended to be shared. In this chapter, we will explore how our deceased loved ones show us love beyond the veil and want us to know they are still with us, around us, and beside us in a ubiquitous way.

The night my father passed, my brother, sister, and I began our drive back to Iowa to comfort our mom. Being the oldest and knowing the most details about what had happened, I knew I needed to allow my siblings to hear the news at their own pace. We hadn't discussed how Mom found Dad. We had only shared a phone call where I did my best to stay strong as I uttered the words, *"Dad's gone."* It was a long, silent ride as we each tried to process what had happened and come to terms with what Dad had done. Feeling his absence was devastating, and yet I clung to the feelings of wanting him to be there to meet us when we arrived. I longed for his presence just one more time, to hold his hand, touch his face, and give him a big bear hug, just like the many times we embraced before. We decided to break up the late evening, five-hour car ride by driving halfway and then staying the remainder of the night in a hotel.

The next morning the sun bounced its rays off the pavement. My sunglasses, while there to protect the UV, were also necessary to hide the tears welling in my eyes as I continued our drive. The fields in Iowa were filled with eight-foot-tall corn stalks, lined up like dominos as we sped past. I've always found it relaxing to stare out the car window as you pass a cornfield. It flickers by, rows precisely aligned with no end in sight. Dark brown, almost black Iowa soil between rows upon rows of bright green corn stalks.

Five hours in a car can feel painfully long, but this ride, even with a night of sleep in between, felt like the Tom Hanks movie *Cast Away;* on a deserted island of loneliness, with no 'Wilson' companion to befriend. None of us could find the words to comfort the other. The silence, at first, felt unbearable but also much needed. I wasn't sure how I would begin the conversation about Mom's discovery of Dad.

It felt as if our mouths were bound shut with duct tape. I don't remember if I broke the ice first, but I remember asking if they wanted more details before we would come face-to-face with our mom. I didn't want them uninformed before they saw her. I felt I owed them that knowledge so they could embrace her gently.

I began to share as best I could from what little my mom was able to recount from her traumatized state. I confirmed with my brother

161

and sister what they already suspected and did my best to relay the news as compassionately as I could.

As the silence returned and we completed the final miles in our journey to my mother's house, we noticed a bright yellow plane to our left flying alongside us. At first, we couldn't understand why it flew so low, but then it became apparent. It was a crop duster. The plane rose, almost like a rocket, to a higher altitude in front of us, then sharply circled back around, facing the opposite direction, and dove back down as it sprayed the corn below. It was a magnificent sight, and we all chuckled at how that plane broke our grim, somber state and filled our spirits with the bravery we needed as we knew we would face mom in a few minutes.

Picture: July 2014, just days before his funeral and one of many encounters with the yellow crop duster. Notice the roofline of my childhood home in the lower right corner of the image.

Mom was in shock, unable to discuss more about how she had found Dad, yet comforted to have her four children by her side. The first few days were overwhelming as we planned his funeral, but the love and shared decisions we made together helped ease the stress.

Most of that week back in Iowa was full of tears and a deep pain

I'd never felt before. It was the type of pain that took my breath away. It was as if my body knew to slow everything down because the pain had to pass through every cell momentarily. Amid all of that agony there were glimpses of hope, love, memories, and signs from heaven. I felt my father was helping to guide our decisions and assisting us as we planned the week. It was a mixture of despair and comfort, knowing he was gone yet feeling his presence was still with us. We cried a great deal but also smiled and laughed at the serendipitous occurrences that took place throughout the week.

I believe our deceased loved ones will do everything in their power to show that they are still with us. The signs I received and those my siblings sensed, felt, and dreamt about that week, were so unbelievably strong and significant that we kept a journal of them all. I love looking back at the moments when Dad showed up in simple, small ways. Like how inexplicable it was that my cell phone rang at the same time, 7:28 am, for three straight days, only to be my aunt accidentally dialing me and no one on the other end. I didn't give much thought to the number 7:28 until my sister mentioned that 7/28 was the day of his funeral. It felt as if Dad was saying he would be with us long after we laid him to rest. There were more signs, much like the daily phone call, but they were more profound than just a coincidence. We sensed that Dad was proving to us that he was safe and at peace. Knowing he was alright kept us moving forward throughout those dreadful days.

As we were trying to decide what we would do with the house and buildings filled with Dad's collection of antiques, vehicles, machinery, and tools, we got an amazing sign. My brother was drawn to an old typewriter in our parents' basement. In the typewriter was a single piece of paper with a note my father had typed. It was a sign from Dad meant to be found by my brother. While written years ago, the typing on the front had significant meaning to my brother. On the back side of that piece of paper was the name of an auctioneer with some details about why my dad was fond of him. The typed note went on to say how much Dad enjoyed the farm auctions led by this particular auctioneer, so when it came time for us to find an auctioneer, we got a few quotes, including one from this gentleman. After we met this man, it made sense why Dad liked him and why that typewritten note was left for my brother to find. This auctioneer valued and sold my father's antiques for three times more than the other auctioneer we were advised to use. Dad knew best.

There was more to the story of the typewriter. Shortly after finding the typewriter that day, there was a knock at the door. It was an unexpected visit from one of my brother's best friends from school. It just so happened that this friend was very familiar with typewriters and had a knack for fixing and cleaning them. He offered to restore Dad's vintage typewriter that my brother had found in the basement minutes before that amazing note was discovered. Ironically his talent with typewriters wasn't the only gift he'd share with us that day. The friend recalled a story about an interaction between his uncle and our father that made the visit extra special. He shared that his uncle had a license plate with the word Ubiquitous, and our dad thought a license plate with the word Ubiquitous was funny and made quite an impression on him. I could picture our dad laughing about the license plate as the story was shared. *But why did my brother's friend choose to share that obscure story? What caused him to recount that particular story?* This sign was not a coincidence. I believe that was Dad's way of telling us he'd always be with us no matter where he was or how far apart we were because he was now *Ubiquitous.*

The additional signs were obvious, especially when the yellow crop duster continued to make an appearance over the week multiple times. However, we still had no idea what the significance of that plane was until we found an envelope of photos Dad had kept. Inside the envelope was an image of the yellow crop duster. It spurred a memory for my brother, who told us how he recalled Dad talking about running into the pilot of the yellow plane one early morning while having coffee at the local truck stop. It was typical for Dad to find a stranger and start a conversation out of the blue. He was inquisitive, and he liked to listen to people's stories. I envisioned Dad pulling up a chair next to the pilot and asking him questions about crop dusting. I could hear his enthusiasm and jovial laugh as he joked, "How long have you been diving from the sky?" We'd like to believe Dad rode in that plane and had the time of his life dipping, diving, and rising through the sky. I imagine for a split second the feeling of the drop. I knew Dad wasn't one to ride roller coasters, but a crop-dusting adventure was something he'd love.

On the final day of our weeklong Iowa farewell to Dad, we packed up the cars and began driving out of town. I looked at my brother riding alongside me in the front seat and said, "Do you think Dad will give us one more crop duster today?" He chuckled and said, "I don't know, but it would be pretty amazing if he did." About four hours into our five-hour drive back to our home state of Illinois, we got the surprise of our lives. Just as we climbed a slow rolling hill, a plane swooped from the horizon flying straight toward us as it rose sharply. It felt so close to the roof of our car I instinctively ducked. It was the final crop duster of our week. We all screeched with the thrill of seeing a crop duster in Illinois. I'd never seen one before that day and have not since, almost eight years later.

I believe that a Higher Power, or Angels, guided me to write this, as it is one of the most important lessons you must gain from this book. They want you to know that it's important for you to accept these gifts because your loved one wants you to know they are alright. These are gifts from beyond the veil and can help in the healing process when you learn to accept them as such. Know that you aren't 'imagining it' when you hear that song on the radio at just the precise time; the lyrics are coming directly from heaven. Believe that there is no coincidence when you sense their presence and embrace it when you feel the joy flow through you with the relief that they are near. They are reaching out, supporting you, and trying to bridge the gap between our realm and theirs in these moments. Allow all your senses to flow through the veil and welcome their presence by letting it be known that you have received their signs openly and freely. Take a moment to hold the enduring touch and absorb all the love surrounding you.

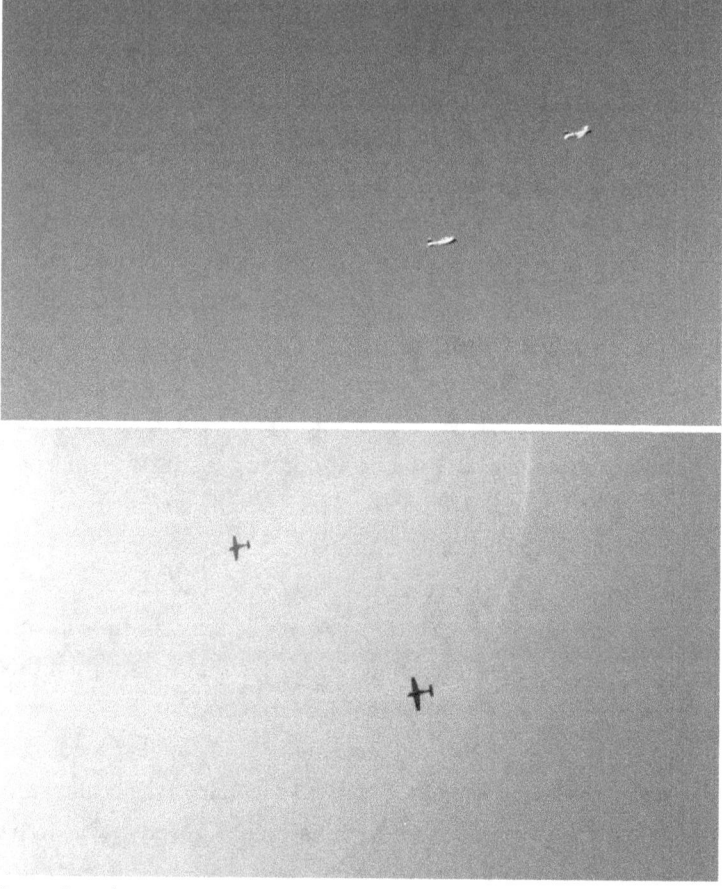

Picture: September 19, 2021. During an emotional moment when I needed a strong sign, not just one but two yellow airplanes swooped down and flew above me for about twenty minutes. Thank you, Dad, for your love and consoling messages when I need them most.

Week of Signs

As I was writing this chapter, I told my daughters about the beautiful signs from their grandfather; he sends me airplanes, especially yellow ones. I regularly share airplane stories with them to remind them how significant they are to me. It's our way of connecting with him on an ongoing basis, and it brings us all joy. My older daughter felt his presence the night he passed and saw signs from him, but my younger daughter is a skeptic and doesn't like to talk about these things. She listens intently, and I know she's thinking about him, but she's also a teenager trying to understand life on her own terms and timeline.

This is why I was surprised to hear my youngest daughter come home from soccer practice last night excited to share a story with me. She began by saying, "You know how you talk about all the signs you get from Grandpa? I don't feel like I've received any signs, until now." She went on to tell us this story.

"I asked Grandpa to send me a sign, but not just any sign. I knew in order for me to believe it was Grandpa, it would have to be something very obvious to me. I decided the strangest sign would be to see a reptile. Last night, I decided that if Grandpa could make a reptile appear in Illinois, I'd believe it was him. Tonight at soccer practice, all of a sudden, girls started screaming and running away from the field. In the middle of the soccer field were two snakes, not just one, but two! I was shocked and started to thank Grandpa, but then thought, well...that's just a coincidence. An airplane came out of nowhere in less than five minutes, flying super low! It was so low that most of the soccer team looked up and noticed how strange it was for this plane to fly this low with no airport around. That's when I knew it was my grandpa for sure."

My daughter was so excited to tell this story to me. She had asked for her sign, which was provided in less than 24 hours. I was also proud of my dad for making her wishes known. Sometimes all we need to do is ask. Our loved ones will do their best to make them appear for us, but we must be open to receiving them. Don't discredit the gift as a coincidence like my daughter started to do. Luckily, my dad wasn't going to let her dismiss him. The joy she got from accepting his gift was priceless.

The same week we talked about signs, my other daughter was cleaning out her closet. She'd been going through a rough time, and it took all of her energy to muster up the effort to clean a closet, but she decided to turn on music to focus for a few hours. This was what transpired for her in the 'week of signs.'

"Mom, I think I may have gotten a sign from Grandpa. As I was pulling stuff off the top shelf of my closet, I found an old shipment wrapper for some piece of clothing I must have purchased online. Just as I opened it up to read the writing on the wrapper, a Billie Eilish song was playing on my Spotify account, and the lyrics, *As long as I'm here, no one can hurt you.* The writing on the shipping wrapper says, "*I'm here.*" I read the shipping wrapper at the exact same time as I heard the lyrics of that song."

I knew with certainty her grandpa was saying he was always *here* protecting her.

Both of my daughters had received beautiful messages from their grandfather within days of each other and shared them with me. But that wasn't the end; as my daughter told me her story about the music lyrics and shipping wrapper, we were leaving to go to an appointment. As she shared the story with me, out of nowhere, the car radio, which wasn't turned on, loudly blared the lyrics, "I'm an angel with a shotgun..." *'Angel With a Shotgun'* is a song written and performed by The Cab, which my daughter downloaded to her iTunes list several years ago. We both jumped in shock because the volume was so loud. I immediately turned down the volume, and for a split second, we couldn't figure out what had happened. Neither of us had connected our phones to the car audio on purpose. Then it hit me... that was my dad. He's the angel with a shotgun. He wanted us to know he was present with us as we talked about his other beautiful signs. He needed to solidify his presence with us one more time. We smiled and thanked him.

I could write an entire book about signs from heaven from personal experiences, but if you still aren't convinced or don't want to take my word for it, I have many powerful stories of signs from the people I've interviewed and connected with over the years. Stories of dreams of their loved ones appearing to tell them something from the other side, gifts of pennies and feathers falling from the sky and dropping in front of them, hummingbirds, butterflies, and cardinals, all making contact with a human in unconventional ways.

If this chapter calls you to seek information about the signs the universe sends you, I highly encourage you to read the book, *Signs: The Secret Language of the Universe* by New York Times Bestseller, Laura Lynne Jackson. Her book made me understand that once I started accepting these wondrous signs as the beautiful messages they are from the other side, I could never *unsee them*. They've been a new gift of sight and perspective I've discovered and cherished ever since.

Healing Moment

Do you receive signs from your loved one? If so, describe the signs you've received in detail.

If you said no to the above question, I want you to ask for a sign right now. Make it specific so that when you receive your sign, you'll know it's your loved one who sent it. You can ask for anything, but know the more specific your ask is, the longer it could take for your loved one to make it happen. I've asked for raccoons as a sign once, and I received the sign within two weeks. The first time was on a television commercial I had never seen before, and then a few weeks later, I saw two live raccoons at separate times while driving in my car. I've not seen a raccoon in over a year, so it's no coincidence that I received my sign multiple times over the course of a month. Be sure to give thanks for the gift. Tell your loved one you saw their sign and appreciate that they provided you with a beautiful message.

Asking For A Sign

Example of how to ask for a sign: *Loved one, I want to know you are safe. I want to know that you are no longer in pain. Please send me a sign to let me know you are okay. If I see a... (airplane, raccoon, reptile, or feather), I will know you are with me. I love you and miss your presence.*

Write down a sign you want to receive from your loved one.

When you receive your sign, write down exactly where you were, how you felt, and what happened as you processed this miracle message. Did you accept that it was a gift from your loved one? How did thanking them for their message make you feel at that moment? I want you to write down everything you remember, so you can come back to read how you felt and experience it over and over again.

12

CONNECT

In the 1990 iconic movie *Ghost*, there is a memorable scene where Demi Moore plays a grieving woman, Molly, whose beloved soulmate, Sam, has died. She is not convinced that Sam, played by Patrick Swayze, is trying to get in touch with her through a psychic woman, played by Whoopi Goldberg. To prove to her he's there beside her, Sam slowly pushes a penny up the door and then hands it to her; as Goldberg's character, Oda Mae Brown, says from the other side of the door, "Sam says it's for luck."

If you've watched that movie, you may recall the emotions you felt as Demi Moore's character realizes there is no other explanation, but to believe her deceased love, Sam, is present and standing right beside her. If only we could be so convinced every time our loved ones send us signs.

We all have the ability to connect with our loved ones on the other side. I'm reassured even more strongly that the signs I spoke about in the last chapter are from my father and other angels who want to make their presence known to me after speaking with the Reverend Sheila Black, an ordained Minister, accredited Medium, and certified Spiritual Healer. She confirmed many of my personal beliefs and affirmed the signs I had received from my father.

After a few mishaps which kept us from connecting sooner, Rev.

Sheila and I finally met. The anticipation of learning more about how I could connect with my father was intense. I believe it was fate that caused our scheduled meeting to be delayed. Upon starting our session together, Sheila shared that she had spoken with a mother earlier that day about her son, who took his life exactly three months ago. The young man was in the military and had hung himself during the isolation of Covid. Sheila shared the events that had aligned for her to meet his girlfriend and eventually his mother. The young man's spirit had been nudging Sheila to reach out to his mother because he had some important messages to share. She explained that Spirits will persist until she reacts to them and lets them know she will assist in their goal. She could still sense his presence as we talked. It was synchronicity that we met on that particular day, and I'd like to believe this young man who Sheila channeled for his mother earlier in the day was helping us to determine what we needed to talk about and include in this book from the other side.

There are ways you can connect with your loved ones that have passed. Rev. Sheila shared how meditation and breathing techniques can help raise our vibration and allow messages and signs to come through more readily. Meditation is a way to disconnect from the noise in our life and go inward to tap into our innate wisdom. Rev. Sheila affirms that it is absolutely key to tuning into the spirit realm. Meditating allows you to hear messages as they come to you in stillness by filtering out the chatter in your mind and creating a clear headspace.

The first step to effective meditation is to clear distractions sur-rounding you through social media, television, and other electronics, so it's important to be completely 'unplugged'. Getting comfortable physically is the next step in preparing for meditation. While many people prefer to meditate while sitting upright, lying down, or even walking while meditating are all acceptable, so you may want to try each to see what feels best for you. Once physically comfortable, you can begin to think about the type of meditation you want to try. It's a good idea to try listening to both guided and non-guided meditations because each can benefit your relaxation process. Another option to consider in determining what type of meditation you like is to look for apps on your phone that offer binaural beats, as this sometimes helps people quiet their minds if they tend to have a lot of self-talk going on. Binaural beats are two tones – one in each ear – that are slightly different in frequency, thus causing your brain to process them at different frequencies and claim to help reduce anxiety, increase concentration, relieve stress, and help manage pain. I prefer transcendental meditation, a technique of repeating a silent mantra to relax the mind, clear thoughts, and gain inner peace. This meditation helps ground me by allowing my thoughts to pass by while I quiet my mind. Any of these meditation techniques are effective, and you don't have to go to great lengths to start. It can be as easy as searching for 'meditation' on the internet and closing your eyes. Over time, and after some practice, you'll find what works best, makes you feel the most comfortable, and quiets your mind.

Breathing techniques are another way to get in tune with our ability to connect with the other side. There are many forms of breathing techniques that you can use, including box breathing and deep breathing. During box breathing, you inhale, hold, exhale, and hold for the same amount of time, usually four to five seconds. As you complete the four breath steps, you can envision yourself drawing the sides of a square or box, hence the technique's name. In deep breathing, also known as belly breathing, you fill your abdomen with air on the inhale, making your belly rise, and as you exhale, you push all the air from your belly, lowering it back to its natural state. You notice your belly rather than your lungs holding the air with each breath. Deep breathing stimulates the vagus nerve, lowering your heartbeat, and reducing your 'fight or flight' mechanism, relaxing your body and mind. Finally, a technique I taught my daughters to use at a very early age was progressive muscle relaxation. You lay on your back, and as you inhale, tighten your muscles, starting with your feet, and hold that tension for a few seconds, then release the tension as you breathe out. Work your way up your body, using your muscles from your calves to your thighs until you reach your face and forehead.

Using techniques like breathwork and meditation will help put you in a heightened state of awareness and energy vibration, allowing your loved one to connect with you and send you messages or signs more freely than if you were stressed, distracted, or vibrating at a low frequency. I learned from Rev. Sheila that the physical world vibrates at a much lower level than the spirit world, which is why they call someone who can bring forth signs from the other side a medium. Sheila also shared that a medium raises their vibration to meet in the middle and help bridge the lines of communication with the spirit world.

Talking with a psychic medium is something that you may be curious about. It's natural for you to want to find ways of validating that your loved one is okay. A medium can bridge the gap between the living and the deceased. I do not doubt that my dad has come through when talking to gifted mediums. However, you must find someone trained only to bring forth positive healing messages and understand grief and loss. Not every medium works for the highest good, so do your research and ensure they are reputable before booking an appointment. Don't just stop at the first psychic storefront you find. Talk to other people for recommendations before you make your decision.

Rev. Sheila tends not to push her beliefs onto other people, especially the skeptics, because it's not for her to worry about whether or not they believe. Still, she does find it sad that people will miss the opportunity to receive a special gift from heaven. I asked her what she says to people who don't believe in signs and synchronicities with those who have passed. "I usually tell people that I don't believe in coincidences, perhaps you do, but I don't. I ask them just to be open and play along with me and see if they can see a connection." It can't hurt to be open to the thought and see if they find an association with their loved ones. She tells them that she believes that the spirit is always around us, and if we ask them for a sign, they will show us one. You just have to pay attention. You must disconnect from all the chatter, sit still, and be open to receiving.

Signs can come in various degrees of intensity. Some are small things that happen sporadically, or some may consistently show themselves over a period of time. Others are real *gotcha moments* where it's hard not to notice their significance. Sheila cautions us that we have to pay attention or we may miss them.

Sheila's dear friend passed away recently, and when she's feeling the absence of her friend, she will often ask her to give her a sign. Her friend provides symbols in the form of hearts carved from nature. Those are what she refers to as little signs. Every rock or knot in a tree that is the shape of a heart is her dear friend saying hello and letting her know she's all right. Larger or stronger signs come in the form of more significance or magnitude. There are times when she misses her mom, who passed away, and wants to pick up the phone to share some great news, and has to catch herself, realizing her mom's not here anymore. One time, in particular, she reached to phone her mother, and upon her realization, her phone rang, and her mom's photo popped up on the screen. "Wow, Mom, you're calling me. I was going to call you," Sheila chuckles as she shares and follows it up with, "I could tell you thousands of stories like this from my personal experiences."

Rev. Sheila continues to tell me about more miraculous experiences of her clients. One had lost her baby in a bad car accident, and as she lay on a stretcher, scared for her own mortality, not knowing whether or not she would survive, she looked up at just the right moment to see a transport truck passing by with the name of her baby painted on the side. Sheila sees no other explanation; "To me, that's an undeniable sign; to others, it's a coincidence."

Rev. Sheila went on to share with me the signs her father sends her. "My dad likes to send me blue jay feathers. When I visited Scotland, where he was born, I was literally tripping over feathers everywhere I went. There were no birds, but I came home with a suitcase full of feathers."

Our loved ones are always with us, and they want us to know they are safe and at peace. *I'm okay. Never give up hope and you're never alone*, are the additional guidance they are providing you with when they show you signs.

Healing Moment

Burge Smith-Lyons is a global motivational speaker, and spiritual and emotional trainer of transformational 'playshops' on relationships, leadership, empowerment, communications, and abundance. I met her through my grief journey and she taught me a technique of talking to a candle, which contributed to one of the first major breakthrough moments for me. At first, I was afraid, and it took me several days to work up the courage to give it a try. I needed to find a quiet space as I didn't want anyone to see me talking to a candle. However, this was one of the most profoundly soothing things I did to begin my healing journey and I didn't start this ritual until almost two years after my dad passed. Since then, I've completed this healing moment several times, and its power is so intense that I've even shared this technique with a few friends during their grief of losing a parent. I have never thought twice about sharing it, even though I remember precisely how scared and strange I felt when I first learned of this technique myself. The reason I feel so certain I'm meant to share this healing technique is because after completing it I felt such relief. Things I had kept hidden came to the surface and were released from my mind, body, and soul.

If you are ready to connect with your loved one, you will need a white candle for this healing moment. If you are ready to connect with your loved one, feel free to put the book down and find a candle now.

Candle Gazing Technique

Choose a place you feel comfortable and light a white candle in a quiet place. You may want to be alone for this healing moment.

I want you to stare at the burning candle gently, and as you gaze into the flame, I want you to say the name of your loved one aloud or silently. Say their name a few times. Then wait...

Wait until you see the candle flicker. You can begin when you see the candle jump or move side to side.

Tell your loved one everything that comes to your mind and ask questions such as, *Are you okay? Are you at peace? Do you regret leaving me? What am I supposed to do without you here? How can I go on without you?* Whether good or bad, you don't need to hold anything back. Tell them how you feel about them leaving you. Tell them how angry, sad, hurt, ashamed, guilty, or any other emotion you feel. Get it all out. Talk as long as you like and leave nothing unsaid.

When you feel like you've said everything you needed to say, sit silently for a minute.

Now it's their turn to speak. Let them know it's their turn and that you are listening. Ask them out loud. *Is there anything you want to say to me?*

Listen, and watch how the flame jumps and moves as you hear their message come into your thoughts. No matter what comes into your heart and mind, it is real. Do not doubt that these are messages from beyond. When no more thoughts flood your mind and they are quiet and have nothing more to say, thank them and say *We are complete for now, and* blow out your candle.

THE SHARING OF

LOURDES

SEPTEMBER 26, 1966 - NOVEMBER 12, 2016

Lourdes M. Santos, age 50 at rest Saturday, November 12, 2016, in Naperville, IL. Born September 26, 1966, in San Juan, Puerto Rico, the loving daughter of Florentino (Maritery) Roces and Lourdes (Enrique) Altuzarra, beloved mother of Andrew Santos and Ashley Santos, and fond sister of Jose (Elaine) Roces. Lourdes Maria Santos was raised in Miami Florida and graduated from Florida International University with a degree in Medical Technology in 1989. Lourdes was an active member of the National Honor Society during her school years. After time spent in the medical field, Lourdes devoted her time to raising her two children, Andrew and Ashley. As a doting and active mother, Lourdes was always involved in her children's school and athletic activities. She loved to read, decorate, and lend a helping hand to anyone who needed it. She will always be remembered for her cheerful presence and her ability to light up a room with her warm smile. A Celebration of Lourdes's life will be held on Thursday, November 17, 2016, at 4:00 PM at Crossroads Church, 3003 South Eola Road, Aurora, Il. 60503.

179

The Story of Lourdes, Mom. Told by Ashley, Daughter.

I walked into the performance arts center of our local high school for the first time in the fall of 2016. I didn't quite know what to expect; it was freshman orientation for the incoming graduating class of 2020. My daughter was a freshman so it was my duty to go and find out all this high school had to offer her. This was the first time I met Ashley. Technically I learned who she was, but she didn't actually 'meet' me. Ashley was a senior and one of a few chosen students who would address the parents and freshman students to provide the idyllic impression of how Naperville North High School (NNHS) would mold new students to be the best of the best.

I remember her standing five foot four on stage with dark curly brown hair. She was mature and articulate and impressed me instantly. It was apparent why the administration had selected Ashley to speak to parents and freshmen students. She was academically gifted and a star athlete.

I recall thinking, *If my girls could be half as confident as this young lady, I'd be very pleased.* She was a successful student-athlete, serving as captain of the soccer team for both her junior and senior years, and later signed with a division one school to play soccer the following fall. She spoke of her academic achievements and how she had mastered time management skills while being an ambitious and extremely active student at NNHS. It made sense that I instantly connected with her because she was someone who I would want my daughters to look up to as a role model during their high school years.

Months went by and I hadn't given much thought about that freshman orientation night, but later that fall, I heard the news about the suicide of a mother of a high school student. That student was Ashley, and that mother was Lourdes. Lourdes died by stepping in front of a Metra train during the early morning hours of a Saturday in November. I remember feeling devastated, dwelling on the pain

Ashley had to have been feeling. Being so young and alone as a senior in high school instantly teleported me back to my high school days and the fear of my own parent's mental illness crisis.

As months passed, stories and articles ran in the local paper about Ashley. I couldn't believe the bravery with which she was speaking out about losing her mom to suicide and how she was moving forward, still reaching her goals of becoming a star student and soccer player. I was once again impressed by her maturity. For someone of her age to have such a profound sense of awareness of her situation and the strength to move forward was unique and riveting to me. *Who raised this wise young lady?* It had to be a very special person. I wanted to learn more about Ashley's mom, Lourdes Santos. I reached out to Ashley over social media and shared with her the connection I felt to her story and wished to meet her to learn how she was dealing with the loss of her mother. I also told her my story to let her know I was also a survivor, and we immediately connected because our stories had many similarities.

Ashley began by telling me her childhood was 'weird' and not as typical as her friends. I could relate, understanding how mental illness plays a role in the instability and lack of certainty children long for and need to feel secure. She shared how she didn't know that her mom was mentally ill until she was much older, but that as a child, she just knew her mom to be slightly different than other moms. She knew her grandmother to be a bit odd as well. She recalls calling her grandma a little 'crazy" in front of her mother and regrets ever saying those words, now that she realizes the genetic link and how much that probably hurt her mother to hear her describe her grandmother that way. She now knows that her maternal grandmother suffered from severe bipolar disorder.

Ashley said her life started with two loving parents and a brother four years older than her. Her family moved from Virginia when Ashley was young because of her father's job with the Drug

Enforcement Agency (DEA). She remembers living in a beautiful home with a pool in the backyard and enjoying 'Friday night pizza parties' as a family. But by the second grade, her parents divorced due to what Ashley says, on reflection, was the result of her mom's mental illness. She and her older brother had to downsize with their mom to a much smaller home they rented. Downsizing became a pattern that Ashley grew to understand. It seemed the natural progression when someone would leave the household. When her older brother eventually left for college, she and Lourdes moved from the small house they shared to an even smaller two-bedroom apartment.

After the divorce, Ashley said she didn't see much of her father because he moved back to the east coast. Her parents would split time-sharing custody between holidays, but Ashley remembers times when her father felt like a stranger to her. Now that Ashley is a college student in her early twenties, she has a much stronger connection with her father. Lourdes' passing was ultimately the catalyst that helped their father-daughter bond.

"My mom was always concerned with what I needed as a child and would find a way to support my dreams no matter what," recalls Ashley when I asked her what she valued and learned from her mom. Lourdes held many jobs throughout her life to make ends meet. She was a medical technician, worked in the hospital insurance department, and was an early childhood translator and teacher's aide. Lourdes tried to return to school to become a teacher to increase her earning potential, but that, unfortunately, amounted to just a lot of debt, and she never finished her degree. Money was tight for the family, and Ashley remembers making sacrifices and getting by on less, but always having food on the table. Her mom was *the hardest worker she ever knew.* Lourdes would work herself to the point of being too thin to ensure her children had everything they needed before fulfilling her own basic needs.

Lourdes was also an amazing cook. Ashley told me that her

favorite dishes were her mother's tasty home-cooked Cuban carnitas, tostones, rice and beans, and egg sandwiches. Preparing food was Lourdes' way of expressing her love. Ashley's friends would come over to be filled with love and full bellies.

Ashley was used to not having the finer things that some of her friends were lucky to possess, but that didn't matter because there was always love in her home. Her mother instilled in Ashley a strong sense of education. Lourdes would volunteer for school activities to be close to her children, and when she wasn't working she attended Ashley's soccer games and her son's baseball games. Lourdes made sure her children got to do all the things they wanted to do regarding academics and athletics. Ashely knew that her mom wasn't able to be at every game like her teammates, but she knew the reason her mom wasn't there was that she was working so that Ashley could partici-pate. Lourdes always found the means to pay for the expensive soccer fees of the elite travel teams in the suburbs of Chicago by becoming an integral part of the comradery that developed naturally between parents of children playing on traveling sports teams. The team and the player's parents became Ashley and Lourdes' extended family.

One of the first realizations that there was something different about her mom was when Ashley was about twelve. Her father had come from the east coast to spend time with Ashley and her brother and took them to a waterpark. Ashley recalls they were having a wonderful time when it was suddenly interrupted. Her brother, a few years older than Ashley, had a cell phone that was pinging endlessly with voicemails and text messages. The same was happening with her father's phone. Family friends were calling and texting, but Ashley didn't understand why. She recalls her father saying they needed to leave because her mom was sick. What she didn't know until she was a teenager was that her mom had attempted suicide while they were away at the waterpark. This wasn't her mother's first attempt. Ashley would later learn, after Lourdes' passing, that she had made two previous attempts. Because she was younger than her brother, her father felt it inappropriate to share this news with her. This would perhaps end up haunting Ashley as she grew older because if Ashley had known of her mom's illness, she might have reacted differently when Lourdes began to show symptoms of her disease.

The summer before Ashley's senior year of high school, things started to spiral out of control for Lourdes. Ashley describes the time as uncertain and unstable. In hindsight, Ashley now realizes her mom was experiencing symptoms of her illness as her actions became erratic and her decision-making abilities diminished. At some point, Lourdes stopped taking her medications which previously had helped stabilize her illness.

Ashley's first indication that something didn't seem right was when her mom began purchasing new cars she didn't need and gave Ashley her existing red Mini Cooper. Ashley came home one day to a matching red Mini Cooper duffle bag sitting on the end of her bed, and inside were the keys to the car! She knew her mom loved that car and couldn't afford to just hand it over, but being a teenager and excited to get a nice car to drive, Ashley says she accepted the gift. She also knew it was irrational when her mom purchased a brand-new SUV and a Volvo convertible despite her financial instability. Still, she had no idea her mom's poor decisions were a sign of something direr. She didn't see the connection that giving away precious items is one of the signs that someone is contemplating suicide.

Buying brand-new cars and trunks full of shopping bags were not typical impulses for a woman who spent her entire life taking such care to ensure her children went to the best schools, had the best education, and could play on travel sports teams. This selfless woman who had sacrificed the finer things her entire life in order to give her children the best opportunities was somehow disappearing in front of Ashley's eyes.

During this same time, Lourdes began dating a man fifteen years younger than her and he was not the caliber of someone Ashley would expect her mom to spend her time with. Ashley detailed how she questioned if it was her mom's way of filling the need to care for someone now that her children were growing up because she couldn't understand any other reason why her mom would want to date this man.

Ashley and Lourdes had lived a frugal life up to that point, and Ashley was starting to worry about her mom's actions and choices. Ashley confronted her mom and asked where all the money had come from. Lourdes said she had won the lottery, but when pressed for more details, she wouldn't divulge to Ashley any more information than to *not worry, I have this under control.* Ashley describes a role reversal during those final months of summer and early fall 2016. Ashley became the parent, and her mom was behaving more like the child.

Ashley recalls the time she and her mom were driving when Lourdes pulled the car over to a stop and started to cry. "My 17-year-old daughter knows more about life than I do." That was when Ashley became scared and knew her mom wasn't just experiencing a difficult phase that would soon pass and the story of the lottery winnings might not be true either. Something was seriously wrong with her mom. Ashley knew she needed more help with the situation, so she called her father that evening. The advice he provided over the phone was, "Make sure she doesn't hurt herself." Ashley thought to herself, *What does that mean?* She did not know about her mother's previous suicide attempts, so while she understood his statement, it wasn't completely sinking in that her mom was in grave danger.

That's a heavy responsibility to place on a teenager with no context or understanding of the complexity of her mother's mental illness. Had she known her mother had made two previous suicide attempts, Ashley may have responded differently. What 17-year-old can fathom their mom is contemplating ending her life? Ashley only knew she needed to keep peace in the house and not upset her mother.

In hindsight, Ashley now realizes her mom's health was spiraling, but she tries not to remember those last six months because that wasn't the 'mom' she knew. "I don't want to remember her like that," she says. "I want to erase those last six months I had with her because it created a bad image in my brain. I want to remember her cooking great meals for my friends, our amazing bond, and our open relationship with each other. I want to remember the little moments like her folding my laundry."

What transpired the night Lourdes ended her life haunts Ashley. "I got home from hanging with friends, and Mom was still up, so I joined her in the living room to watch TV It was a bit odd for Mom to still be up at midnight, as she'd usually ask me just to wake her to let her know I was home." Ashley recalls it was getting late and decided she needed to go to bed as she had plans in the morning. "I'm going to bed, mom." Lourdes responded, "Come give me a hug." But instead of wrapping her arms around her mom, Ashley simply replied, "I'll see you in the morning," and went to bed without hugging her goodnight.

The following morning, Ashley awoke by a knocking at the front door. "*Mom will get it,*" she thought. When the knocks continued, she wondered, "*Maybe she's out for groceries?*" Ashley finally got up, and as she looked down the hallway toward her mom's room, her dog Bailey was sitting in her mom's doorway, not at the front door where all the commotion was going on. Little did Ashley know Bailey would be her best companion and saving grace through the next chapter of her life.

Ashley opened the apartment door and in the hallway stood two Naperville police officers. One of them asked... "Where's your mom?" Ashley was confused. "Can we come in for a second?" As her stomach dropped, Ashley thought something had happened to her friends from the night before. The police officers asked her to have a seat and then delivered the kind of news no one is ever prepared to hear. "This is never news we want to deliver," the police officer said.

Ashley felt a punch in the gut as she immediately knew intuitively that her mom was gone. She opened her mouth, spewing the words out loud before the officers could tell her, "Is my mom dead?" The police confirmed her greatest fear as they told Ashley how her mother had gone to the train station in the early morning hours and taken her life. Ashley says she completely freaked out and the rest of the day was a complete blur. Her whole world unraveled within ten minutes of waking up on November 12th, 2016.

Ashley lives with the regret and guilt of her actions that night and questions herself. "What if I had hugged her? Could I have stopped her from making that our last night together? I missed the last opportunity to hug my mom. That messed me up for a long time, and I had to work through it with a grief counselor."

Ashley has rewritten the story for herself. She would like to believe that as she slept that night, her mom came into her room, kissed her cheek, and told her goodbye. There was no note, but there was evidence of the plans from the searches made on her computer. The Metra train schedule and a search on "What happens to your debt when you die" were a few of the last searches. Ashley didn't know that night that her mom was planning to file for bankruptcy the next morning. Lourdes' debt had become a significant burden to her. A dear friend of Lourdes was planning to take her that Saturday, the day she passed, to discuss the bankruptcy filing. It pains Ashley to this day that her mom couldn't see she had support and there was a way out.

Knowing how her mom would have wanted Ashley to handle things, she made the brave and conscious choice to 'move forward.' "She wouldn't have wanted me to crumble." Ashley knew how much her mom wanted her to achieve her dream of playing college soccer. For Ashley, moving forward became her mantra. She spoke out in the local newspaper about her mom's death with a strength I can only imagine was fueled by Lourdes's motherly imprint. It's not about moving on, because this experience completely altered who she was as a person, and her life would never be the same. Her courage and belief that her mom was still a driving force for her got her through the days, weeks, and months following her death. Ashley finished her senior year, continuing to play soccer along with her scholarly achievements. This is what Lourdes would have wanted, and it was the one thing Ashley knew she needed to do for the both of them.

After graduating high school, she fulfilled her childhood dream of playing division I soccer with impressive statistics. Today, Ashley is comfortable with sharing the importance of caring for your mental health and identifying the signs and symptoms with her fellow stu-dent-athletes. She has taken the time to discuss her personal story with her teammates. She uses her knowledge of her mother's illness and loss to impress upon her teammates the need to care for each other and themselves. She's working on her master's and plans to become a math teacher. She hopes she can be the teacher her students and everyone in the school want to talk to when they have doubts and feel unworthy. *Even if I suck at teaching math, I can impact young lives. I want my students to come to class feeling comfortable; they can talk to me about anything. I will make that promise to be a role model, mentor, and advocate for my students.*

"She wouldn't have taken her life if she knew I couldn't continue without her. How I was raised shaped me into where I needed to be at that point. God knew I was going to be fine. He knew I would move forward, become better and stronger and do something with it."

Everything happens for a reason.

Tattooed across Ashley's rib cage are the words, *everything happens for a reason.* A symbol of her mom's favorite phrase. She uses that phrase to keep her moving forward and hopes that one day she will be even braver at sharing the lessons she's learned from an amazing mother whose teachings were powerful while she was alive and in her death.

"Be grateful for the time you have with your mom. I want to help people gain that perspective without going through the tragedy I had to go through."

Ashley offers some profound advice. She feels strongly about having someone to talk to outside of your family. Having a consistent person, a professional, to check in with regularly is important. It needs to be someone you feel comfortable with and can offload things to without feeling like you're a burden to them. She believes the stigma of suicide is loosening up, so hopefully, more people are willing to get the help they need. She relates the importance of the support she received for processing her emotions following her mom's death and credits the sports psychologist she was provided with throughout college. Mental health has become a part of the training program for athletes where Ashley attends school, it's a much-welcomed shift within her soccer program; all athletes these days should have this type of support.

13

EMERGE

*"No one is actually dead until the ripples
they cause in the world die away."*
—TERRY PRATCHETT

Stage Five - The Emerging Phase

How we emerge from the depths of our loss determines how we move forward in life. As I mentioned earlier, we have one of two choices: we can become bitter, and allow remorse, shame, and guilt to devour us whole, or we can choose to become something better, a transformed human being who lives with a veil lifted. The choice is ours.

Bitterness leads to self-destruction and agony. No one benefits from living in a state of anger, resentment, and shame; not us, nor the people around us. I'm guessing you've met someone who likes to complain about everything in life. They drain every ounce of energy from you and are no fun to be around. That is what prolonged bitterness will do to someone. Betterment, on the other hand, leads to finding a new purpose and a new emergence of our life after loss. When a person has chosen to make something good from the depths of devastation, it's almost inevitable that it is profound and transformative.

You've been through the stages of Yearning, Educating,

Surrendering, and Empathy. Now we come to the Emerging phase. This is the only time I'll say that being a survivor of suicide has a benefit. What I mean by this is all of us survivors have a fresh set of eyes. Things we took for granted before are no longer hidden in the peripheral. Our senses are heightened to new levels. We hold an amplified awareness and responsibility along with these enhanced attributes. With our recently discovered clarity, we now hold the potential to change the narrative on mental health globally. Who better than the wounded and grieving inhabitants of the earth to transform the way cultures across the globe view suicide and mental illness? We all can agree that we never want anyone else to go through the tragedy we have endured. This newfound lens on life is what makes our position one of power. And that power is meant to be used for good in the world.

When I shared the step of empathy earlier, I wanted to make the point that we each hold a metaphoric gift in our hands: our compassion for helping others. As I suggested, our emotional tie or connection to others is only activated and fulfilled when we take action and respond to the empathic call. The gift we hold is one that not only helps the person we give it to, but also helps us. We tend to believe that by being empathetic, we are only serving another in need. However, it's actually much more complex and beautiful. Being empathetic toward another is a reciprocal process. We gain as much, if not more when we reach out to someone in need and authentically connect with them. There is no need to learn what to do to show empathy, as you have the metaphoric gift of knowing pain which will guide you if you just listen and respond.

Besides the basic physical needs of food, water, shelter, and sleep, there are a few additional key things we desire as humans: acceptance, acknowledgment, love, and dignity. While Maslow's Hierarchy of Needs may be more theory-based and most certainly studied and researched, I like to simplify what I believe are the key components of basic human needs. In my opinion, it's as simple as having someone tell you these three statements and ask one question when they lean in to help. *I see you, I hear you, I understand you, and how can I help?* Compassionate empathy is the emotional tie that connects us to other people and encourages us to take action in order to truly emerge. We must not only show how we care for others, but we must act to benefit from the reciprocal effects of empathy. This is why becoming better, rather than bitter, is the gift you now possess from having clarity after a tragedy.

This present can be empty or hold a blossoming growing flower. You get to choose. Just as Ashley chose to move forward knowing that it was what her mom would have wanted her to do, you can choose to take steps toward your personal growth.

When we can accept the gift as it is intended and gain a little wisdom from our loss, we crack open a door to allow a sliver of more light into our space for healing. Ashley could open that door by remembering a motto she shared with her mother, "Everything happens for a reason." After Lourdes passed, it had an even deeper meaning. For Ashley, it symbolized her mom's destiny and provided a reason behind her mom's death. She knows now Lourdes' passing can be perceived as part of a bigger picture that is playing out in her life.

Ashley believes there is meaning and purpose that is to come from this tragedy. She prefers to look for the silver lining and focus on her mom's positive influence on her life rather than the devastating end. The ending is insignificant to the bravery, courage, and strength her mom possessed and the love her mom created in the world. In Ashley's view, how Lourdes died has no relevance and does not define her mom's life. The two are completely incompatible, which provides her relief from some of the emotional distress over suicide. Her positive view and perspective, given how much she's suffered, are inspiring. Obviously, this mindset has helped Ashley through her healing process and has positively impacted how she's processed her grief. She's been able to connect the positive meaning of her loss with events that have taken place since.

Ashley has stepped through phase four, Empathy, and has been able to pay it forward. During college, she met and became best friends with a girl who would go on to lose her father to brain cancer. Ashley knows now that her losing her mother was the reason her new best friend was put in her path. She was meant to be put in this friend's life at precisely the right time in which to provide the support, compassion, and love her friend needed. Having already gone through the experience of losing a parent provided Ashley with tools to support her new friend.

The concept of "everything happens for a reason" is powerful in the healing process. It gives a sense of closure and helps alleviate some pain. It is in times of tragedy and adversity that we experience our biggest growth. Aristotle, the Greek Philosopher, believed that *everything happening to you today has a purpose.* It allows you the opportunity to learn and transform into the person you were meant to become all along. When you have a reason for things happening to you, a shift in your thought pattern can empower you in life. It can provide a reason to help ease the burden and pain, which allows us to heal. Sometimes, during the lowest points in life, we gain the courage and strength to emerge as better.

Grab hold of the belief that there is a bigger meaning in life and that God, Universal Source, has a plan in store for you. By believing that a loss is not meaningless, we see the picture not as it is right now but as it could be when all the pieces are finally put together. One day, some of the pain, struggle, and chaos will make more sense in your life.

Opening your heart and mind to Spirituality and Mortality

Have you ever wandered into a forest and lost your sense of direction? An unfamiliar terrain can feel pretty frightening. That is how we sometimes feel through our grief journey. With each turn, we feel less sure of ourselves and our ability to find our way to safety. Just as we need to look for higher land and seek distinctive signs when trying to find our way out of a forest, similarly, we can look to a higher power and signs to keep our faith that we will come out of the woods and emerge from the aimless wandering of despair. There are ways that can help us emerge which require us to expand our thinking.

I attended a Death Cafe recently. It's a concept that was new to me, but after reading about what a Death Cafe was, I was intrigued. A Death Cafe is a quorum of people gathered to discuss spirituality and mortality. At first, it sounded a bit strange to me why anyone would want to meet up with strangers to discuss death, but then I realized the power of this experience. There is strength in numbers and in the commonality of a group coming together with thoughtful reflection on a topic that is frightening to most people.

I can only speak for American culture, but we don't really like to talk about death. Talking to someone after a death is one of the most awkward experiences, far outranking some other difficult topics such as divorce, illness, and sexuality. I've yet to meet anyone other than a funeral director who feels comfortable discussing death. If you're like me, you freeze up a bit when you hear someone has died.

Yes, we feel sad and concerned, and we send our condolences to our neighbors and friends when they lose their spouse or their child, but we do so in an awkward sort of way, like having to hold our breath underwater when all we want to do is gasp for air.

The first time I went to the funeral of someone outside of my family, I was barely out of college in my early twenties. I was very naive about the condolences and funeral etiquette. My co-worker had lost her teenage son in a motorcycle accident, a grief that would be unimaginable to me until I had my own children. I felt this terrible sense that I wouldn't know what to say to her. I was right. As I leaned in to hug her, I said what no mother wanted to hear after losing her son, but it slipped out of my mouth. "It will be alright." No, it won't be alright. How could I have said that? She will never be the same, and nothing will ever take away the pain of losing her son so young. I felt like a complete idiot at that moment, and she let me know it with a hurtful look. A mistake I vowed never to make again.

From that day on, "I'm sorry for your loss," was etched into my brain. It keeps me from opening my mouth and blurting out, "It'll be okay, I know how you feel; it was God's will," or "At least he's in a better place." None of these are helpful to someone grieving, yet are often shared unwittingly by friends and family. It's often an easy mistake to say something that sounds innocent and harmless, but until you've lived through a loss and heard those sayings from the receiving end, you may not know how insensitive and hurtful they are. I certainly don't mean to tell someone amid their grief that I know what's best for them or how to envision their loved one during their anguish, yet those sayings insinuate that I do. I have no right to tell them how they should mourn or feel when I certainly don't have any authority to make such claims. In addition, what might be comforting to me, may not be to someone else.

I find it's much better to share a story that was special to me about the deceased. I sometimes rehearse it in my head, so I don't make a mistake. I understand why I put so much pressure on what I say and how I respond to someone's grief because so many people do it so poorly. Someone can diminish death without realizing it by saying, "You'll get over it. Time will heal. It's for the best that he's gone." As the recipient of these sorts of comments, we feel completely unseen.

We internalize and try to interpret the meanings because someone has just made us feel like we need to "get over it and move on." Yes, death is natural, so we may begin to think, "Maybe I shouldn't feel this way? Why am I not able to cope like everyone else?" We begin to feel disenfranchised grief, which doesn't fit into society's normal ways of expressing the loss, and we are left feeling completely alone in our grief.

Grief is complex no matter the situation, but add the layer of trauma and the dark riptide swallowing you and leaving you breathless, which comes with suicide, and the impact of those thoughtless words becomes magnified. I'm going to assume if you're reading this book, you, unfortunately, know what I mean when it comes to the vastness of emotions stoked by hearing poorly worded comments. You may have had words said that felt like a dagger was drawn by someone you knew, who meant no harm, but still felt like a knife was deeply plunged and twisted into your heart. We never forget those words and the gut-wrenching feelings they invoke, but we can reach a point where we release the negative emotion attached to it and are no longer painfully affected by the thoughts and feelings. That is the significance of Emerging.

Societal, cultural, and familial norms play an important role in how we grieve. Because these norms do not accept suicide as a respectful way of dying, we are left feeling shame and guilt. Neither of these are helpful to our healing process. What is deemed *acceptable* to most is death due to old age. If someone has lived a long, fulfilling life, we aren't nearly as upset or grief-stricken as if the person died in what we perceive as prematurely or 'too young.' What if we could accept that our life expectancy timeline is not nearly as important as how we live in the present moment each and every day?

Death is a major life event, just like births, graduations, weddings, and anniversaries. We hold ceremonious events for each occasion including death, yet it's extremely difficult and disturbing to talk about death until after it happens. It's no wonder we are ill-prepared to have these types of conversations. If we shared our beliefs, ideas, concerns, and fears about death more openly and freely, perhaps we would have better grief responses, feel less prickly, and soften how we react to what we perceive as negative comments. We would also give our loved ones a better idea of how we'd like our death to be memorialized, celebrated, and acknowledged.

According to the National Funeral Directors Association, not many people plan their own funerals. The younger you are, the more likely you may think people *should* pre-plan their funerals. 15.8 percent of Americans aged 18 to 39 say you should pre-plan it before age 40, but only 7.9 percent of people over age 60 agree, according to the NFDA. (https://nfda.org/resources) I interpret this data to mean that the younger we are, the less likely we are to fear your own death and think it's a good idea to plan for it, but as we get closer to the 'old age' mark, we don't want to speak of what is to come.

The Death Cafe taught me that perhaps we *should* talk more openly about death. We all will die someday, yet we keep that part of our journey guarded. We talk about religion and the afterlife but not about the act or nature of death. Instead, the act of dying is something to be feared. Would talking about death more regularly while we are healthy help us cope when it becomes inevitable? Maybe it would help us process the death of our loved ones when the time comes. The more I talk about something, the less uncomfortable it becomes and the less worried and anxious I am about the topic. I can point to several fears that once I exposed them, shed light on them, and challenged them, they no longer were as fearful and some even completely vanished.

A local woman was dying of metastatic breast cancer, and she chronicled her final years on Facebook. In the end, it was very difficult to read her posts. The fear and devastation she felt over never seeing her family again and missing her children's weddings, and the birth of grandkids was heart-wrenching. Seeing the outpouring of love and support that showered over her through the posts was such a beautiful tribute to her. Strangers shared their appreciation for her telling her story and sharing her darkest fears about dying. It takes immense bravery to admit our ugly, most vulnerable feelings deep within.

I met a death doula only a few years ago. Most of us are familiar with hospice and end-of-life palliative care, but a death doula is slightly different. A death doula is a non-medical professional who helps the dying and their family through the emotional and spiritual process of death. They may even help people with the administrative affairs they want to clean up before their death. It's that kind of support that I can see great benefit in having someone trained in grief counseling and spirituality that seems extremely beneficial.

Why do I search out and investigate so many things related to death? Why does my mind want to find new ways of thinking about suicide? Because knowledge brings understanding, and understanding brings peace of mind and healing. All the knowledge I'm able to gather and pass on to you is because I've been willing to be open to discover things I did not understand. I've allowed myself to seek awareness while being extremely vulnerable and uncomfortable. For it's in my discomfort and acceptance of things I don't understand that I grow and expand.

Knowledge + Discomfort = Acceptance + Growth
– CINDY TANK-MURPHY

I share these ideas, such as death cafes and doulas, to help open your mind to finding new ways of learning and understanding your loved one's death. By improving how we emotionally process death, we can help heal from the trauma of suicide. These new ways of approaching and learning about our own mortality can be a healthy way of releasing the ugliness associated with suicide. When you expand your thinking and open up to more than you first considered, you alter limiting beliefs and allow yourself to accept, comprehend, and handle your grief more comprehensively. It may be a bit uncomfortable initially, especially if your loss is recent. Give yourself time to work through the phases that come before the Emerge phase. Practice the phases of Educating, Surrendering, and Empathy for the length of time you are comfortable with, and when you feel ready, tackle Emerging. Only you will know when the time is right for you to move to this phase.

If you felt any bitterness while reading this chapter, you are not ready, and that is alright. No one expects you to move through these phases in a set amount of time. It took me a few years to get to this place, and I still have more to learn, grow and experience. I continue to push my limits of expansion. You will know when it's time to move into the next phase. It will feel right to you. Once you've acted on your empathy for others and feel more compassion for yourself than guilt or shame, you are ready to acknowledge your enormous progression. Step into and own your beautiful transformation. I congratulate you on obtaining this level of healing. The willingness to ask more questions and see grief from other perspectives will ultimately help you grow leaps and bounds toward your compassionate transformation.

Healing Moment

You are ready to emerge. You have accumulated a wealth of new insight, perspective, and ways to embrace your transformation from tragedy. In this next activity, we are going to explore your gifts. We will uncover what you have gained from this tragedy. We always have the ability to choose to be grateful, even in the most difficult and painful situations.

What is the gift you've been handed through this loss? Think about what you have learned since losing your loved one. Is there a lesson you've gained along your healing journey?

List three opinions or perceptions that have changed, shifted or grown within you?

How will you use what you have just discovered about yourself for good? Are there ways you can use your knowledge to help your community?

You get to decide how you choose to live tomorrow and the day after with the new knowledge you've learned about yourself and the gift of clarity you've been given. Will you choose to share your knowledge and gift with the world? I encourage you to explore how you can use your new perspective to improve your own life, someone else's life, and bring new meaning to your loved one's struggle and death.

We honor our loved ones by making their lives matter. We can become mental health advocates by sharing our stories and teaching tolerance and understanding to those around us. It's our responsibility not to waste the gifts we now possess, but instead utilize them to change the narrative no matter how big or small the impact. I like the analogy of adding a drop of water to the collective consciousness. Each drop creates a ripple effect that spreads further than we imagine. Your voice, our collective voices, can encourage change and create new values, beliefs, and attitudes.

SETBACKS

*"Grief is a nasty game of feeling the weakest
you have ever felt and morphing it into the
strongest person you will have to become."*

- BRIDGET MOTTL

In the first two years after my father's death, I would replay over and over in my head how I envisioned my mom finding my dad. Even though I wasn't there and didn't witness his final moments, I had nightmares and felt the trauma as if I were. The image of his limp body slumped over a chair, his face unrecognizable, would come to me when I closed my eyes to lie down to sleep. I'd hear the gunshot, and it would jolt me into a panic. It was as if I could feel what he must have felt in those final seconds of his life, my heart racing like it was *my* finger on the trigger.

As I've said before, the road to healing is never linear. It winds and twists, and just when I felt joy and happiness going for a walk outdoors, the next day, I would find his sweater and be frozen on the bedroom floor in a puddle of tears clinging to his cardigan.

Sometimes the triggered setbacks came out of nowhere and would catch me by surprise. I scared myself at how explosive my reactions were for things that would never have bothered me before my dad passed, but they now shook me to my core for some unforeseen reason. I've been with friends sipping wine on a Friday night, watching a television show or movie, and feeling triggered or react-ing to someone's ignorant remarks or actions. My prickly response has pushed people away and even caused me never to want to be around certain people again. They have no idea how deep my wounds are, or why I was triggered, and they take my eruption personally. I can't blame them, I'd probably react the same to my inexplicable and unusual behavior, but those same people, who I thought were friends, never knew what I was going through, nor did they care to ask me if I was alright.

On my 24th birthday, my co-workers and I witnessed a suicide from our fifth-floor office window. A man jumped from the top level of the parking garage directly across the street where I had parked my car earlier that morning. Some of us witnessed him fall to his death. I remember at first, I was frozen and unable to process what was happening. The trauma of suicide hit me like a freight train. I felt like I was submerged under water, gasping for air, only to plunge to the surface and try to regain my breath. I left the office early and went home for the rest of the day, unable to celebrate my birthday, as all I could think of was the image of the man. I wondered what he was going through. I wondered what he thought about as he smoked his last cigarette from the rooftop before he stepped out onto the edge.

The emotions and thoughts are absorbed into the cells of our body, and our minds aren't capable of erasing all the images which it records non-stop. Even if we don't remember, our body still holds the memory somewhere within us. That is why it is hard to control the video loop playing over and over in your mind.

If you witnessed your loved one's death or found your loved one after they died, I am so immensely sorry. There are no words to console you or provide comfort, but I want you to know you don't have to experience this unimaginable nightmare alone. Begin by speaking to a therapist, counselor, psychologist, or someone who can provide healthy advice on how to work through the trauma you've experienced. There are techniques such as eye movement desensitization and reprocessing therapy (EMDR) that the World Health Organization recommends as a treatment for post-traumatic stress disorder (PTSD).

You will improve over time as you work through the tools you've learned in this book, but I also want you to recognize that you will have setbacks. Setbacks are normal, to be expected, and part of the process. They remind us that we are still healing and need to take time and care for our healing. We can't expect our trauma to be alleviated quickly or without constant focus and practice. I like to think of setbacks as mini reminders that we still need to provide ourselves with grace and self-care consistently. Let your setbacks be a reminder that each day you are improving and to take it slow, learn from them, and eventually, you will grow your healing potential.

You might be feeling like a victim, injured, and may have lashed out at someone for no reason other than how much you were hurting inside. It's no excuse for your actions, but I want you to be gentle with yourself. If you can understand how your pain impacts those around you, honestly assess your emotions, and determine whether they are impacting your relationships, then you can begin to course correct, bringing your feelings back in check. We are human; we make mistakes. What matters is how we respond to those mistakes.

I used to wonder when the triggers I would experience in my recovery would go away, and I'd be back to my 'old self,' but then I'd contemplate how I could ever be my 'old self' again. What I now realize is that I am changed forever. I will always respond differently to certain things that didn't matter to me before my loss because my life story has changed drastically. I can hear people share something ignorant now and say to myself, *Oh, that person's words really stung, but I don't need to react to their words like I may have in the past.* Controlling my responses to things that trigger me has been a hard lesson to learn, but I am much better, and you can become better too.

Once you embrace that you are forever changed, and things won't just go back to *normal*, you accept that those triggers don't have to control you or your response to them. When people say things to you, you have a choice to either react negatively or instead, you can pause, take a deep breath, and count to ten before you say anything in response. This technique can help you calm yourself, and within ten seconds of your pause, you may realize what made you feel prickly inside isn't that bad after all or isn't worth potentially hurting someone else's feelings.

I was surprised to learn that after Dad's suicide, friends didn't want to be around me because they didn't know how to act or what to say to me. People I used to count on didn't call, didn't reach out, and didn't acknowledge the grief I was feeling out of fear of saying the wrong thing, so they said nothing at all. My husband admits he has bitter feelings about some of my friends who disregarded my feelings during that time. Over time I grew to understand their discomfort was due to their own insecurities and fear, and I saw how my situation was too overwhelming for them. Going through my grieving process has helped me reconsider that they weren't trying to be mean. They just didn't know how to react.

If you've lost someone close to you to suicide, I imagine you've had a similar experience. I hear this often from people who say their friends and even family members found it too difficult to speak to them. It's not uncommon for people to disappear after you've been through a suicide loss. They may still be in your life, but choose never to talk about your loved one, and will tense up when you try to talk about it with them. If you are experiencing this type of abandonment, I'm sorry for your added pain. I want you to understand that their lack of knowledge of what to say or how to help you has scared them away, but know you will find new connections and perhaps even deeper ones as time goes on.

I believe people sometimes come and go in our lives in order for us to learn valuable lessons. While I still love to reflect on the companionships that no longer exist, I've learned the friends that stuck around were the connections I want and appreciate today. I've connected with new friends, those who have had similar tragic life experiences, which have led them to evolve like me. Having gone through similar life-changing circumstances, we can connect at a deeper, heartfelt level of friendship.

I prefer to spend my evenings at home with my husband and daughters, watching a movie or playing board games now because I value more intimate and stronger connections. I don't miss conversations about the latest accomplishment of their children or the complaints about the coffee shop employee who made the wrong order last week. It doesn't mean I don't cherish friendship. It just means that superficial conversation is not as meaningful to me anymore. Going through a devastating situation gave me a new perspective, and things that I thought were important now have less significance, and that's progress.

Having experienced such a loss, you may begin to see life differently. Authenticity and genuineness become characteristics you start to appreciate more through this new lens. You may no longer find yourself gaining pleasure from material objects or craving acceptance from any source; instead, you search for purpose and what is meaningful to you in the world.

Setbacks can and will still happen frequently, and we shouldn't be ashamed of them or blame ourselves when sadness, guilt, or remorse hit us smack in the face. What is important to remember through the healing process, is not to doubt ourselves and be honest with what makes us happy. I believe we all have been called to act on our instinct to help one another and spread joy and love. When we don't have the capacity to help one another, we feel insignificant.

A setback can come at any time during your life and doesn't just happen in the early phase of our loss. Setbacks can hit us when we learn of another suicide death, confront a sentimental memory, or can happen on special dates or anniversaries. They can also appear as if out of nowhere due to the stress of life. It could be as simple as not being ready to pack up and donate your loved one's clothes or as complex as returning to work to realize your job no longer makes you happy. Setbacks are not limited to emotional responses to negative influences. They come at all times, even when we are celebrating a momentous achievement or occasion. We might instantly be brought to tears because we wish our loved ones were there to celebrate with us. The best thing you can do is treat each situation as if you are feeling it for the first time. Allow it to flow through you, and don't try to stuff it down or keep it inside. Allow the tears, anger, and fear to pass without judgment about how long the emotion lasts.

Two years after Dad passed, I struggled to maintain my professional and personal life and didn't want to do my job anymore. My job had become too stressful in combination with the grief I was still trying to deal with, and the job I used to love no longer challenged me, gave me a purpose, or made me feel accomplished, so I chose to leave. I walked away from a job I used to think defined me. When asked what I did for a living, I used to be proud of my career, but after Dad's death, it wasn't nearly as important or significant in my life.

I felt that everything I had accomplished before his death was all a farce, and none of it mattered. I started seeing the world around me differently and realized how sheltered and ego-centric my life had been. I began to question everything about myself; *what is my true purpose in life?* I certainly knew it was no longer climbing the corporate ladder, having a bigger home, driving nicer cars, or accumulating objects. I had been in total denial, asleep, for several years, thinking this was the best life had to offer. These things seemed worthless to me. I needed to find answers.

Life was too short to continue living small, insignificant, and voiceless. My perspective of who I was had been forever tainted. I went from feeling successful in my career, marriage, and parental responsibilities, to feeling unimportant and lacking any real substance in most areas of my life. There had to be more to give and gain from life.

Two outcomes could have taken place when I had this epiphany about my life. One choice was to curl up in a ball and just accept that this was my life from that point on, living it out in an unhappy, disgruntled manner until I made myself sick, collapsed, and died. Or the second choice was I could seek to find my true passion, what gave me joy, and regain the voice I had lost along life's journey. I knew I was still a great wife, mother, and employee, but what more could I offer the world? Determined to make a difference, I chose the second option. My desire to find a new purpose in life brought me to the place I am today. I'm a much stronger, less judgemental person because I chose to wake myself out of a slumber. I decided to learn from what happened and redefine what my life could be like in the future.

Setbacks are natural, but don't let yours become an excuse to stop living a fulfilling life. Take the time to reflect on how the setback challenged you and how you might be able to overcome those feelings if they arise again. It's absolutely understandable and acceptable to have times when you feel emotionally triggered or fall back into a slump. Be gentle with how you respond to those setbacks, and know that they will pass and become less frequent as time progresses.

Healing Moment

One of the ways to overcome setbacks is to expect them, the discomfort that comes with them, and learn from them. You are dealing with emotions you've never experienced before, and that takes practice in figuring out what caused the triggered feelings and how to make it better the next time. Just like anything you learn that is new to you, the more you do it, the better you become.

This exercise will help provide some self-reflection on how you currently deal with your setbacks and will help you practice for the next setback, which is bound to happen. Answer the questions honestly and to the best of your ability without blaming or judging. Remember, this is a healing moment.

Have you recently felt triggered by someone, something, or an event? How did you react? What did you say or do? Do you feel you handled it well or could use more practice?

Was your reaction to keep it to yourself or express it externally? Could your reaction have potentially been hurtful to you or someone else? If so, what do you think was the cause for your strong negative reaction? Can you pinpoint what made you upset, angry, fearful, or irritated?

If you could redo the situation with the new knowledge of what caused you to react as you did, would you do something different this time? What might you say differently? Or are you comfortable with how you handled the situation?

You're in the grocery store when a song that reminds you of your loved one starts to play. You feel your throat clench up. You want to run out of the store. You find the nearest restroom and break down sobbing.

   a. You are upset that something so simple as a song made you react this way and deeply hurt you.
   b. Everyone in the store must have noticed your response because you looked foolish.
   c. You realize this is a typical setback, and it's okay to have this emotional response. It will improve over time, and you promise to be gentle with yourself the next time something like this happens again.

If you answered C, bravo! You are teaching yourself how to heal and keep pushing through any setback that comes along.

When you can use self-reflection as we did above, the next time you feel a setback response occur, you can start to see patterns. Finding those patterns will help you know when to pause, count to ten, and decide how to react before any impulsivity starts to take over. Every time you accomplish this technique, you become better able to manage how you respond to even the most difficult situations.

15

ANNIVERSARIES

If you've had to celebrate a birthday, anniversary, holiday, gradua-
tion, wedding, or any other special occasion without your loved one,
you may already know what I'm about to tell you. These once-beauti-
ful milestones are not the same without your loved one and might be
some of the most difficult days of your year. This is a typical response,
but one I wasn't prepared for when those days arrived. Knowing the
sorrow, I had to overcome; I want to discuss how these significant
milestones impact us emotionally. I also want to help prepare you
for the challenges you may face when they arrive in your life.

The first big milestone that sent me into a tailspin was my dad's
birthday, which came less than two months after he passed on September 9th. It would have been his 66th birthday. I hadn't given it
much thought of how I'd react until I woke the morning of the 9th.
I had no idea how hard it would hit me. The wave of grief came
flooding back as if I just heard the news of his death all over again.
I couldn't get myself out of bed, so I called in sick to work, canceled
my appointments, and allowed myself time to grieve and recover. I
was shocked at how I responded to the day. If someone had told me
I would have had to relive his death over on his birthday, I wouldn't
have necessarily believed them. It never occurred to me his birthday
would trigger my emotional state to reach such an extreme.

The next occasion without my dad I had to endure was the Thanksgiving holiday. As we gathered to celebrate, I tried to be in the present moment with my husband, children, and in-laws. Still, I couldn't help but think how everyone around me was happy and celebratory while I was completely miserable inside. I wanted to shout out, "How can you all eat, laugh, and give thanks when I've just lost my father!" Nothing felt like it had in years past. On most Thanksgivings, after lunch with my husband's family, we'd visit with my dad in the evening. The first year that didn't happen had me feeling angry and wanting to boycott the holiday altogether. I kept wondering *how come no one else could see how unacceptable this was and how it would never be the same?* I had to pretend to be fine on the outside while I was completely shattered inside.

In those first few years, almost every holiday, tradition, anniversary, and milestone stirs up feelings of emptiness and resentment. It feels thoughtless and disrespectful to celebrate when someone has died so tragically. It can feel as if there is nothing to celebrate.

I had no idea I would react the way I did. I wish someone had warned me and told me how to prepare. Given the opportunity to rethink how I wanted to spend his birthday, I may have chosen to do something that would have helped me grieve while honoring him on his special day.

Since that first devastating birthday without my dad, I've learned there is no right or wrong way to pass these milestones, and I've learned that no two milestones show up the same way. For instance, a few years after Dad passed, I handled his death anniversary fairly well, but the following year, I was flung back to the day he died once again. It didn't make sense. I did so well the year before, so why did I have such a negative emotion the following year? Unfortunately, that's the thing about life events like anniversaries and holidays. We can't predict how we will react, so it's best to think about them ahead and plan how you want the day to go. These dates will come whether we like them or not, so it makes sense to do them in a way that supports your healing.

You may not know what to plan or how to prepare for these days. Be gentle with yourself and plan to clear your calendar if you aren't sure how you might react. Over time you will find new routines and rituals that honor your needs and your loved one's. Whatever you choose, it doesn't need to be anything elaborate or cumbersome. The key is to think through what would make you most comfortable and how you'd like to enjoy the day. Focus on the positive experiences you'd like to take part in, like lighting a memorial candle, going on a walk to a favorite place you enjoyed together, or listening to a favorite song, and most importantly, how you want to feel. Your feelings will be of the utmost importance and deciding how to create new associations and habits with the event will ensure you feel connected with family and friends for years to come.

Let's explore some examples of how others have found ways to prepare for these milestones and how people have turned what could be a very sad occasion into something that honors their loved ones.

You may want to be surrounded by friends and family who understand what you are going through. Having people around can help take your mind off the strong emotions you experience throughout the day. Don't be afraid to reach out and ask for this help. You also may need to tell your loved ones that you would like them to be with you and explain to them why having them near you is an important and common response for survivors when faced with a birthday or anniversary. We can't assume they will realize why this is a difficult day for you. It's okay to talk about how you are coping, what's troubling you, and how you are dealing with the emotional stressors of your recent loss, but be sure to communicate this is how you plan to spend time with them. This will give them time to prepare for a conversation they may be apprehensive about having. Remember that not everyone deals with suicide grief the same way and knows how to handle difficult conversations that may make them uncomfortable. The more upfront you are with how you want to spend the day the better equipped they will be to hold that space for you. It's also perfectly fine to tell them that all you need from them is to listen. This will remove some of the pressure they may feel about your requesting them to spend the day talking through your grief.

I mentioned earlier that I spent my dad's entire birthday in bed. I didn't want to talk to anyone. If I had the opportunity to do that day over, I wish I had anticipated my response so I could have saved myself some of the misery and hassle that unfolded. It would have been much easier to clear my calendar if I had planned ahead to take the day off work. Because I hadn't planned to spend the entire day alone, I had several uncomfortable conversations that morning with my boss, my cleaners, my husband, and my children to let everyone know that I didn't want to be disturbed.

My day in bed was the reaction to my not planning ahead and feeling completely overwhelmed when I was triggered. I didn't allow myself to move through my emotions; instead, I kept the feelings bottled up. The next year, after learning this, I made sure to look at the calendar a few days before and figure out what things I could move around before his birthday which would allow me to spend his special day doing things that would bring me joy while remembering his love and fatherly guidance. I encourage you to add a few self-care activities, like taking a walk outside, soaking in a tub, and eating a healthy meal.

The one-year anniversary of a death is one of the more significant milestones we must endure. It is a new date that has been added to your milestone calendar and one that can be extra difficult. Each year will be different than the next and you may find some are easier than others, but know it's alright if you have a deeper reaction one year as long as you recognize you are always making progress and moving forward no matter the amount of times you stumble on your grief. You may take two steps back, but I promise you can take three steps forward, and if you continue to work on the steps in this book, you'll progress forward one day at a time.

An 'Angelversary,' is an event that honors the deceased on or around the anniversary of their death. I've shared how Morgan's story was part of the impetus of my healing journey, so I was honored to be invited and attend Morgan's 3rd Angelversary at Morgan's church gymnasium. It was the first time I had attended someone's death anniversary, so I had no idea what to expect. Christine, Morgan's mom, had planned every detail down to the music selection, craft projects, bracelets, and t-shirts for everyone to wear in Morgan's favorite color, purple. This particular event was part celebration of life and part suicide prevention. Morgan's Angelversary was a fun, packed event where young people gathered to remember and honor a dear friend. I found Morgan's Angelversary therapeutic and healing for everyone who attended. The suicide prevention and "being kind always" message was important to Christine since many teens were in attendance and many of Morgan's friends. Her goal was to encourage the crowd as well as provide tips on what to do if you or a friend is experiencing a crisis. A large "remembrance wall" with photos and messages to those lost to suicide flanked one side of the gym. Prizes, food, and sweet treats, many of Morgan's favorite things, were handed out, and the attendees engaged in fun crafts, games, and dancing, mixed with heartfelt memories.

Sharing stories was one of the most impactful parts of the day. A DJ who donated his time to play the music for the dance contest testified to losing someone to suicide. He shared a story of the night he DJ'd a Homecoming dance with the help of a teen employee. That young employee ended his life later that evening after the Homecoming dance. The DJ shared his great remorse that he had not seen the signs of struggle the teen was dealing with as they drove home together that evening. In hindsight, he realized he could have said something on that long drive home. He shared what he would have done differently if he had the chance to do it all over again and how each of us can be more vigilant when someone shows even the smallest signs of loneliness and isolation.

Throughout the Angelversary, everyone was filled with education, conversation, memories, and fun. At the end of the event, participants were allowed to write a message to Morgan, share how much they missed her, and say their goodbyes. By celebrating Morgan's life in this manner, her friends, relatives, classmates, and family could express their emotions and gain a sense of closure to their loss. When we lose someone without getting to say goodbye, we experience ambiguity, uncertainty, and have many unanswered questions. Closure happens when we can process the loss like a puzzle, putting pieces together until we feel we've completed the full picture. The Angelversary helped soften an extremely difficult day for everyone who knew Morgan. It was a safe space filled with joyful activities and allowed the participants time to process and heal collectively as a community.

Creating meaningful and positive emotions around anniversaries and holidays can help replace the negative feelings attached to them. When you plan how you want to feel and what you want to do to honor these special occasions, you begin to associate positive sentiments with them in the future. By connecting joyful, loving experiences to these dates, new memories are created along with the fond ones you already cherish.

Healing Moment

Let's begin the planning process for the next upcoming milestone you will be experiencing without your loved one. Imagine the next anniversary or holiday that is to arrive and reminisce how you used to share that day, and then move into how you now want to observe it. Think about how you might respond to the upcoming event. Even though you don't fully know what emotions might come to the surface, let's explore some types of responses you could have so you are prepared and not surprised if your emotions don't align with how you think you will react. Planning with some ideas of how you anticipate what you want or need will help you have options when the day comes.

The next occasion I will need to prepare for is...

_____

_____

_____

I will honor my loved one by...

_____

_____

_____

I will practice good self-care by...

_____

_____

_____

Here is a list of ideas to help you choose how you want to celebrate an Angelversary, a birthday, a favorite holiday, or any annual event you plan in honor of your loved one.

- Visit their final resting place
- Take a nature walk
- Plan a special dinner with family
- Make an appointment with a therapist to talk about how you feel
- Plant a memorial tree
- Support a charity or volunteer
- Post a Facebook Tribute
- Light a candle
- Create a photo memory book
- Write a letter to them
- Scatter some of their ashes somewhere special
- Watch videos and look at photos
- Go to work to keep yourself busy
- Cook their favorite meal
- Release butterflies or lanterns
- Partake in one of their special pastimes or hobbies
- Play your favorite music or a special song
- Get a tattoo
- Take a trip
- Dedicate a bench in honor of them
- Adopt a pet
- Try something you've never done before
- Take a class to learn a new skill or talent
- Go for a run or exercise to release endorphins
- Do something creative like paint, garden, crochet, or play a musical instrument

It doesn't have to take a lot of time or effort to plan how you'll spend the day, but being in control and knowing you have options will make you more likely to have a better experience when the day arrives.

If you want to create an event or celebration to honor your loved one, it's a good idea to begin thinking about what you'd like to do so that you are prepared and feel the success of your efforts to honor their memory. There are many ideas and resources online that can help you with planning such events. No matter how you spend your day, be sure it's what *you* need and how *you* envision it unfolding so that *you* feel the healing. The most important thing on all these anniversaries and holidays is to be caring, kind, and loving to yourself.

THE SHARING OF:
TYRONE

Tyrone Lecelle Good was born June 17, 1956, in Pittsburg, PA to William Good and Anna Bell Henderson. He departed this life Monday, June 22, 1998 at Allegheny General Hospital, Pittsburgh, PA.

Tyrone was educated in the Pittsburgh school system and graduated from Allegheny High School. Formerly, he had been employed as a painter and laborer with the City of Pittsburgh until he became disabled.

Tyrone had a great love and talent for playing the drums. He expressed this talent performing at various churches. Tyrone was known throughout the Northside community and will be remembered for his gifts, a 'green thumb' in gardening, his kindness, generosity, and a great conversationalist.

Two brothers preceded his death, Harold and Jerome Good. Tyrone leaves to mourn his passing a loving companion, Joan Pollard, children; Tyra Lynn, Tyrone Jr., Omar Phillips Good. Parents William and Anna Bell Good; three brothers, Billy, Michael, and Anthony; four sisters, Dorothy Good, Rosa Travillier, Cassandra and Deborah Good, a host of nieces, nephews, cousins and friends.

The Story of Tyrone, Common-law Husband. Told by Joan, Common-law Wife.

As I waited to meet Joan for the first time over a video conference line, I thought back to what she told me over the phone a few weeks prior; she wasn't sure about sharing something so vulnerable and personal in a book. Joan lost her first love, Tyrone, to suicide over 20 years ago. She's since married and Joan senses her current husband would be uncomfortable knowing this story. Talking about Tyrone's death is not something she's even disclosed in full detail with him, yet she's chosen to meet with me and share her story in detail.

Joan was feeling vulnerable and nervous about what she was about to reveal. "Cindy, no one has ever asked me about my story. My family doesn't want to know all the details because it's too hard," she told me as we began to get to know each other. I shared with Joan, I wanted to hear her story. I felt it was time for her to share, and I was willing to listen. For a woman of deep faith, who was about to tell me something her own family was afraid to hear, I felt extra pressure to get this story right and not miss an important piece of information or make a mistake. I was honored she wanted to unveil the darkest moment of her life to me, a stranger.

Joan's speech is slow and altered due to the traumatic brain injury she suffered at the hands of her former common-law husband, Tyrone. It's not noticeable enough to instantly detect she's been injured, but it's something she points out to me to let me know she finds it hard to find the right words. She stutters as the words are slow to come out. If she hadn't mentioned this to me, I might have at first thought she was taking her time to choose her words carefully, but as our interview progressed, I could tell how hard she was working to find the right vocabulary.

Joan and Tyrone met when she was just 17 years old, and he was 18. She gave me a timid grin when I asked what made her fall in love with Tyrone. I could see the innocence of her 17-year-old self reliving the moment she first met him. He was not like the other boys his age. He was an entrepreneur from a very young age who dressed the part of a businessman wearing clean, fitted shirts and wing-tip shoes. He didn't own a pair of sneakers back in those days and that was a complete turn-on for a young black girl wanting to find a man who would sweep her off her feet. She was dating his friend when she first met Tyrone. Together, the two young men had picked her up to drive her home one day. Tyrone came back to see her that same evening, and from that moment on, they were inseparable. "He was a bit of a bad boy, and I was the good girl who fell for him." She let out a big chuckle when she shared that with me.

Coming from a family of twelve kids, Joan felt accustomed to having support and a tightly connected family. She grew up in a loving Christian home but says she started to drift from her faith when she and Tyrone became pregnant and moved into the same home to raise their daughter.

It wasn't long after their family was established that Joan realized Tyrone's business ventures were not all legitimate. He owned an ice cream truck, painted for a living, and played drums in a band, but those things were never steady enough to keep the family afloat. His livelihood also depended on him selling marijuana on the streets of Pittsburgh.

Around the same time she had their first child, it became clear to Joan that Tyrone was a possessive man. Knowing he was now the father of her child gave him a sense of entitlement toward Joan. She could feel something shifting from their dating relationship into their home and family life. There was an 'I now own you and our child' type of sentiment. Joan loved him and was willing to spend her life together despite his controlling nature. She was raised to believe it was important to keep a Christian marriage intact no matter what, even though they weren't legally united in matrimony. To Joan, having children and living together was a marriage in God's eyes. But as soon as she had her first child with Tyrone, there was a subtle shift that would foreshadow what was to come in the future.

Joan shared how she gave little thought to officially tying the knot with Tyrone. People were living together out of wedlock and raising their families no differently than if they were married. She didn't see her and Tyrone as anything but a married couple and within a few years, a son came along. In her mind, they were a complete family.

Joan played the dutiful wife and mother. She became fond of caring for her children and being involved with them. She took her kids to birthday parties, school events, and trips to the park. She had found mothering to be her greatest gift. Her mother was a preschool teacher and had valuable advice to give her daughter. "Joanie, don't you start a job until your daughter is in kindergarten." Her role was to be the caregiver, and she enjoyed every moment of it.

By his mid-twenties, Joan says, Tyrone started to become angry and bitter due to the difficulties of raising a family in the inner city, and Joan realized he was battling the demons of depression. He was making a living by selling marijuana on the street, and his mental state would shift abruptly, easily turning hostile.

Tyrone's lack of direction didn't seem to interfere with Joan's focus. She was ambitious and set her mind on improving her life. She dreamed of making a better life for herself and wanted to improve her quality of life. Much of her ambition was forced upon her due to the lack of stability with Tyrone's business ventures. His emotional battles caused personal strain as well. Joan eventually went to college and earned her associate's degree, looking for a way to increase her earning potential. She would later go on to work toward her bachelor's degree.

As Joan continued to ladder up in her life, she kept moving forward for herself and her children. She found the Lord by attending church regularly and became 'saved' in her faith. Joan attempted to cut ties with Tyrone by moving to her own apartment, but Tyrone wasn't going to give her up that easily, and she was still tied to him emotionally and physically. She and Tyrone had a third child together even though they were separated as a couple.

Joan's love for the Lord continued to be her guiding light through their rocky relationship. Tyrone would attend church occasionally with his family, and it didn't take long for the Pastor to learn of his drumming talent. He began playing drums in the church. In the eyes of the church, them living together out of wedlock was a sin. Eventually, her Pastor sat them down to discuss their living situation. Joan began to feel pressured to make their marriage official in the eyes of God, so they began taking pre-marital counseling classes at the church. She was asked to select her wedding invitations when Joan abruptly felt a rush of doubt come over her. As she skimmed through the wedding invitation book, she couldn't find a single announcement in the entire book that fit the sentiments about her relationship with Tyrone.

She had run out of excuses for herself and her children as to why she was still with his man. She had finally fallen out of love, and she knew she needed to stop the wedding plans. Tyrone's drug-dealing lifestyle had always conflicted with Joan's morals. He was no longer the man she wanted to be married to for the rest of her life. The push to become married had actually been the kindling to her fire of wanting more for herself and her children. Her strong faith helped her realize it was time to end the relationship.

It took three more marriage counseling sessions with her Pastor before Joan finally got the nerve to say she no longer wanted to marry Tyrone. His head dropped, and he was despondent. Her Pastor told her they could no longer live together if they weren't going to marry. Joan wanted desperately to obey the Lord, so she agreed. She called her sister and Joan began to pack her home to move in with her sister immediately.

Tyrone did not handle the split well. Sinking to a low like no other before, he made a final plea for help to Joan. "I love you, and I need help, please, Joan!" His lips moved, but she no longer heard anything coming out of his mouth. She had finally reached her breaking point. The chapter of Tyrone and Joan had ended.

He was using the drugs he was selling on the street, and it was no longer just marijuana that was in demand. Narcotics like opiates, cocaine, and heroin were now the drugs being pushed in Pittsburgh, and Tyrone was keeping up with the times.

It was Father's Day weekend, and Joan's siblings were celebrating with a picnic. It had only been a few months since Joan had moved out once and for all. She went to Tyrone's home to pick up her oldest son, who was living with his father while attending high school. She had allowed this living arrangement, agreeing he could stay there until school was over, and then move back with her. She invited Tyrone to join them at the picnic. It was not only Father's Day but also Tyrone's birthday, and she didn't want to see him home alone, but he declined. The drugs and depression had taken a toll on his body, and his 5'5" frame was withering away. Joan could see the obvious depression on Tyrone's face.

No matter how bad things got with Tyrone, Joan always ensured her children respected their father. She believed he was still a good man. As a mother, she had chosen never to speak negatively about her children's father in front of them. Underneath the drugs and bad behavior, she knew he loved his children and needed to be near them.

The family party was filled with laughter, singing, and praising the Lord. It was a joyous occasion, one that Joan vividly remembers. After the family gathering, Joan dropped her son off at Tyrone's home and reminded him that he needed to pack up his belongings as the following day, he'd be moving back to Joan's home to live with her for the summer just as they had planned.

Joan arrived as scheduled on Monday and promptly woke her

son to pack his bags. As their son got up to collect his things, Tyrone and Joan went downstairs and sat on the sofa to talk. Soon her son came down, dropped his bag, and Tyrone told him to go out to the car to fetch something. Giving a typical teenager response to just being woken up, like a bear from his winter slumber, he made a snide remark, but Joan stopped him and said, "listen to your father."

The teenager respectfully responded and went outside. As soon as he left, Tyrone reached between the cushions of the sofa he and Joan were seated on and pulled out a gun. Fear instantly pulsed through her body. This wasn't the first time Joan had seen Tyrone with a gun. A few months earlier, Tyrone had left her stunned and appalled when he revealed a different gun. "What are you doing with that?" she demanded. When Tyrone brushed it aside, Joan snuck the small pistol away from him, hid it in a sock, and packed it up in a box, thinking that was the only weapon he had. Joan says she was now faced with the hard truth that he possessed a second gun and was about to use it.

This time, Joan didn't question why Tyrone had a gun. She got up and ran! She darted from the family room toward the dining room, but the gun fired, and Joan fell to the floor. She was hit twice in the side of her head. As she lay on the dining room floor bleeding, she could still sense her surroundings and knew what was happening around her. Enduring the pain but unable to get up, she could see Tyrone laying on the floor near her, his head hunched over as if he was asleep in her mind. He had shot himself at close range and was gone.

Joan's son, who had been catching up with some friends in the street after retrieving the items for his dad, heard the gunfire and knew instantly that it had come from the house. As soon as he heard the shots, he ran as fast as possible to his cousin's store nearby to get help. "Help me; I heard shots coming from the house. My mom and dad are inside!"

Police and paramedics arrived on the scene, and Joan was

surrounded by people she knew. She could hear them as they hovered above her, but she had no way of communicating back to them. "We love you, Joanie. Please stay with us!" Through her shock and disbelief, Joan heard the police pronounce Tyrone dead.

The family was frantic as word spread quickly that Joan was hospitalized with gunshot wounds to her head and that it was Tyrone who had fired the shots. Their tight-knit family began praying for Joan's recovery and ascended to the hospital. Joan's daughter had returned from college for the summer, and rushed to the hospital, not knowing what had happened. Upon arriving and hearing all of Joan's family members asking staff and relatives, "How is Joanie? Is she going to be okay?" the lack of any mention of her father told the horrifying truth. She burst out crying. She knew her father was gone.

In hindsight, Joan can recall several warning signs and the presence of the Holy Spirit in the weeks and days leading up to the event. She felt that God was looking out for her and protecting her. Medically speaking, it's a miracle that she survived. To her, she was protected by her Lord and Savior.

Joan had a long road to rehabilitation. Doctors told her family, "if she makes it, she will be in a vegetative state." There wasn't a positive prognosis for her recovery, but slowly Joan miraculously proved them wrong. Through therapy, she began to respond, first by nodding her head, and eventually, her speech returned. A few weeks following the shooting, Joan had no recollection of the shooting or what had happened to Tyrone. At a follow-up appointment, the Doctor asked if she remembered getting shot. She didn't. The memories slowly started to come back to her. It was slow and took time, but eventually, she started to recall what had happened and Joan was ready to face the truth. She asked her sister, "What happened to me?" Her sisters sat her down to tell her that she had been shot and Tyrone had been shot too and was dead. She turned to her daughter and cried, "I'm so sorry, you had to go through this all."

Joan feels sadness that Tyrone wasn't able to get the help he needed for his depression, but she doesn't feel remorse or blame herself. She knows she was honest, loving, and had been through thick and thin with him. "He was sick, and no one was able to help him; they kept pushing him away." Ultimately, he lost his will to live the moment Joan moved out. She had been the only constant in his life besides his kids, and he could see they were growing up. Soon they, too, would be deserting him. It was more than he could take to be alone.

Joan has only small signs today of her injuries. Her speech is still altered and she has numbness on her left side, particularly in her hand. The bullet fragments are still lodged in her skull because there were too many to clear out during surgery, but she's able to walk, talk, drive, and even has married (for real this time!). Many people never believed she'd come this far.

Miracles of forgiveness exist throughout this story. Joan tells me she forgave Tyrone for shooting her. No bitterness or anger has settled into her heart, "because I know he was sick." She still talks to his family, and she loves them dearly.

During our meeting, Joan shared intimate details about her life and relationship with Tyrone. I could tell how much she loved him by how respectfully she chose her words to describe him. This was a man who tried to murder her, and yet she refers to him as a loving father. Yet he was also a man who planned to take his life. Joan and I talked for over two hours. It was her chance to finally tell the complete story to someone willing to listen. Her family was close to the situation and couldn't hear her perspective without judging her or her feelings. I was someone safe. Toward the very end of our conversation, I said to Joan, "Wow, you are a true miracle." Without hesitation, she responded, "We all are miracles."

16

SYMPTOMS

*"The strongest people are not those who
show strength in front of us, but those who
fight battles we know nothing about."*
- UNKNOWN

It's my opinion that we often lack the understanding of how someone with great success in their profession can be fighting a battle inside. We assume that because they have clawed their way to the top, accomplished stardom, or possess such charisma and elegance, they must have things under control in all aspects of their lives. We place them on a pedestal admiring their achievements and we forget that they deal with the same emotional baggage all of us carry throughout life.

A person's outside appearance doesn't always match what is going on inside. Former Miss USA, Cheslie Kryst's death by suicide was a complete shock to many. Her outward positivity didn't reflect what she must have been feeling inside. It's hard to reconcile the stark difference between that contrast. When Robin Williams died by suicide a month after my father, no one could understand how a comedic icon like him could take his own life. We see this time and time again when someone famous dies. People begin to question how someone who appears to "have it all" could do such a thing.

There is a myth that mental illness only affects certain people. The truth is mental illness is not discriminatory and affects celebrities like the rest of the population. The disease doesn't go away once you are successful or because you are famous. It's not what we see on the outside that determines whether or not something could be lurking on the inside. In my research and after talking with people, I often hear things like *He was a happy person. There's no way he was depressed, he was so funny, or she never acted depressed; she was a great student.* I don't blame people who have this thought because there is a lack of understanding of mental illness as a disease.

Depression is often not something you can see from the outside because people can hide their thoughts, feelings, and emotions easily behind a facade. It's also easy to be confused about what major depressive disorder or anxiety looks like compared to normal mood changes we all experience. In addition to that, it's not all black and white. There is a myth that a person is either mentally healthy or mentally ill; in fact, we all fall somewhere on that continuum. We each have moments of sadness, anger, guilt, and lack of energy, which don't necessarily mean we have a diagnosed illness, just as someone with a mental illness can still experience happiness, clarity, and live a healthy life.

Mental health is so complex, I imagine it's difficult for even a professional to understand all the intricacies of someone affected by an illness. It's not crystal clear to us amateurs when symptoms cross the line of becoming a severe problem.

Sometimes we name the emotions as something less intimidating because we are afraid to call them what they are. We describe a person or their symptoms as "broken-hearted," "emptiness," or "deep despair" in an attempt to not label them something more insidious as mental illness. It's out of fear that we don't want to label these symptoms and physical ailments as mental instability. We've been taught since we were little kids that we are supposed to be able to control our emotions. When that control of our emotions is taken away, it can be scary.

Some startling statistics suggest that almost half of adults in the United States will experience a mental illness within their lifetime. According to Mental Health Aid First Aid, only 41 percent of Americans with a mental disorder in the past year received professional health care. If mental illness is this prevalent, why are we blind to it, and why don't more people seek help? My guess is two of the reasons include ignorance and stigma.

Ignorance stems from the lack of knowledge and the fear of the unknown. We sometimes purposely push aside things we don't understand because we feel knowing *more* might somehow be worse than knowing *nothing* at all. We don't do as good of a job of coaching and educating ourselves on the signs and symptoms of mental disorders as we do other diseases. If I asked you what the signs or symptoms of a heart attack are, you could probably list off a few that you've heard. For instance, chest pain, shortness of breath, and a sore shoulder or arm, to name a few. If I asked you the same question, but in the case of depression, you might not think of some of the common signs as readily.

The other obvious reason people don't seek help is the stigma associated with mental illness. There are a few other stigmatized diseases, such as AIDS, venereal diseases, and leprosy. Still, none are more discriminated against in the health care system than mental disorders. We are uniquely positioned to help increase awareness and lift the stigma when we know.

Let's uncover the symptoms of mental health and start to have an honest talk. Here is a list of overarching symptoms from the Mayo Clinic website for three diagnoses in order of major depressive disorder, generalized anxiety disorder, and bipolar disorder.

- Feelings of sadness, tearfulness, emptiness, or hopelessness
- Angry outbursts, irritability, or frustration, even over small matters

- Loss of interest or pleasure in most or all normal activities, such as sex, hobbies, or sports
- Sleep disturbances, including insomnia or sleeping too much
- Tiredness and lack of energy, so even small tasks take extra effort
- Reduced appetite and weight loss or increased cravings for food and weight gain
- Anxiety, agitation or restlessness
- Slowed thinking, speaking or body movements
- Feelings of worthlessness or guilt, fixating on past failures or self-blame
- Trouble thinking, concentrating, making decisions and remembering things
- Frequent or recurrent thoughts of death, suicidal thoughts, suicide attempts or suicide
- Unexplained physical problems, such as back pain or headaches
- Feeling nervous, restless or tense
- Having a sense of impending danger, panic or doom
- Having an increased heart rate
- Breathing rapidly (hyperventilation)
- Sweating
- Trembling
- Feeling weak or tired
- Trouble concentrating or thinking about anything other than the present worry
- Having trouble sleeping
- Experiencing gastrointestinal (GI) problems
- Having difficulty controlling worry
- Having the urge to avoid things that trigger anxiety
- Abnormally upbeat, jumpy or wired
- · Increased activity, energy or agitation

- Exaggerated sense of well-being and self-confidence (euphoria)
- Decreased need for sleep
- Unusual talkativeness
- Racing thoughts
- Distractibility
- Poor decision-making — for example, going on buying sprees, taking sexual risks or making foolish investments
- Depressed mood, such as feeling sad, empty, hopeless or tearful (in children and teens, depressed mood can appear as irritability)
- Marked loss of interest or feeling no pleasure in all — or almost all — activities
- Significant weight loss when not dieting, weight gain, or decrease or increase in appetite (in children, failure to gain weight as expected can be a sign of depression)
- Either insomnia or sleeping too much
- Either restlessness or slowed behavior
- Fatigue or loss of energy
- Feelings of worthlessness or excessive or inappropriate guilt
- Decreased ability to think or concentrate, or indecisiveness
- Thinking about, planning or attempting suicide

I realize this extensive list of symptoms can feel overwhelming and confusing. It's also difficult to comprehend them when so many are opposite variations of low mood symptoms, like fatigue and slowed thinking and speech, as well as symptoms that reflect high-intensity mood, like the decreased need for sleep, restlessness, and racing thoughts. It's no wonder it's hard to understand the signs when they can be confusing and contradictory. Many of us have experienced at least a few of these symptoms at some point in our lives. We've probably even neglected these feelings with little thought about the impact on us or the effect they may have caused someone else. We have been taught to hide many of these feelings or act the opposite even if we are experiencing them. Sayings like, *suck it up, it's all in your head, get over it,* are not helpful. They are hurtful and dismissive to the person experiencing depression. When we hold those feelings in for long periods of time, they cause discomfort, disorder, and disease. We need to be taught to release these emotions through healthy means and methods.

All humans have the basic instinct to survive. Self-preservation is innate, in fact, it may be the most powerful human trait we possess. I believe suicide results when a person's mental state crosses the line between human instinct and the will to survive. It's the intersection where pain crosses the boundary of a typical human reaction. The road of choice becomes self-harm because it far greater exceeds that of our survival instinct. When you think of it this way, it's hard to envision just how f*cking hard life can be.

Sometimes people are afraid to address mental health challenges by name and don't want to accept the correct definition of illness, but we must call it what it is. People who are suicidal are not wanting to die because of a broken heart or hopelessness, a failure of self, a selfish act to gain attention, or any other way people try to explain or even deny the cause. These are terms we make up to explain what is inexplicable to us. When a person experiences a break from their usual mental state, they are no longer able to sense their natural instinctive state of survival. They've crossed over to a state of the emotional brain where dying is the better option (in their minds) for them. It's a stronger instinct to die than to continue in the current painful state of being. Their perceived suffering is far greater and outweighs their perceived survival.

I once read a comparison of suicide to a person who jumps from a burning building. The person on the top floor of a burning building does not want to die, nor does a person who is suicidal. It's not as though all of a sudden death is appealing, but instead, the person about to jump from a burning window is just as terrified as you or I would be to fall to our death. What's different is that falling from the building becomes slightly less horrifying of the two terrors. This analogy helped me comprehend just how terrible someone in a suicidal state must feel. I can't imagine having flames burning you to the point you decide jumping to your death is a better option.

Once we can try to understand the intensity of what our loved one was feeling at the time of their death, we can feel empathy for them in a new way. When we step into someone else's shoes, we can begin to speak on their behalf. We can help address the myths and stereotypes that shadow those in need and create the stigma that keeps people from reaching out for help.

How do we address this as a society and make a change? We talk about it openly and compassionately. When we can remove the negative emotions and stigma from the disease and have honest conversations about our own mental health with doctors, family, and friends, we allow those around us to see what true strength is. Strength is asking for help when something feels off. We are emotionally more susceptible to triggers in life, like divorce, job loss, financial loss, and personal conflicts when we don't ask for help. Strength is seeking professional support, whether it be a counselor, social worker, spiritual leader, or physician.

If you or someone you know is showing any of these signs, please seek professional help. I know it can feel overwhelming and scary to talk to a doctor about these signs and symptoms, but please don't allow fear to keep you from getting help. It can also be easy to talk yourself out of going right away and instead wait until morning because you may think that the ER is busy and you aren't deserving of their attention. Please don't let that happen. You deserve medical help no matter the time of day, the severity of your symptoms, and the trepidation you might be feeling.

Call or text the National Suicide Prevention Hotline / Suicide and Crisis Lifeline at 988.

- ❖ For International crisis numbers: https://findahelpline.com/i/iasp
- ❖ Drive to the nearest ER or Behavior Treatment facility
- ❖ Dial 9-1-1 or your local emergency center.

17

SAM

Scrolling through my Instagram feed, I came across a handsome blonde haired, blue-eyed man holding up a blue post-it note that reads, "5 things my suicide attempt taught me."

I've been following Sam and his movement to "erase suicide from this planet" for a few years now. When I first came across Sam's posts on social media, I got chills throughout my body, which is my sign to pay attention because this is a message being sent from heaven. At first, I only knew Sam as the guy holding up a post-it note with a positive affirmation, a personal life lesson, or a horrific statistic about suicide. I've realized this man is an amazing miracle, and his movement is changing lives. He's written a book, *Recklessly Alive*, which details his emergence from a suicide attempt to living a life full of expression, self-care, and resiliency. Sam speaks at events telling his story and empowering his crowds to have honest conversations about mental health and suicide.

While writing this book, I've tried to cover everything I could think of that would be on your mind. I've included things I questioned about my father's suicide, and as new ideas evolved, I researched and explored new ways of thinking about death and dying. It occurred to me one more thing I needed to embrace in this book was the perspective of someone who had fought the demons and lived to tell how they felt in those moments when all they wanted was to end it all. I decided I needed to talk to Sam. I want you to hear in his own words what his darkest moments felt like and what led up to his decision to want to die. I knew it would be healing for me, so I felt this chapter would also be healing to you. Understanding what Sam felt on that fateful day and how his blurred mind had impacted everything leading up to that day is important for me to share with you. I believe this chapter will not only provide you with some much-needed understanding, but hopefully, you'll begin to know that suicide is indeed an awful disease and one we need to irradicate from this planet, just as Sam's movement works to imagine "a world with zero deaths from suicide."

Sam was just as compassionate and friendly on our video call as he appears in his social media presence. His warm, welcoming smile and sincere, honest eyes hide the fact that this intelligent, soulful man had once contemplated what he was about to share with me. I'm thankful he was willing to tell me his story and share as best as he could articulate how a suicidal mind works.

As I began to share the purpose of my book with Sam and what this chapter meant to me, he relayed how he has seen how different the grief of a suicide loss is compared to any other loss from the people he'd met in his speaking engagements. He admitted that when he started doing his work on suicide prevention, he didn't have the perspective of having lost anyone close to suicide. That has since changed.

> *"Many of my talks are sponsored by families who have lost some-one to suicide. My book editor lost her daughter to suicide, and she says it's a loss unlike any other. I've become close with a family from Illinois who lost their son. They tell me they wish their son had died in a car accident because that's a death they could accept and get through. They say the hardest part is the fact that they didn't know*

he was suffering and didn't know how to help him. They talk about
ostracization (which accompanies suicide) and how no one knows
what to say, so nobody says anything. They tell me the hardest part
is how they have lost so many friends."

I nod my head in agreement with him as he shares all that he's
learned over the years about suicide loss. He is genuinely compassionate toward the people he's met along his journey. As we talk, I
find myself thinking it's inconceivable that this brilliant man once
stood in his bathroom, ready to end his life.

Sam was twenty-three in November of 2011 when he set his death
date, Christmas day. He says he had intentionally made plans and
gave himself an ultimatum.

"Either I was going to do this on Christmas day or never think
about it again. I had battled suicidal ideation for almost ten years
at that point, and hadn't ever really received help with my feelings
of wanting to die. No one had ever talked to me about depression
and suicidal thoughts. There weren't any stories I had heard about
people getting through it."

At that point in his life, Sam had only heard about suicide when
someone famous passed away. "I had no foresight beyond the pain I
was experiencing," Sam shared. Sam was just two years out of college
when he felt his life had completely "bottomed out," as he calls it.
Burdened with tons of student loan debt and working on a music
teacher's income, he hated his life. He felt it was meaningless. On
top of the financial pressure, Sam had ended the relationship with
his college girlfriend months prior to his personal ultimatum. He
recalled how he was sinking in quicksand when his first year teaching
job in a small town in rural Iowa ended for the summer, so he moved
back home to live with his mother in Minnesota. Once inside his

childhood home, the memories of an alcoholic, verbally abusive father came flooding back. According to Sam, he had vowed he'd never drink when he went off to college, having seen the damage it caused his family. But some things we despise end up creeping into our lives no matter how hard we try to avoid them. Binge drinking on weekends was a right of passage with his twenty-something-year-old friends. The drinking didn't help his situation since alcohol is a depressant; it only worsened the lows.

Sam explained how his mind constantly lied to him, telling untruths about himself, things he would never tell another human being, yet he didn't see these lies as anything other than the truth. Sam gave me some examples of the lies a suicidal mind tries to tell itself:

> *You're stupid. No one truly loves you; how could they? You are worthless, ugly, and disgusting. You'll always be alone. You've made mistakes your entire life. Look how dumb you are; you can't even figure out how to get yourself out of this mess. Why would anyone want to be around you? If you were gone, no one would even care. They certainly wouldn't notice that you were gone. In fact, they'd be better off if you were gone.*

For someone who hasn't experienced suicidal ideation, it's hard to imagine your mind telling yourself these hateful things repeatedly, the same stories of unworthiness. Try to picture waking up in the morning, and the first thing your lying mind says to you is:

> *You overslept again, you f—ing idiot! What are you going to tell your boss this time? Why even bother going to work now? Everyone knows what a f*ck up you are. Just stay home where no one can bother you or hurt you. They don't want you there anyway. You just mess everything up. Always have and always will.*

For someone experiencing suicidal ideation, this type of one-way conversation takes place every day, constantly degrading, humiliating, and breaking the person down. It can render them completely helpless, unable to get out of bed and do the most basic self-care. For others, the nonstop chatter is background noise while their body sprints to the bathroom, begins showering and brushing their teeth, and heads out the door to work. To the external world, there isn't anything wrong. The person appears healthy, present, and engaged when in reality, they are living on autopilot, appearing to be functional, all the while the demeaning, degrading echo is playing over and over in their head like a looped recording.

Sam explains it best to me when he says that over time his brain got so warped that he could not see reality. He described how everything gets distorted by this warped version of what's happening around you, none of which is true. He likens it to how someone with anorexia can be wasting away, their body withering, yet when they look in the mirror, their distorted perception believes they are fat. A suicidal person looks in the mirror and sees no value in themselves, someone whose life if a complete disaster and not worthy of love or of life. The emotions and voices are intense. He continues to explain that on top of that, you aren't seeing the love of your family clearly because depression numbs all pleasure and things that you enjoy.

The pain is so strong there is only one thing you want – to make it stop. The only way to stop the agony is to end it. The only way you know to end it, is to cease your existence. Nothing is rational about this pattern of thought because nothing is rational in a suicidal brain. If you've never been shown how to stop the constant stabbing of despair, it's understandable to think there isn't one.

Sam explains, "Imagine a pain so deep that you wouldn't care what happened to your friends and family. It's that intense. The flipside of that distorted mindset is that you also feel like such a burden. I was 100% convinced my family would be better off without me. People always talk about suicide as the most selfish act anyone can ever complete. I hate that. I fight against that so hard. I say if anyone could experience the amount of pain I was in that day, I don't think they would say it's a selfish thing; they would say, 'Oh, I get it.'"

Sam believed in the most twisted way that he was helping his family. He had deliberately thought about how Christmas day would be difficult for his family with him alive. It couldn't be any worse with him gone. The holiday meant nothing to him.

Sam continued to share, "It's a tough, tough illness. Yet we don't talk about it as an illness, so you don't even know you're sick, right? You don't understand that your brain is lying to you."

Sam paused from sharing his personal experience of his mental state leading up to and during the moment he wanted to end it all. I told him my philosophy from the previous chapter about the point at which someone decides to end their life and how I believe they've crossed the line from their rational brain and instinctual will to survive, to their emotional brain and their will to live no longer exists.

I asked him, "How do you respond to people who say there wasn't a mental break or the deceased didn't suffer from any illness? Instead, some believe they were shamed or guilted into their own death because they did bad things. Or they couldn't live without someone in their life." After a few seconds, some deep breaths and exhales, Sam turned his neck from side to side as if to say, *I don't know how to answer that question politely.*

He responded, "Until you've been there, it's impossible to explain. Until you've lived it, it is impossible to understand what that person was thinking and feeling...their reasoning or logic...you can call it whatever you want, but I'm 100% in agreement with you. Mental illness is to blame."

If we think about the terms people use to explain why someone died by suicide, words and phrases like *guilt-ridden, loneliness, ashamed, scared, cried for help, fixated on the negative, made poor choices, and out of*

242

control come to mind. These are also words that describe symptoms of mental illnesses. By using words that diminish the fact that a mental illness is most likely to blame, it lessens and undermines the seriousness of the illness.

I shifted gears and asked Sam questions about when he began having suicidal thoughts around the age of thirteen. I wanted to understand how he dealt with those thoughts at such a young age. "It must have scared the sh*t out of you."

"Yeah, so there are two types of suicidal thoughts: passive and active. For the most part, they were passive when I was younger. They were self-esteem driven. I didn't like myself. I didn't like the way I looked, the way that I sounded. So the thoughts were, I wish I didn't exist. If given a choice to flip a switch and not exist, I would have taken it, but I didn't really want to die. In high school, I never had a plan. Occasionally I had active thoughts, and as they got worse, more and more, it evolved into active thoughts. That's when the thoughts started to turn to *if I was going to end it, how would I do it?*"

Sam, like so many people who live with suicidal thoughts for long periods of time, became an expert at hiding it. Perhaps you can relate to this from your own experience with your loved one. You may have said things like, *I didn't see it coming. She was such a funny girl. He had everything going for him. I would never have guessed he was struggling. They never shared any feelings of sadness with me,* when you talk about your loved one's passing. It is because your loved one became good at hiding their thoughts from you. They didn't want you to be burdened with their ugly thoughts.

Sam said, "People don't want to appear weak, broken, or crazy, which is why they fight so hard to hide what is going on inside. They become experts at disguising the symptoms." Couple the deception of a person who's sick with a society that has a distorted perception of mental illness, and it's no wonder we don't see it coming. Sam explained how it is much more complex than someone habitually crying in the shower. The mask hides any physical symptoms which might otherwise be present with other illnesses. It's impossible to know someone is struggling internally unless they tell us. Sam believes this is why it is so important to break the stigma so the afflicted can honestly, bravely, and easily seek medical treatment as they would for any serious disease.

"No one wants to admit they hate themselves. It's embarrassing and demoralizing to admit the thoughts, and if it's not met with empathy, it can actually backfire and make a person feel even worse for bringing it up in the first place."

Sam explained the reason for his perfectionist tendencies. A counselor once told him he was the type of person who scared him the most because no one would ever suspect he was struggling in silence due to all his success and accomplishments. Sam admitted one of the ways he coped with the pain was to overcompensate through his achievements. No one would have guessed Sam was having thoughts of dying if everything was perfect in every other aspect of his life. He adapted by being meticulous with every aspect of his life and never showed any sign of weakness. He thought that if he could only be good enough and help enough people, this would all go away.

This theme of overcompensation bled through to his work life as well. He would work multiple jobs, staying busy to keep his thoughts at bay. It was when he was still that the feelings would rise and attack.

Keeping excessively preoccupied is a theme I'm familiar with in my own family. I watched my dad stay busy because it was in the quiet moments that the demons were the loudest.

As we kept talking, Sam brought up one of the strongest symptoms of his depression, which was his extreme irritability. Looking back to the times he was in the depths of his depression, he said friends and family members commented on how difficult he was to be around. Irritability is a key symptom that we don't always correlate to mental health. We associate sadness, loneliness, and excessive crying with depression but not agitation, anger, and extreme frustration as signs when these emotions are just as prevalent as other symptoms.

Sam said the depression kept him from enjoying most social gatherings, and he wasn't fun to be around either. "I was secretly trying to push people away because I didn't want people to get close enough to know what was really going on," Sam shared. It's a vicious cycle that feeds into the mental lie that *I'm not worthy of friends or being loved.*

I remember my daughter going through this stage in high school, losing every friend she had because kids don't understand the strug-gle of a mentally ill person, nor are they inclusive when it comes to people who are different than themselves. Her closest friends shut her out when she would retreat, needing her own space and safety, which ironically was when she needed them the most.

Sam hadn't known anyone personally who died by suicide before he made his own attempt. It wasn't until after he started to share his own story that he learned of people close to him who had also struggled and contemplated suicide.

It saddened and even angered me to think how if he had been aware of people he loved and trusted who had made it through the darkness, it might have changed his own perception of what he was going through. Had he seen someone recover from their disease and get to a stable place, he would have known he could do the same.

We must be brave. Our willingness to discuss mental health freely and openly, like we do with other diseases, will save lives.

Sam was amazingly brave to step up to advocate for mental health, but it didn't come easy. He was about to be called on by the stron-gest nudge, God. It came the year the school he taught at lost three students, a teacher, and a principal, all within eighteen months to suicide. Sam told me how he couldn't stay silent any longer. Up until that point in time, Sam had only told two people his entire life his secret. Now he was being asked to tell the world. He thought, "Someone has to start telling stories about this, even though I didn't want it to be me. In fact, I begged God for it not to be me." His mission has become a lifeline for youth. His focus is to get stories of life beyond suicide in front of as many people as possible so that they can know that there is hope and that it is possible to get help and move past the mental anguish of suicidal thoughts. Sam continued, "I truly believe that the number one prevention of suicide is telling stories of survival."

I couldn't agree more. It's my duty to tell not only my father's story and honor him, but also I must share how my daughter has fought for her survival.

Sam's diagnosis hasn't changed and he still struggles, but he now has several tools to manage his disease and knows the signals for when he needs to dial in more aggressively with therapy. He attributes talk therapy as giving him a safe place to work through his thoughts and feelings. Physical activity and exercise have been his biggest survival tool, along with a newfound inquisitiveness. He shares how he began to question after certain events why he'd feel suicidal. By questioning why that event caused him to have those thoughts again, he's begun to put the pieces together of his triggers. Sam talks openly about how medication hasn't been as effective for him as it is for many, but he's tried his share of drugs to provide stability. It takes time and effort, but he's thriving today, having learned a healthy way of life that works for him.

FORGIVENESS

"Forgiveness says you are given another
chance to make a new beginning."
- DESMOND TUTU

Your first thought as you begin reading this chapter may be that this is going to be a chapter on learning how to forgive your loved one for what they did. It's understandable to think that would be a natural part of the healing process. They left, abandoning our futures and dreams. What they did was something hurtful in our minds. As we work through the healing process, we often feel we need to find a way to forgive them. It's natural to want to forgive our loved one for the act which took so much away from us.

This might surprise you, but I don't believe our loved ones need to be forgiven. Let me give you some context, so you understand what I mean. When my grandmother developed breast cancer, and it took her life, I never thought once that I needed to forgive her for getting cancer. The same is true for your loved one's illness. My Dad doesn't need my forgiveness for developing an illness he didn't ask for and no doctor could cure.

I'm thankful to Sam for helping me see this slight distinction and valuable lesson. When I interviewed him, there was a moment when I asked, "What did you say to your mother when she learned you had attempted suicide? Did you ask her to forgive you?" My words cut like a knife. I could tell by his facial expression and physical jerk as if to say, "Wait a minute...what are you accusing me of? Do you think I meant to hurt my mother?" He was quick to correct me, and I'm so glad he did because I agree 100% with him.

Sam went on to say, "I don't believe I have anything I need to be forgiven for. I didn't choose to have this disease. I couldn't stop the suicidal thoughts on my own."

I go back to my analogies of cancer and heart disease. We don't blame a loved one who has a serious heart condition that is life-threatening, and we certainly wouldn't feel the need to forgive them if that disease caused them to die from a heart attack. Did I need to forgive my grandmother after she died of cancer? No, I don't blame her for getting sick. Who else has died and I've had to forgive them? No one. Sam makes such a valid point that I can totally understand why he was offended by my comment, and it's no coincidence how he responded to me in that manner so that I could share this point with you.

Suicide was the final symptom of your loved ones' terrible disease. I'm sorry it took their life. I'm sorry it left you in this immense grief and emotional state. You may need to forgive the act, but your loved one doesn't need you to forgive them. It was a disease that caused their ending. They want you to pick up the pieces and keep living. They want you to fulfill your dreams and the dreams you shared together. Your loved one wants you to live your life for both of you.

Your next question may be, then, who needs forgiveness? If you haven't figured that out yet, my friend, it's you. You need to forgive yourself. Forgiveness is necessary to release any feeling of blame, guilt, or shame you are carrying due to the suicide. The act of forgiveness always benefits the person on the giving side, and often it is felt more impactful by the giver than the person on the receiving end. For this reason, I like to think that when you forgive yourself, you gain double the benefit. Forgiving yourself helps you grow and leads to healing because you allow yourself to let go of past thought patterns, freeing you from what's been holding you back. Choosing not to forgive yourself traps you in the past, not allowing you to move forward. Self-forgiveness helps us reconcile how we see ourselves after we've experienced blame, shame, or guilt. You were never intended to hold onto these strong emotions of shame, guilt, or blame for what happened, and when you realize why you are worthy of self-forgiveness, you can see clearly just how deserving you are to be *free.*

I want to be clear though, asking yourself for forgiveness does not imply you did anything wrong. It's not about you needing forgiveness for sins or wrongdoings. You may feel like you did something wrong, but I'm here to help you reframe that. What I'm going to ask of you has nothing to do with blaming anyone for anything. It's quite the opposite. You will forgive yourself for holding onto blame, guilt, anger, or shame related to your loved one's death. This is about self-compassion, self-love, and allowing yourself to move forward.

I spoke honestly about my initial struggle with blaming myself for not taking stronger action when I thought my father might be suicidal. What I shared was that I realized that beating myself up for his illness and my lack of action wasn't an effective way to continue living my life. Instead of punishing myself for a disease that I knew little about and even the doctors didn't have a cure for, I needed to reframe the experience. When I could rationally accept that I had little to no experience with mental illness or what suicidal ideation was, how could I be to blame? Even if I was professionally trained in medicine or psychology, I still couldn't cure him alone. And on top of that, I can't change the outcome now, so nothing positive comes from me holding onto self-blame.

What I could do for myself was find a loving and compassionate way to reframe my experience. In doing so, I also accepted my self-forgiveness because I could see how holding onto the blame was a means of punishing myself for his death. I began to use self-compassion techniques to do this. My blaming thoughts were replaced with caring statements. I replaced the blaming thought, "If I had come back to visit him the weekend he died, he'd still be alive" with, "I'm not responsible for anyone else's actions."

I began to realize everything I had done out of love for him. I had spent time talking to him on the phone when I knew he was lonely. I mailed him cards and visited whenever I had the chance. I encouraged him to seek treatment. I was a loving daughter. I listened to him talk about the crippling pain in his back, and his unsuccessful attempts to get disability benefits. I even wrote letters on his behalf to help him when his lawyers failed to assist him. When I realize the number of things I did to help him get through some of his most difficult times, I can feel assured that I was doing everything I could and knew how to at the time. Taking the time to reflect on what I had done for him allowed me to stop blaming myself for not "saving him." None of us have the power to save anyone, nor is it our responsibility. If we loved deeply and we cherished our time together, we served our loved ones well.

I did my best to help you, Dad. The concern I had for your safety, and the talks when I'd ask you to seek help were all my way of showing how much I loved you. I recall the interventions when you wouldn't listen to our pleas. I remember the follow-up calls I made to the hospital staff therapist, who sat our family down and told us you needed to agree to admit yourself voluntarily or they couldn't help. I even contacted a local healthcare provider seeking to get you admitted to a program. You began some therapy and told me you thought it helped but eventually decided you didn't need it anymore. I never stopped trying to include you in family gatherings, even when you said no time and time again. When I visited you, I sat and listened. I tried not to judge. I did my best to understand your situation.

I was taking this new perceived experience and growing from it. This was my way of finding self-forgiveness. Today I carry little if any blame for his death. I give credit to some of my therapy for getting to this place, but I had to do the work. No one could do it for me. I have since taken additional steps to grow. I decided to attend Mental Health First Aid training, and I am certified in QPR, a suicide awareness and prevention training. I felt it was my responsibility to learn more so that I would be better prepared for future situations in which I was faced with a mental health crisis.

I am thankful to my inner wisdom for realizing and knowing the importance of reframing, gaining clarity, and growing from tragedy.

Healing Moment

Take a few minutes to reframe the negative comments you have been telling yourself. Focus on the positive things you did for your loved one and write them down. Use my example above to assist you in writing down how you showed up in a loving and caring way. Remembering all the things you were to your loved one will help you to forgive yourself for feeling guilt or blame for what happened. Your loved one doesn't hold you responsible for their actions, nor should you.

Next, I want you to write down something you wish to forgive yourself for. An example might be if you want your loved one to know you didn't understand or know how to help them. "I forgive myself for not having the tools to know what to do to help you."

Now that you've forgiven yourself, we can move into the final stage of healing. You've come a long way through this journey. You have worked through the Yearning, Educating, Surrendering, Empathizing, and Emerging phases. Each one has challenged you to think differently, seek new meaning from your experience, and recognize that there is always a way forward no matter how difficult and grief-stricken you may be. You've learned that this journey is not linear and that there will be setbacks, obstacles to continue to overcome, and anniversaries and life events to prepare for along the way.

The final phase of your healing is to take what you've learned and share your story so that others can follow in your footsteps. We walk this path together, and along the way, we share the same fears, obstacles, challenges, and, most importantly, we share the same hope. Through our hope and courage, we open our hearts to help pull others along the same path.

19

SHARE

*"Loving ourselves through the process of owning
our story is the bravest thing we'll ever do."*
- BRENE' BROWN

Stage Six: The Sharing Phase

Congratulations! You've come to the sixth and final phase of your healing. You should be proud of yourself. You've spent time reflecting, learning, and stretching yourself, and maybe a few of your past beliefs have shifted slightly or even changed dramatically. This is hard work, and we are about to honor and acknowledge your accomplishments, but first, let's explore why sharing your story is the valuable final phase.

As the quote above from Brene' Brown, a nationally renowned author and researcher who has studied courage, empathy, shame, and vulnerability for decades, expresses, you can't get to this phase without putting in the work of self-compassion and self-love. Hopefully, you've felt a shift in your emotional well-being by this point in the book. It may be small, but any progress toward seeing yourself moving forward is progress to be celebrated.

We've explored how paying it forward with empathy can provide you with a new focus while also honoring your loved one. As you emerge with a sense and understanding that there is a greater meaning in life, your heightened awareness and outlook propels you to the next step in your transformation: to own your story and begin sharing it freely.

My vision of half a million individuals transforming their lives annually to eliminate the stigma of mental health wouldn't be complete without this phase. Without sharing our brave stories, how would those who will experience a suicide loss in the future learn to walk this rough terrain? They need to hear our journey to show them there is a way through the dark and treacherous path. I have purposely shared stories throughout this book because I knew they would do the same for you. Christine, Jon, Ashley, Joan, Beverly, Keri, Rev. Sheila, Sam, and I have shared our stories with vulnerability so that you could heal. I thank each of them for having the courage to speak their truth, seeing my vision, agreeing to help, and graciously accepting the calling to be a beacon of light. It's now your turn to do the same. You don't need to have your story published in a book to make a difference.

Your impact can be felt significantly the next time you hear about a suicide in your community because you have the tools and the strength to reach out to someone grieving. It could be writing a handwritten note, making a phone call, or attending a funeral to share your condolences with a suicide survivor. These gestures are respectable ways to show your support and let someone know you can understand what they are going through. But I challenge you to go even further in your commitment to being a part of the ripple effect we will create. You are now equipped to have difficult conversations with friends and family members struggling with the grief process, just as you were when you started this book. You can share your philosophy and teach them how best to assist people grieving as you experienced. Let them know why it's polite to say, 'died by suicide' vs. 'committed suicided.' Share how you were impacted when someone made a gesture of pulling a finger trigger to their head. Help a friend having a mental health crisis by listening to them without judgment, asking them if they want to harm themselves, calling a crisis line, and then getting them to a professional for immediate help if you suspect they are contemplating suicide or they tell you they are.

There are so many ways you will make a positive impact. Our collective ripple effect will eventually erase the stigma of mental health. I can't wait to see how you show up in this world.

At the beginning of this book, I told you that I found healing in telling someone else's story. I could tell Morgan and Christine's story more easily than I could tell my own at first. It was safe. That was where I could start. But as time went on, I began to share my own story more and more. Little by little, I was amazed at how many people opened up to me. I began to wear it more as a badge of honor instead of the badge of shame and guilt I had once carried for so long. By becoming vulnerable, I allowed others to speak through their insecurities.

I challenge you to find one person you trust and ask them if you can share a story that is difficult for you to share. Explain to them that you feel called to share this story with them because it's impacted you greatly. Ask them to listen without judgment. Tell them one story from this book or if you feel brave, tell them your whole story from start to finish.

Continue to tell your story to more people you trust until it starts to feel less scary. You might be surprised to hear they have a story similar to yours. They may have lost someone close to them to suicide but have never shared their story with anyone. You can now provide a safe space for them to reciprocate by sharing their story. When this type of connection is made, you create a very powerful and healing process. Share your personal story and freely own it.

Healing Moment

Write the story of your loved one as seen through your lens. This story is meant for you. Write it with raw, unbridled nakedness. You can take as much time as you need. Your story may not be ready to be told completely, but you can begin with what you know thus far.

In the space below, journal the love you shared with this person. Write about the times you experienced that love and the loss you feel inside. This is your token. This story will be healing to you, and if you choose to share it, I'm certain it will also heal those who read it or are willing to listen to you share it.

You have so much to give this world. Your voice is one that needs to be heard, now more than ever, if you choose to tell your story. You have lived through something so devastating and when you come out on the other side of this, you can encourage and inspire people. You may never know how many people you will touch, but I guarantee you will make at least one significant impact and that's all you have to do to call your transformation a success.

BUTTERFLY

*"Perhaps the butterfly is proof that you can
go through a great deal of darkness and
still become something beautiful."*
-UNKNOWN

Have you ever watched a butterfly flutter by and wondered how and why it started as a caterpillar? When I see a butterfly, I smile, knowing it's a beautiful symbol of my transformation. We all experience life like a caterpillar, inching our way along, consuming things like the caterpillar consumes leaves until metamorphosis begins. For caterpillars, it's a very scientific process. For humans, it sometimes takes a jolt to awaken our awareness of the need to transform. You've been given that jolt in the most unimaginable way. Yet, you have wrapped yourself in a cocoon of knowledge, under-standing, compassion, and healing that allowed you to emerge as a beautiful butterfly.

I hope that as you come to the end of this book, you've begun to realize every opportunity life provides to us, no matter how difficult, is meant to transform us into something better. Seize this moment and realize you hold the power to create something greater for you and anyone you touch. It's what you make of a moment like this that matters. You are worthy of growth, health, happiness, and peace. You deserve all of it.

Yearn, Educate, Surrender, Empathy, Emerge, Share

Let's review the six steps to healing that I've laid out in the chapters throughout this book. Each one of them is important, in its own way, to aid your overall well-being. These steps led me to the self-awareness and self-care tools I needed to gain the strength to live beyond the loss of my father and transformed me with compassion, understanding, and hope in the process. When I chose to listen to the nudges and say yes to things that felt scary, I was permitting myself to heal. The self-discovery led me to a wisdom much deeper than I even knew existed inside of me. I hope you have found the tools to continue to step forward each day, even if the steps are small at first. You have a life full of promise waiting to be seized and tapped to its fullest potential. You now have the key to unlocking your strength to live.

Yearn

Yearning is a natural response to your grief. There will be things you'll crave to know and search desperately for answers. Yearning needs to be attended to so as not to cause long-term emotional stress over time. It can become unhealthy when it constantly gnaws away a part of you, leaving you feeling like the raw tips of chewed-off fingernails, sore, bruised, and unsightly.

It is your decision when you begin to move from the yearning phase and into a place of acceptance and knowing. Until you accept that there will be unanswerable questions, you will find it hard to get past this phase. You must be ready and willing to release the burden to continue forward.

It's okay to take some time in this stage because aching for the past is natural, but please know that you won't move forward completely until you are willing to let go of all those questions holding you back. Getting stuck in this phase will impact your daily functioning and can become emotionally unhealthy. Releasing your need to search, question, and ruminate is a brave step. Hand your yearning over to the Universe, to God, however that looks and feels to you. Envision it and set every intention to dissolve it.

Educate

When you increase your knowledge and expand your understanding of mental illness and what your loved one might have been going through, you gain confidence and some comfort in knowing the disease caused your loved one's demise and not something you did or didn't do. The realization that your loved one wasn't in control of their thoughts and actions because their mind was not functioning as it should, telling them lies, you begin to view their death as less of a personal decision and more of an illness that was left untreated.

Educating yourself also allows you to be an advocate on behalf of your loved one if you so choose. You are now more informed than the average person and can use your knowledge to help others and lean into your experience to start an open dialogue and potentially save someone's life.

Surrender

The Surrender stage is about acceptance. Nothing you did in the past, do in the present, or could do in the future will bring back your loved one, which is why surrendering is necessary.

Remember, surrendering is not giving up. It's merely accepting they are gone and that life and love are still ahead of you. Realizing you must continue to move forward is healthy for you and those you love. When you understand what your loved one wants for you, it's easier to step into the surrender phase.

You may choose a creative way to initiate your surrender moment symbolically, whether by asking for spiritual guidance, writing a letter, practicing gratitude, or creating a memory book as a token. An act that represents your surrender moment can be healing and cathartic.

Empathy

According to Brene' Brown, "Empathy is listening, holding space, without judgment, emotionally connecting, and communicating that incredibly healing message of you're not alone." It's hard to find a better way of expressing this stage than those words. You will gain so much from practicing empathy for those around you.

We tend to think that being empathetic helps the person we are supporting. However, it's a reciprocal process. We gain as much, if not more, when we reach out to someone in need and authentically connect with them. There is no need to learn how to show empathy, as you have the metaphoric gift of knowing pain which will guide you if you just listen and act.

Emerge

Breaking through the trauma and resurfacing is the step of emerging. Choosing to be better instead of being bitter over your situation will catapult you into this fourth stage of recovery. Being better always leads to healing, whereas being bitter will only cause you more discomfort and pain and trap you in a vicious cycle of destruction.

Aristotle's philosophy that everything happens for a reason

provides a powerful insight to shift or reframe your experience. Reframing our story more positively also allows us to forgive ourselves and practice self-compassion, which all leads to the final stage.

Share

When you have confidently processed the four stages before the sixth and final stage, you are ready to become a messenger of hope. You will impact lives in ways you may never truly comprehend. Sharing your story and the stories of others like you provides safety for those still hiding within the shadows of their suicide story.

Our thousands of voices will collectively rise to a level that it will be impossible for anyone to feel shame or stigma associated with mental health. It will empower the 53 million people living with mental illness in the U.S. to break free of the victimization and demonization of their illness and seek positive treatments without fear of being stigmatized. Your voice will change the narrative, and the landscape, and will ultimately save lives.

Now that you've read all six steps of healing, waded through stories of loss to recognize you are not alone, and learned techniques for self-care and connection with the other side, your metamorphosis is activated. The butterfly has become a symbol of hope and transformation. Just like the transformation from a caterpillar to a butterfly, there are stages that have to happen for the changes to occur. It doesn't happen overnight. It is a miraculous process.

The terrible experience of losing my father to suicide and doing everything in my power to save my daughter turned into something miraculous for me. I believe it can and will do the same for you. It led me to find a way of honoring my dad and gave me the direction I needed to support my daughter. That roadmap is in your hands now. You now have the opportunity to create your ripple moments which will add to the collective rise of consciousness. Spread your wings and fly.

Healing Moment

"Like a yellow daisy growing from drought-ridden soil, you are a survivor."
- CINDY TANK-MURPHY

A Grounding Practice

I want to leave you with one last healing moment. This grounding technique helps calm me when I'm anxious, putting me at ease. Whether I perform this ritual first thing in the morning or as a way to calm myself after a stressful day, it helps me connect with my values, my vision and energetically align myself with the earth.

The grounding technique allows you to be present, removes stress and chaos in your life, and connects you to your body. When you initiate this grounding practice, you will feel less frantic, helpless, and distracted and more aligned with your goals, power, and strength.

Practice this grounding technique daily to feel connected and at peace.

Close your eyes and take a deep breath in through your nose, holding for a second before releasing the air out through your mouth on exhale. Repeat this deep breathing five times, releasing any thoughts and allowing them to pass by.

With eyes closed, picture yourself looking up to the sky, envisioning the clouds parting and a bright light shining down upon you. This light heats the top of your head and begins to wrap itself completely around your entire body until you are covered in white light, glowing from head to toe.

As the white light encompasses your body, picture yourself grow-ing roots from your feet or your root chakra (the tip of your tailbone). These roots grow deep into the earth's soil, through the rocky depths toward the earth's core. As the roots dig deep, they spread wide and attach to the earth's center.

The roots attract a water source in the center of the earth, and the water begins to rise through the roots toward your feet and root chakra. Visualize the water flowing up inside your body and filling every inch of space within you until it reaches the top of your head and begins to overflow like a water fountain, pushing out any negative thoughts and emotions.

You are now completely grounded between heaven and earth. You are now centered, balanced, secure, and indestructible.

Repeat this mantra three times before slowly opening your eyes.

I am a Survivor. I am brave.
I love myself for owning my story.

Acronyms for Yearn, Educate, Surrender, Empathy, Emerge, Share

You're an Exceptionally Strong, Empathetic,
Evolved, Survivor

EPILOGUE:
STABILITY

Twenty years ago, when I first felt a nudge to write a book, I never would have guessed my journey was preparing me to write *this* book. The topic of suicide was not something I would have chosen; it chose me.

Now, almost two years from the day that I sat down at my computer and wrote for six hours straight, I reflect on what has transpired. I have so much to be grateful for, which includes my family, our health, and my personal growth.

My siblings and I have made significant strides in our collective healing. We've been lucky to have each other. We have each gone through our own grieving process, and in the act of healing have created a closer and even stronger family bond. We've supported our mom emotionally, physically, and spiritually in our own unique ways, and helped her to gain the care she needed. My mom has shown her tremendous strength by improving her own mental health struggles. She has a wonderful medical team treating her, bringing relief and peace of mind.

My husband has been my rock and the one person I've always been able to lean on. The past five years have been the most challenging of our lives. I am eternally grateful for him and his steadfast love. Watching the constant mood swings, from mania to depression in our oldest daughter and the wake of destruction it caused left us scarred and bruised at times, yet better in many ways, for we know it was our love and persistence that saved her from the depths of her personal pain.

It has been a year since our daughter's last suicide attempt. A year since her last inpatient stay at a behavioral health hospital. The difference was finding a medication that finally worked for her. Her demons have settled into a safe, manageable state, allowing her to look forward to returning to her college studies while growing her understanding of her lifelong illness and her ability to reach her potential. 'Proud' is an understatement for how I feel about her deeply empathic nature, maturity, intelligence, creativity, and powerful strength. She has dedicated herself to volunteering as a mental health advocate for youth. I know she will change lives and impact those who will resonate with her journey.

My other daughter, who has lived through these tumultuous years as a bystander, watching her sister struggle, has grown into an amazing young woman. She's just starting her college adventures and regaining her friendship and bond with her once difficult-to-love sister. She's had to transition from child to adult with the unfortunate reality of having distracted parents at times. She's been scared, challenged, and wounded, as have the rest of us, yet she's been a consistently devoted, dependable, loving, and uplifting member of our household. Her presence holds us together. She lights up every room she enters, which has been vital through our darkest days. I have no doubt she will be a great addition to the medical profession.

As for me, I take each day as a gift. I know that life will continue to challenge me, and I'm not invincible to future grief. However, I believe I am strong enough to move forward no matter what life has in store. I've learned that my desire to help others gives me my greatest joy. Through Reiki and my vision of the Compassion Transformation Method, I hope to provide healing to those grieving and in pain. I have grown in ways I never imagined through my determination to seek light, hope, peace, and joy.

Writing this book has been both a healing and an informative process. I learned how valuable telling my story was in closing the wounds of grief, shame, and guilt. I didn't know when I started down this path that I would gain an invincible strength, find my voice, and learn that I have been a mental health advocate for a long time without even realizing it.

Life is complex, tumultuous, and unique to each of us, just as it's simple, amazing, and familiar in many ways. The beauty in that is we all possess *free will*. We get to choose how we show up in every situation, event, and even tragedy that comes our way. We can choose to run away and hide when things are tough, or we can choose to face the challenges head-on. And when we achieve the latter, we grow, become resilient, and evolve.

I hope you will continue on your path to healing, take every moment in your life to see the beauty and courage of what you've overcome, and recognize your strength as a gift. We only get one chance at this experiment called life. I want you to live it with the utmost love, joy, and peace you deserve.

We never will be the same, but we can be whole again.

I look forward to hearing from you if something you read helped you gain a better understanding or relief in your healing. I have started a Facebook page to showcase additional tools, healing techniques, and offer words of comfort and encouragement. I offer Reiki healing both in person and from a distance, specifically designed for grief and survivors. I also provide a checklist you can download from my website that will help you ask those important questions if someone you know may be contemplating suicide. You can find my website and contact information in the resource section at the back of the book, where I share additional websites, songs, books, suicide prevention hotlines, and support for you to continue your healing. I am currently in the process of doing one-on-one coaching and taking a limited number of clients who are truly wanting to heal and find the gift amidst their loss. My door is always open.

I believe our world is ready to pull back the curtains and address mental health head-on. I am encouraged by the strength of survivors who bravely tell the untold stories of those who are no longer with us. It is my hope that one day our world will see no difference between illnesses of the body and the mind. That *health* will refer to our whole human condition, encompassing the mind, body, and soul. And that we always treat each other with love and kindness.

Love, Hugs, & Joy

PERSONAL NOTES

Acknowledgments

Christine Schmidt

Christine started a non-profit organization after losing her daughter, Morgan, to suicide. *It's All Love, Only Love Coalition* has educated students and parents on suicide prevention and the importance of always being kind. Christine felt that the coalition gave her an outlet to help others when she could no longer help Morgan. Christine is a mother, an author, a Christian, and a survivor.

Burge Smith-Lyons

Burge is a best-selling international author, diversified motivational speaker, personal development trainer, a spiritual relationships communication counselor, and hypnotherapist. Whether it's a large-group corporate training, leadership development, relationship enhancement, or teen and younger children self-esteem and suicide prevention, she's creating win-win situations with mind-body-spirit healing, transformation, and growth. She has taught thousands of adults and children since 1985 on six different continents. She built the Conscious Leadership Academy for hundreds of children in Liberia with her non-profit, *the Healing Forest Foundation*.

www.Healingforestfoundation.org

Wendy Hayum-Gross, MS, LCPC

Wendy is a licensed clinical professional counselor and co-owner of *Grow Wellness Group*. She works with individuals and couples going through transitions in their lives. Her counseling style comes from a holistic wellness perspective encompassing the entire person, mind, body, and spirit. Wendy helps people find their strengths, values, and truths in a warm, relaxed setting.

https://growwellnessgroup.com provides varied services such as house clearings, wedding ceremonies, and celebrations of life, amongst other services. For more information and testimonials, please refer to her website.

https://beonewithspirit.com/

Sam Eaton

Sam is a best-selling author, speaker, and founder of *Recklessly Alive*, a suicide prevention organization sprinting toward a world with zero deaths by suicide. Sam has spoken at over one hundred events throughout the U.S., where he shares his story of battling depression and suicidal thoughts.

https://www.recklesslyalive.com/

Dr. Yasmine Saad

Dr. Yasmine Saad is a two-time international best-selling author and top-rated NYC licensed clinical psychologist with a national and international reputation. She uses ancient eastern wisdom to cure modern western problems. Her method empowers clients with a clear sense of direction in just one encounter. She is the founder of *Madison Park Psychological Services*, a premier therapy and assessment group in NYC, awarded the best business in its category by *Three Best Rated* for the past 4 years. Dr. Saad's expertise has been featured on ABC, NBC, CBS, Fox, HuffPost, and many more media outlets.
Yasmine Saad, Ph.D.

Robin & Sandra

These two women have been devoted to my same mission and vision of helping youth since I first met them in the summer of 2016 at a Women's Network entrepreneurial workshop in San Diego. We teamed up with the vision of raising $10,000 in 10 hours for foster children and achieved our goal in no time. Since that momentous accomplishment, we've shared both tears of joy and grief together. We founded an organization, *A-List Hero*, to help teens struggling with mental health and traveled to New Zealand to share our vision of hope. We've held space for one another during our individual challenges, supported each other's dreams and aspirations, and believe that together we are able to move mountains. I've learned invaluable life lessons from our friendship. They've taught me that love transcends all things. They are my angels here on earth.

Reverend Sheila Black

Rev. Sheila is an ordained Minister, accredited Medium, and certified Spiritual Healer. Her sessions can be offered in person or virtually. She is a compassionate medium, providing healing, uplifting, and evidential messages from your loved ones in Spirit. Her healings are profound and can be life-altering, whether in person or remotely. Rev. Sheila also teaches developmental classes and has enjoyed her spiritual practice for the last eight years. She sees clients as a medium and healer, and offers spiritual guidance and consultations. She also

References

Suicide Statistics AFSP (American Foundation for Suicide Prevention)
* https://afsp.org/suicide-statistics/

International Association for Suicide Prevention
* https://findahelpline.com/i/iasp
* https://www.iasp.info/

World Suicide Prevention Day
* https://nationaltoday.com/world-suicide-prevention-day/

Pandemic Increases Depression Research:
* https://www.npr.org/sections/health-shots/2020/09/02/908551297/pandemics-emotional-hammer-hits-hard

Jamie Raskins Son Tommy Death:
* https://repraskin.medium.com/statement-of-congressman-jamie-raskin-and-sarah-bloom-raskin-on-the-remarkable-life-of-tommy-raskin-f93b0bb5d184
* https://www.washingtonpost.com/local/md-politics/rep-jamie-raskin-and-wife-sarah-share-moving-tribute-remembering-their-son-tommy-raskin/2021/01/04/0ef01b30-4ee3-11eb-83e3-322644d82356_story.html
* https://raskin.house.gov/2020/12/congressman-raskin-announces-loss-son-tommy-raskin

Benefits of writing

- https://hbr.org/2021/07/writing-can-help-us-heal-from-trauma
- https://www.urmc.rochester.edu/encyclopedia/content.aspx?ContentID=4552&ContentTypeID=1
- https://www.apa.org/monitor/jun02/writing

Benefits of practicing self-care

- https://www.usatoday.com/in-depth/news/investigations/surviving-suicide/2018/11/28/suicide-prevention-tips-true-stories-how-survivors-cope/1112169002/

Death Cafes

- https://www.aarp.org/home-family/friends-family/info-2021/death-cafes.html

National Funeral Directors Association

- https://nfda.org/resources

Inside Japan

- https://www.insidejapantours.com/us/japanese-culture/samurai/

NAMI (original article with quote in Chapter: Hospitals)

- https://www.nami.org/Blogs/NAMI-Blog/June-2017/Supporting-Someone-with-Borderline-Personality-Dis
- https://www.nami.org/home

Non-Medication Treatments

- https://mhanational.org/science/non-medication-treatments-mental-health#:~:text=Things%20like%20therapy%2C%20brain%20stimulation,symptoms%20of%20certain%20mental%20illnesses.

Mental Health First Aid and Crisis Trainings

- ✤ https://www.mentalhealthfirstaid.org/
- ✤ https://www.thenationalcouncil.org/about/
  mental-health-first-aid/
- ✤ https://qprinstitute.com/

5 Surprising Mental Health Statistics - Mental Health First Aid Organization

- ✤ https://www.mentalhealthfirstaid.org/2019/02/5-surprising-mental-health-statistics/#:~:text=In%20the%20United%20States%2C%20almost,equivalent%20to%20 43.8%20million%20people.

Mental Health Disorder Statistics, John Hopkins Medicine

- ✤ https://www.hopkinsmedicine.org/health/
  wellness-and-prevention/mental-health-disorder-statistics

The legal status of suicide - 20 countries it's illegal and attempters are prosecuted and jailed for it.

- ✤ https://pubmed.ncbi.nlm.nih.gov/26375452/

Homelessness & Mental Health: "The Never-Ending Loop: Homelessness, Psychiatric Disorder, and Mortality"

- ✤ https://www.psychiatrictimes.com/view/never-ending-loop-homelessness-psychiatric-disorder-and-mortality

Time Magazine article on teens and anonymous apps: "5 Things Parents Should Tell Kids About Anonymous Apps"

- ✤ https://time.com/2921467/
  parents-kids-anonymous-apps-whisper-secret/

"Signs The Secret Language of the Universe" by Laura Lynne Jackson
- http://lauralynnejackson.com/

CDC 2018 Causes of Death - Rankings by age / Suicide Statistics and Prevention
https://www.psychiatry.org/patients-families/suicide-prevention
- https://www.cdc.gov/injury/images/lc-charts/leading_causes_of_death_by_age_group_2018_1100w850h.jpg
- https://www.americashealthrankings.org/explore/health-of-women-and-children/measure/teen_suicide/state/ALL

Statistics of increased suicide amongst people who have lost a friend or family member to suicide & genetic link studies:
- https://psmag.com/social-justice/are-people-grieving-suicides-more-likely-to-attempt-suicide-themselves
- https://www.health.harvard.edu/mind-and-mood/left-behind-after-suicide
- https://cronkitenews.azpbs.org/2020/08/31/suicide-family-genetic-risk/
- https://www.hhs.gov/answers/mental-health-and-substance-abuse/can-the-risk-for-suicide-be-inherited/index.html#:~:text=There%20is%20growing%20evidence%20that,the%20risk%20for%20suicidal%20behavior.
- https://www.news-medical.net/health/The-Genetics-of-Mental-Disorder.aspx

Statistics of how hospitals are ill-equipped to care for mental health patients.
- https://www.modernhealthcare.com/node/266611/printable/print

- https://www.modernhealthcare.com/article/20181114/
  NEWS/181119973/hospitals-are-ill-equipped-to-treat-be-
  havioral-health-ecri-finds
- https://www.healthline.com/health/mental-health/los-
  ing-someone-to-suicide?fbclid=IwAR11qA0MI52xF2S7M-
  jIHhnOZrp3LOuCSS8d0Fxfc0cfoHrLaydYbsy0vgc0
- https://www.recklesslyalive.com/meet-sam

Mayo Clinic List of Symptoms

- https://www.mayoclinic.org/diseases-conditions/
  bipolar-disorder/symptoms-causes/syc-20355955
- https://www.mayoclinic.org/diseases-conditions/anxiety/
  symptoms-causes/syc-20350961
- https://www.mayoclinic.org/diseases-conditions/
  depression/symptoms-causes/syc-20356007

Article on why writing is healthy

- https://www.health.harvard.edu/mind-and-mood/
  writing-to-ease-grief

Complicated Grief

- https://prolongedgrief.columbia.edu/for-the-public/
  complicated-grief-public/overview/

Research on Traumatic Bereavement by Barle', Wortman, Latack

- https://www.researchgate.net/publication/281537466_
  Traumatic_Bereavement_Basic_Research_and_Clini-
  cal_Implications

Burge Smith-Lyons

- www.Healingforestfoundation.org
- https://essenceofbeing.com/

- https://theconsciousleadershipacademy.com
- https://burgesmithlyons.com/

Wendy Hayum-Gross, MS, LCPC
- https://growwellnessgroup.com

Reverend Sheila Black
- https://beonewithspirit.com/

Yasmine Saad
- www.madisonparkpsych.com

Sam Eaton
- https://www.recklesslyalive.com/

Resources

Chapter shared in the compilation book, *Ignite Your Wisdom.*

Website: www.thestrengthtolive.com
Facebook: https://www.facebook.com/TheStrengthToLiveBook
Instagram: @thestrengthtolive
Email: cindy@thestrengthtolive.com

Mental Health First Aid Training
* ✤ https://www.mentalhealthfirstaid.org/

QPR Certification
* ✤ https://qprinstitute.com/

NAMI National Alliance on Mental Illness
* ✤ https://nami.org/

Signs: The Secret Language of the Universe, by New York Times Bestseller, Laura Lynne Jackson

Averee, Singer/Songwriter and Mental Health Advocate
To download her music from Spotify, use QR code.

https://open.spotify.com/artist/4sIT6x1MgDcvdYIFsZEytd?si=M-dzbATXgR-6fq6Qlzv6uBQ

Essence of Being
- ✤ www.Healingforestfoundation.org
- ✤ https://essenceofbeing.com/
- ✤ https://theconsciousleadershipacademy.com
- ✤ https://burgesmithlyons.com/

Grow Wellness Group
- ✤ https://growwellnessgroup.com

Be One With Spirit
- ✤ https://beonewithspirit.com/

Recklessly Alive
- ✤ https://www.recklesslyalive.com/

Madison Park Psychological Services
- ✤ www.madisonparkpsych.com

Evolution Counseling
- ✤ www.evolutioncounselinginc.com

Find a Support Group in or outside of the U.S.
American Foundation of Suicide Prevention
- ✤ https://afsp.org/find-a-support-group/

SAVE Suicide Awareness Voices of Education
- ✤ https://save.org/what-we-do/grief-support/

National Suicide Prevention Hotline
- ✤ 988 in the United States
- ✤ 800-273-8255 / 800-273-TALK

International Crisis Lines
- ❖ https://findahelpline.com/i/iasp

Crisis Text Line
- ❖ Text HOME to 741741

The Trevor Project
- ❖ 866-488-7386

Trans Lifeline
- ❖ 877-565-8860 Canada: 877-330-6366

Veterans Crisis Line
- ❖ 800-273-8255 press 1

For International crisis numbers:
- ❖ https://findahelpline.com/i/iasp

About the Author

Best-selling author, international speaker, and mental health advocate, Cindy Tank-Murphy offers a unique perspective on the much-needed conversation around overcoming the grief from suicide and the mental health epidemic around it. Trained in Mental Health First Aid and certified in QPR, a suicide prevention technique, Cindy believes we can eliminate the stigma associated with mental illness through awareness and open dialogue that will ultimately save lives.

Cindy's life was forever changed on July 22, 2014, when her father ended his life, and she was left with a choice to make. She could allow shame, guilt, and sorrow to swallow her whole or seek better understanding through education and a new version of herself through vulnerable self-discovery. Thankfully, she chose the latter, which began a massive shift in her healing journey, one that has had a profound and lasting impact on her future and called her to be a compassionate voice regarding mental health.

In the years that followed her father's suicide, Cindy began to notice similar signs of depression, anxiety, and dissociation in her teenage daughter. Her mother's intuition knew she needed to seek the right expertise and treatment for her daughter, or she might find herself reliving the devastation of suicide all over again. As someone who has both experienced the emotional impact of suicide from someone who has succeeded, and the anguish of keeping it a bay from someone who is contemplating it, Cindy understands the fear that comes from both ends of the spectrum and acknowledges it from a perspective that enables her to be a supportive lifeline for others.

Her gift is her desire to help others heal by exploring their own stories and finding compassion and understanding amid the sorrows of suicide. Her personal experience, perspective, and passion for sharing her experience make her an ideal mentor and a compassionate voice for those struggling emotionally with suicide loss or dealing with someone they love battling mental illness.

Through her dedication to raising awareness and providing support, Cindy gives a compelling and personal account of how she began the healing process and provides supportive steps to help her readers do the same. In her debut solo book, *The Strength To Live*, she shares how to move through your grief and find the hero in you on the other side.

Cindy lives in Naperville, IL, with her husband and two daughters. She enjoys traveling, humanitarian work, writing, practicing Reiki healing and radical self-love, meditating, and spending time in nature. Her background has empowered her to become an advocate to help those who are grieving from suicide. She can be reached at cindy@thestrengthtolive.com. For more support and information go to www.thestrengthtolive.com

www.thestrengthtolive.com
cindy@thestrengthtolive.com
TheStrengthToLiveBook
thestrengthtolive